HELLGATE
— WORLD

MW01009741

Through My Eyes

91st Infantry Division in the Italian Campaign 1942–1945

Leon Weckstein

Hellgate Press

Central Point, OR

Through My Eyes:
91st Infantry Division in the Italian Campaign 1942–1945

Hellgate Press
an imprint of L&R Publishing, LLC
P.O. Box 3531
Ashland, OR 97520

(541) 973-5154

info@hellgatepress.com *e-mail*

Editor: Janelle Davidson
Book designer: Constance C. Dickinson
Compositor: Jan O. Olsson
Managing editor: Constance C. Dickinson
Cover designer: Steven Burns

Weckstein, Leon, 1921–
    Through my eyes : 91st Infantry Division in the Italian campaign, 1942–1945 / Leon Weckstein. — 1st ed.
       p. cm. — (Hellgate memories World War II)
    Includes index.
    ISBN 1-55571-497-8
    1. Weckstein, Leon, 1921– . 2. World War, 1939–1945—Campaigns--Italy. 3. World War, 1939–1945 Personal narratives, American. 4. United States. Army Biography. 5. Soldiers—United States Biography. 6. United States. Army. Infantry Division, 91st--History. I. Title. II. Series: Hellgate memories series.
    D763.I8W43 1999
    940.54'215'092—dc21
    [B]   99-20888

To those incredibly courageous dogfaces of the 91st Division, living and dead, with whom I had the distinct honor and privilege of serving, and to fighting infantrymen everywhere. They are a special breed.

Contents

Illustrations

Following page 102

Photographs

The author on leave in Italy

The second chow line, after our soldiers were fed

Working with a heavy mortar platoon at an OP

The first day of combat

Dead Germans in front of a Gothic Line dugout

Getting howitzers to the front

Mud everywhere

White phosphorous shelling

The author and J. P. Dunnagen

Company G near Pianoro

Rounding up prisoners in the Po Valley

Being awarded the Legion of Merit

Foreword

Leon Weckstein and I both served with the 363rd Infantry Regiment, so the roads we traveled up the bloody boot of Italy were very much the same. Leon was an intelligence sergeant with 1st Battalion Headquarters; I was a Private First Class and served with a rifle platoon in Company E, 2nd Battalion. Except for the three weeks I spent in a field hospital recovering from wounds I received at the Arno River, I went the entire route with the 91st Division. We were two of those rare birds of World War II, soldiers who returned home with the same units they trained with in the States. We were survivors because Lady Luck rode on our shoulders all during the time we were in combat. As the late novelist James Jones put it, "It's largely a matter of luck that decides whether or not you get killed. It doesn't make any difference who you are, how nice a guy you might be, or how much you know, if you happen to be at a certain post, at a certain time, you get it." Leon and I escaped that post and that time.

As this book shows us, it's the infantryman who has to go in and face the rifle, machine gun, and mortar fire. The artillery can shell the valleys and the mountains, and the Air Force can bomb the roads and destroy the towns, but it's the infantryman who must move through those valleys, climb the mountains, capture the towns, and stagger up the roads, forever pursuing the enemy.

Through My Eyes chronicles the evolution of a soldier from a frightened young innocent to a seasoned veteran of war. As the book progresses, we follow these young draftees through basic training with all its absurd orders, through the final stages of overseas movement, and into the terrifying first days of battle. The 363rd Infantry spent ten months in combat, an absolute eternity to those men who had to endure the heat of summer, the rain, mud, and sleet of autumn, and the bitter snows of winter. When the war finally and mercifully ended, "we had waited and prayed for it so long that the remarkable news was accepted calmly and passively, with only a strange numbing relief as the prime emotion." Only then did the nerves begin to calm down and the knots in the stomach slowly unravel.

At the top of Il Giogo Pass, where troops of the U.S. II Corps initially broke the Gothic Line, there's a monument to the dead of the 363rd Infantry Regiment. It stands along State Road 503 just a few yards from a small restaurant with the ominous name, *l'uomo morto* (the dead man). On the monument are the names of over 500 young men who were cheated out of a life. The place is quiet now and the stillness extends even down into the valleys that are covered with a fifty-year growth of pines. To stand by the monument and look out over the mountains and hear the wind sigh through the grass and to remember these men is to feel a hurt that is beyond all healing.

This book tells us about those men, and it does it magnificently.

ROY LIVENGOOD

Historian, 91st Infantry Division Association

Preface

Seven A.M. The clock radio interrupted my sleep with the sound of somebody's damn horn concerto blaring harshly in my ears. How could the program director be so insensitive so early? Anything except horns at this hour would have been acceptable. I reached over faster than I should have and put an end to that insanity in a hurry. Ten, very brief, minutes later, I opened my eyes properly, slowly, as I felt for the elusive buttons of the TV remote that connect me to the morning's news. Obviously, I had pushed right. A bugler was in the midst of sweetly sounding taps as "Good Morning America" somberly reminded me that today was November 11, 1997, Veteran's Day.

It had become my habit for too many years to avoid the bittersweet memories, allowing myself only a few introspective seconds on that special holiday to smugly and selfishly meditate on how great it was to still be alive. Usually, I'd allot time for just one or two hastily derived thoughts of my old infantry comrades, those I had last seen in Italy before I was lucky enough to be shipped home, thoughts I could quickly fritter away with the last application of my shaving cream before they managed to get the better of me.

Maybe it was something in the dolefully compelling tones of the announcer on that particular day, but I found myself suddenly and unwillingly caught up in the intended sentimentality. For some reason, I began to recall how many men I knew who still sleep permanently there beneath the sacred soil that had become a vast American graveyard near Florence and how many continue to haunt me even now as I attempt to brush aside this ephemeral sadness. They didn't make it; why did I? Was there any sense to it?

Since the war, I've chosen to subvert the worst memories of those many hideous war incidents and gradually shunt them to a more distant strata of my brain. But, it took many years and many nightmares to mitigate all that unforgettable butchery. Only during the last ten years have I even allowed myself to attend a war movie which, surprisingly enough, was too realistic for me. Titled *A Walk in the Sun*, it was about a platoon of infantry in Italy. Even that masterfully produced film conjured up too many unsettling memories.

I challenge the old cliché that time heals all wounds. I'd be infinitely more content to put the whole thing to rest once and for all, if only I could.

As I looked in the mirror that morning and saw that corrugated, seventy-seven-year-old face doing its best to conceal a brain that thinks it's still twenty-nine, a strong need impelled me to write something enlightening about those unsettled times. I especially wanted to convey the terribly savage part I witnessed as well as the more pleasing part the congenial Italians played during those never-to-be-forgotten years between 1942 and 1945.

So little has been written about the people, how they faced the immense tragedies inherent in their hunger, the almost daily demolition of their cities, the slaughter of their kin. All of this they stood up to with unbelievable spirit, humor, and remarkable stoicism. Examples of human dignity such as theirs requires a considerable amount of reporting, much more than the subject has been given to date and more than I personally could ever contribute. Yet I feel that what I have seen is extremely important and well worth adding to the, unfortunately, limited number of memoirs of this historic Italian era.

Certainly, it would be sinful to ignore the real-life drama of the infantryman's role during those traumatic years. For the main part, my chronicle is the honest truth as indelibly remembered from a span of more than half a century. It is easy enough to recall the delightful as well as the horrible situations of those turbulent times, so of necessity these memoirs will include just about everything, the sentimental, the sensual, and, sadly, the morbid. Names will be named, except where my narrative tends to deride or scandalize.

Much of the detail that helped me recall dates and locations was taken from the *History of the 363rd Infantry* compiled by Captain Ralph E. Strootman and published by the Washington Infantry Journal Press in 1947, for which I offer my sincere thanks. That portion of my memoir relating to my part in having possibly saved the famous Leaning Tower of Pisa from destruction is verifiable.

There are valid documents of my actions as well as witnesses who are, hopefully, still alive.

I tried not to be redundant, but the stark drama and recollections I have attempted to convey can in no way come close to recapturing the entire story of bravery, humor, and hell instigated by this war, or any war I suppose. I ask the reader's forgiveness if I have found it too easy to get carried away with emotion.

It was the soul-shattering, life and death events that occurred near the crest of Monticelli during those decisive four days of the summer of 1944 that grow increasingly vulgar and more obscene as they continue to smolder in a very secret section of my mind — for as long as I will live. Nevertheless, I chose to dig deeply into my white-lipped memories of acts splendidly heroic as well as barbarously profane, so you could join me as an armchair witness to the furious battle for the Apennines as I saw them.

For lack of a camera at that time, only these printed words can serve to recreate those amazing experiences I've attempted to relate in this book. I clearly saw them through my eyes then and, I promise you, with only the tiniest sprinkle of self-indulgence and pride do I relate them now.

Acknowledgments

My greatest appreciation goes to my best friend, Mimi, who by an odd set of circumstances also happens to be my affectionate, loving wife. Without her patient reassurance, these pages would be blank, non-existent, since it was she who taught me to like myself enough to muster the chutzpah to dare write this wartime autobiography.

Without the technical support of my son-in-law, Barry Chass, and my stepson, Dennis Passovoy, computer wizards who helped me contend with a fearsome new word processor, I'd probably still be working on chapter two. Please, guys, accept my too often unexpressed but heartfelt gratitude.

Very special, sincere thanks go to Dan Striepeke, Ron Friedman, and Carole Kirschner for their advice, counsel, and encouragement when I needed it most. And I certainly owe a huge debt of gratitude to Gigi Orlando, owner of the very Italian Café Roma in Beverly Hills. He sparked my enthusiasm to begin my book because of his fiercely emotional accolades regarding the Pisa adventure.

The author also gratefully acknowledges Bill Maulden and the Watkins/Loomis Agency for their permission to reprint select WWII cartoons featuring Willy and Joe, probably the world's most famous and popular pair of "dogface" infantrymen. They will forever remain every WWII GI's memory of guys he slept with, chowed down with, and fought alongside. "Maulden," as he was fondly known to the multitude of American fighting men, created more than a bit of sorely needed light to brighten many of our otherwise indescribably dark days. Thank you again, Bill Maulden.

Chapter 1

Drafted

"Let's get married." Hundreds of thousands of panicky youngsters tremulously whispered those supposedly consoling words, almost daring each other, while all around them a very anxious America watched the gathering clouds of war, which just about scared the hell out of everybody. I was no exception and also wed, having to say heavyhearted good-byes soon afterward to my wife of a few months at the urgent and irreversible request of the terrifying Selective Service Board.

It's of passing interest to note that well over half of those quickie weddings ended in divorce later, beating the fifty-fifty odds.

I was drafted out of the then-Jewish section of Los Angeles in November of 1942, along with every other poor frightened Brooklyn Avenue shlep the fearsome Board could round up, including my forty-nine year-old, five-foot-one-inch father-in-law. We looked very much like an anxious and mangy Dirty Dozen. Each intimidated one of us carried to our unknown destiny a small dilapidated suitcase filled with toilet articles, sox, a change of underwear, and whatever else could make us feel that we hadn't totally lost touch with what used to be reality. Almost everyone had a small paper bag that included the all important nosh lovingly created by mother or wife, a hard salami sandwich, kosher pickle, and slice of marble cake. God forbid we should go hungry!

It might have been easier on me than the others. I had spent several years in an orphanage as a kid and had been kicked around pretty good by that time. As I watched some of the others, I couldn't help but notice their frightened white faces, their moist eyes. It's not that I was a hell of a lot braver; I was probably almost as scared as they were. All I had going for me was my previous experience of early separation and, as a result, a bit less fear of the unknown.

Aware that the draft would get me sooner or later, I had first attempted to volunteer for service with the Navy, then the Coast Guard.

"Your eyesight is lousy!" they both reminded, rather than informed, me. "Go home and eat lots of carrots. Don't bother us again for at least six months." I wiped my glasses with a tissue and went home to wait. I didn't know for what, at the time.

I was really a very dumb twenty-one-year-old, going on sixteen socially, and sincerely believed that if they turned me down, so would the Army. They didn't. The incredibly ironic thing was that I ultimately became known in the 363rd Infantry Regiment as Eagle Eye Weckstein and was awarded one of our country's highest medals, the Legion of Merit, mainly for my unusual ability to see things others couldn't. Ultimately, I gained fame among the big brass for my curious talent to spot targets and direct fire at the enemy from perilous forward observation posts.

I took the Navy's advice and did eat a carrot or two, but what the generals of the 5th Army would later learn was that it wasn't necessarily my eyesight or corrective eighteen-dollar lenses that mattered. The simple fact was that I really did have unusual powers of observation, particularly a latent aptitude for discerning a camouflaged Panzer tank or a dug-in machine-gun position before anyone else could. Even as a child of eight, I could see a garter snake slither through the fall leaves long before the other kids did. There is no magic here. Some of us have it, but most don't.

A hundred or so of us sad sacks piled gloomily into the train headed for Fort Ord, California. I was about to learn a very valuable lesson from that first train ride to our staging area in Monterey. An imposing, official-looking sergeant rounded us up as we were about to depart the train station in Los Angeles. "Anybody here ever been in the Boy Scouts?" he yelled.

"I was!" My hand went up.

He had his pigeon. "What's your name?"

I told him, and he said "You're going to be the acting corporal for this group. See that they don't drink too much or get too rowdy. Make sure they stay on the train. We'll put it on your record."

Yeah, sure they would. Needless to say, I became a most despised official trying to uphold his orders. I couldn't see a way to back out gracefully and realized too late that I'd been had. I would never again volunteer for anything. My typical, naïve reaction left me frustrated to the point of evaluating everything a bit more seriously from then on. It was just the beginning of my real-world education.

After a few days of being indoctrinated at Fort Ord, we received our first olive-drab uniforms and clumsy GI shoes from the hard-bitten quartermaster sergeant. Generally sized ridiculously wrong, these formidable trappings were unceremoniously selected and handed out to us by German prisoners of war (POWs), who probably took some solace in the illogical distribution.

Then, after the cursory physical exams which consisted mainly of bending over with pants ridiculously draped at half-mast and coughing to test for hernias, we were once again stacked onto a train headed north to Camp White near Medford, Oregon, some seven or eight hours away. This time I was more than happy to be rid of my silly title of acting corporal as well as the attending reference to me as Corporal Chickenshit. I swore that, from now on, it would be the real thing or nothing.

Looking around that melancholy, smoke-filled train compartment, I realized that the over-animated expressions and loutish clowning around I had noticed a few days before had now begun to turn dour, moody. Bottles of cheap bourbon were being passed around freely, quickly making glassy-eyed buddies out of complete strangers.

Who could blame them? We were all going off into the vast unknown, urgently missing home already, and wondering if we would ever again see our loved ones. The unsettling matter of where and how we'd wind up was terribly unnerving.

I recall that the prime sensation that gripped me was one of loneliness. My father-in-law had been routed to a medical unit because someone finally took note of his age, which was funny as the man couldn't stand the sight of blood, so he was put in another compartment in a different part of the train, and now the feeling of total abandonment was complete.

Soon a real honest-to-god corporal passed through the train when we reached the Oregon border, calling off each man's official designation and naming the company he would be attached to once we arrived at Camp White. I found that I was now assigned to 1st Battalion, Headquarters Company, of the 363rd Infantry Regiment, 91st Infantry Division, destined to be a clerk-typist, of all things. That post seemed logical since I had taken a year of typing in high school. But wow! That word *infantry* was scary. The only saving grace were the words *headquarters* and *clerk-typist*. Weren't those guys always behind the lines? How in the hell could you type anything with bullets flying past you?

I would find the surprising answer to these questions during the a year-and-a-half journey down the long, muddy road that would lead from here to the killing fields, those rutted, mine-laden olive groves and craggy, snow-covered mountains awaiting us in Italy. Of course, we had no knowledge at that time of just where we'd wind up.

Military trucks carried us from the train to our barracks in a pouring rain that must have been specially ordered by the Army to start the punitive process of turning us into desolate, wretched recruits since the deluge didn't let up for over sixty soggy days.

To this day, I can't help thinking that our company commander at that time, Captain Glen C. Long, took the gung-ho infantryman's usual pleasure in watching us pale-faced weaklings squirm in misery as we lined up in the oozing mud at company formation before dawn, shivering, soaking wet, and feeling terribly sorry for ourselves on that first dreary morning. As it turned out, this would be the ritual we'd be forced to start with every day. This method of attempting to make men out of us continued for months to come as we didn't have the pleasure of seeing the sun begin to shine again until January.

We soon learned that the cadre sent to Camp White in advance of our arrival to whip us into shape were previously rough-and-tumble 1st Cavalry noncommissioned officers and commissioned officers, most of whom had come out of Fort Bliss, Texas. That bit of alarming news quickly began to sink in when those seasoned roughnecks began to put us through our paces.

First Sergeant Joseph Higdon from Waco, Texas, usually ran the show with firmness and a no-bullshit attitude. As a pusillanimous tenderfoot, I was forced to both despise and respect his professional, soldierly temperament for the next year and a half, until he was transferred to a rifle company. Later he was killed while gallantly attempting to be a one-man army trying to destroy well dug-in enemy positions at the dreaded Gothic Line. From what I had witnessed and will relate in the pertinent chapter, he went down bravely shooting from the hip John Wayne style before he was cut down.

With all his gruffness, he was always fair in his treatment of me, the so-called Jew-boy in his outfit. Most of the other Southern-bred, hill-country noncoms referred to men of my faith in much more derogatory terms. Fortunately, that attitude changed rapidly after the real shooting began eighteen months later, but that's another chapter.

For the next few years, I was unwittingly to become thoroughly educated in Americana. Fresh out of Los Angeles' Belmont High in 1938, I could never have guessed that what I had often wondered at, or seen on the magic movie screen, was real. One might call them hillbillies, horse soldiers, or Li'l Abners, even rednecks, but I was learning from these men that the United States of America was made up of a very broad range of citizens, not necessarily at all like me.

Chapter 2

The First Ninety Days

Let the neophyte soldier beware! The first ninety days you spend in a military camp are designed to be a crash course in learning to hate. You can bet your combat boots that they're going to do their damnedest to make you as miserable as possible, as fast as possible. Maybe you were a sweet-natured kid before you got here, but this isn't Elm Street, son. It never was and never will be, and the top sergeant sure ain't going to love you like your mama.

I could almost hear the chortle of those macho, hill-country horse soldiers, rubbing their calloused palms together in glee at a secret powwow just before we innocent inductees arrived.

"Let's make this lily-assed batch of rookies wish they were never born!"

"Yahoo!"

"Yee-hah!"

Make no mistake that these were one tough bunch of hombres whose strange new language was one totally unknown to Berlitz. We had to quickly get accustomed to the hysterical barking noises of military commands, typical of sounds made only by non-coms and angry German shepherds. "Teh, shah!" (attention), "Harray, heh!" (parade rest), "Rah, fay!" (right face), "Patoo, bow fay!" (platoon, about face), "Hoewa, har!" (forward march), and so on, were some of the many, repetitive stentorian shouts you're clobbered with and are expected to understand from the first moment you arrive.

The quicksandlike mud and puddles of standing brown water were dishearteningly everywhere, and you'd damned well better get those grimy, slime-filled shoes cleaned up for inspection by — when? Well, you never knew. We found out early that inspections of your bed, your foot locker, and you could occur just about every day, and if everything wasn't exactly, and I do mean precisely, up to snuff, they'd take the greatest pleasure in teaching you an abhorrent new trade called latrine duty. But if you were lucky, you might instead only have to do a few thousand push-ups in the nearest pool of slime.

The blanket on your bunk had to be as tight as a drum. If the inspecting officer couldn't bounce a coin off your blanket to his satisfaction, he would delight in dumping blanket, sheets, and all on the floor, preparatory to your second and third attempt. It was the same for your footlocker, a small, wooden trunk in front of your bunk. We were shown only once how to keep everything we owned in perfect order within its limited space, and the punishment for a sloppy footlocker was the same, its contents dumped on the floor to be redone as often as necessary until you made the inspecting sergeant or lieutenant ecstatic with your neatness.

The day came too soon when they handed you a rifle, and you'd better fall madly in love with it. Those were their words then, mine eighteen months later. Even though the klutzy, yard-long contraption seemed to weigh close to a hundred pounds in your, as yet, frail condition, you were expected to learn to toss it around like a kid's balsa-wood toy.

"Rah-sholdaa, hah!" (right shoulder arms), "Peezeh, hah!" (present arms).

It quickly became apparent both to me and the drill sergeant in charge how flabby our city-boy muscles were, after an hour of close-quarter drill with that miniature cannon. Sadistically, it seemed, his next pleasure was for each of us to take apart every miniscule piece of that M-1 rifle and learn to put it back together in about three minutes, blindfolded. If you lost this game too often, you could find yourself fumbling with those elusive tiny parts until the bugle blew taps, thus missing dinner.

After all this petty soldierly crap, you'd learn after a while that it was better to try to be agreeable, to hate them quietly, but to do what they wanted in order to avoid the myriad barbarous punishments these professionals had so cleverly gleaned from the days of the Spanish Inquisition.

If it weren't for an unusual sweetheart of a guy, Sergeant Myron Sheldon, who hailed from Sleepy Eye, Iowa, I think I would have been driven over the edge, to transfer to something more akin to the Boy Scouts, or to a Section Eight nut house. That wise, handsome young man was the exception to the rule. In charge of the thirty inductees in my part of the barracks, he ran it with surprising evenhandedness as well as a firm, closed fist when needed. He taught us well without being ridiculously overbearing and helped me personally get through those initial grueling months with fewer mental scars and bruises. I later attempted to emulate him, in many ways, after earning my own stripes.

I missed him sorely when he transferred to the paratroopers the next year. After the war ended, I wrote to him, mainly to brag but in a subtle way. Still a brash twenty-five-year-old, I had the chutzpah to gloat about my awards and my part in the war. However, I also wanted to let him know the depth of my attempt to imitate his inspirational leadership. I wasn't sure that he was still among the living. So many weren't. Happily, I received his reply, which was typical Sheldon, barely touching on the serious wounds he had received when he jumped in the invasion of France and saying that he was OK now, working on something or other in Sleepy Eye. I think of him often and hope that his life has been good.

As if things weren't bad enough, the dismal rain continued, seeming as though it would never end and doing nothing for the pallor, morale, and soggy, shapeless uniforms of all the alarmed draftees like me who, by this time, probably feared that Noah's ark would soon make an appearance. Was it possible we'd continue this nightmarish basic training, two by two, in a camp on Mount Ararat? Rain or not, like it or not, the complete regimen of infantry basic training continued nonstop throughout that cold, miserable winter.

Private First Class Lloyd Gallegos of Denver taught me to handle my rifle properly while lying prone in the oozing mud. It completely amazed me that the way you wrap those leather straps around your arm could be so critical in order to shoot straight.

I suppose that, not wishing to take any chances of my shooting up one of my own, the Army provided me with a pair of repugnant GI eyeglasses to help make me a better marksman. They should also have provided me with a government issue field towel to wipe them with because the damned things would fog up immediately with my perspiration. Later, we were given a balm of some kind to wipe them with to avoid that persistent cloudiness. I don't know which was worse, the supposedly corrective balm, which didn't do a thing to help, or my steamy sweat. I tried my best not to wear those glasses, even though the Navy would be horrified to know that. Yet, somehow or other, I managed to earn my sharpshooters' medallion eleven months later. In retrospect, I understand now why I had tried so hard to learn to shoot well then. Somehow, I had correctly foreseen that my ass was going to be on the line, as later chapters will demonstrate.

Rudely awakened at five A.M. with shouts of "Up and at 'em," "Get your ass in gear," or "Last one in formation gets to do latrine duty," you try your damnedest to get your bunk and your body in inspection-passable condition as fast as possible. If you weren't out of your bed as soon as the last notes of the bugle sounded, you would find that you and your bunk were tipped over, your body greeting the new day from the level of the cold, rough wooden floor. Standing reveille in the miserable rain, then finally eating breakfast at 5:45 A.M. took a hell of a lot of getting used to.

One of the Army's glaring accomplishments that remains in my mind from those punishing early days was that they always managed to fill our tables with more than enough to eat. For breakfast, there usually were heaps of fried eggs cooked over-medium, and I'd eat six or more. Sometimes there'd be pancakes and, almost always, the ubiquitous Spam main course. Never one to be a religious fanatic, I didn't seriously mind that it happened to consist of a concoction of forbidden ham and whatever else they had chosen to doctor it with. I ate it and almost learned to enjoy it.

Several times a week, we'd be lavished with something our old cavalry men called shit-on-a-shingle. Totally alien to Jewish kitchens, this concoction of chipped beef served in a thick, gooey white gravy on toast appeared disgusting to my frightened ethnic eyes. I might have tried to taste it once or twice but, in the short run, could never get past the sight of it.

We'd go through our training routine for the rest of the day, then after what seemed like endless years later, we'd end up in the privacy of our bunks, physically and mentally worn to a frazzle. Only after the lights were turned off did we begin to sense relief or have time to suffer the terribly gnawing homesickness of violent separation. In the darkness, no one could see your tears or read your mind. I cannot say that I didn't lose sleep, often fearfully wondering if, amidst this hopeless chaos, I'd ever see home again, realizing only too well that many of those around me wouldn't. But who? Dead tired as we were, sleep fortunately came quickly more often than not.

The day came when the rain finally ended after almost three soggy months. It was then that I began to show the first signs of outgrowing my immaturity as I became more and more the accomplished rookie, looking and feeling more like the man the Army posters promised I'd be. Those forced marches, running with full field packs, lengthy calisthenics every day, and push-ups couldn't help but have a noticeable effect on my previously soft and feeble body.

Less frightened by blustering minor officials now, I was ready to move ahead.

Chapter 3

After the Rain

One of several important turning points in my three-year career as a soldier occurred when it became my turn to pull KP. The term is an abbreviation for kitchen police, which is deceiving because to police simply means to keep in order or supervise. In actuality, it was just another word for clean-up duty.

After only a few hours of sleep, two other lowly buck privates and I had to report to the kitchen for duty at the ungodly hour of 2:30 A.M. Greeted by the surly mess sergeant in charge, we were shown a pile of crockery and flatware and told to put out place settings on the ten-foot barbecue-style wooden tables, all twenty of them, over 200 place settings in all. Occasionally these dishes would merely be stacked near the chow line as if for a buffet, but not this morning.

Every so often, we'd have to stop and clean up the culinary garbage, wash and scrub the pots and utensils as Sergeant H_____ ordered us to, then empty the cooking grease into forty-gallon drums to be recycled into soap or something, who knows what, for the war effort. We'd have to be damned sure that the food platters would be ready and on the tables when the company came in to eat at 5:45 A.M.

Dog tired as we were, there would be no relief for the KP crew. We had yet to clear off the tables when the men left, see to it that the dishes, flatware, and huge, steel cooking containers were thoroughly washed again and the whole room swept clean and readied for inspection. Then a ton of potatoes had to be neatly peeled for the next meal.

God help us if the mess sergeant didn't pass those occasional spot-check inspections. We'd be sure to be uncordially invited to do it all over again tomorrow. If he found a fleck, the tiniest spot, you could bet he'd bellow like a Banshee and make your life a living hell. His motto was, "Private, better give your heart to God, 'cause your ass is mine!"

The rest of that terribly long day followed with a similarly sadistic procedure after the final meal was served. You'd think we would have earned some time off after that, but no. We'd have to fall in at reveille the next morning just like everyone else and drag ourselves through some new form of training punishment that had been gleefully prepared for us by the company commander, more fiendish fun and games to be played out in the muddy fields near the Rogue River in the vicinity of Camp White.

After kitchen duty was over very, very late that night, I showered and fell onto my bunk feeling badly beaten by the GI system. Yet, as miserable as my body felt, my brain began to do some serious thinking. I was mad as hell and wasn't going to take it anymore. But yelling it out the window would not be practical in the barracks and would only succeed in getting me another day in the mess hall.

Only privates did KP, and in no way did I want to continue to be a lowly private. But how was I to achieve such a herculean promotion to corporal after only three months in the service?

It occurred to me that, since the battalion already had a couple of clerk-typists and I had recently been reassigned to the battalion's intelligence and reconnaissance (I and R) section, it might be wise to study like crazy, learn to read a compass better than anyone else, and work doubly hard at map reading. I would do things the Army way, by the numbers. Only then would it be possible to get a promotion and end my frustration with KP and all the other so-called police duties.

From then on, when the others were playing poker, I studied. The trick of reading and understanding compasses and azimuths, for me and most all of the men in the company, had to be almost as hard as learning Greek, but I was determined. I had always been lousy at algebra, and any kind of math scared the heck out of me, but I feverishly put my mind to learning the compass until I knew its clever little ways backwards and forwards. I'd make it pay off.

Within two months, I had become quite adept and felt ready to teach my simplified system to non-coms, officers, or anyone, without the slightest fear or stage fright. The lieutenant in charge of my section, as well as the company commander and his staff, couldn't help but become aware of my achievement. First, I managed to work the miracle within my own I and R squad, making good use of the time we would otherwise have to spend with regular field maneuvers. The blackboard in our recreation room served as my podium, and I made myself as obnoxiously obvious as possible.

"Weckstein?" Captain Long's stentorian voice with its Texan phrasing always sounded like a question to me, ending as it always did on the higher note. "I'd like ya'all to do a class in map reading every morning at 1100 (11:00 A.M.) for all the company non-coms and enlisted men? Any problem with that?"

"No, sir! No problem, sir." As if I had an iron poker up my butt, I made it a point to stand as straight as a ramrod, stating the obvious with conviction and sending him an extra snappy salute that West Point would have been proud of.

Success! I knew full well that I was edging closer to earning those two significant and invaluable stripes I'd been busily bucking for.

I taught all comers at least two or three times a week, and strangely enough, it turned out to be more satisfying for me than for the men who attended my blackboard lectures and field trips. These efforts soon earned me those elusive stripes, the ones that would — thank God and amen! — keep me off the KP roles permanently. It also placed me in line to take full command of the ten men in my section, if I had it in me to become their sergeant, but that had to be earned another way, the hard way, almost a year later.

Wait a minute. These were no five-foot-six-inch kids I could push around. Strapping, hardy, back-country lads, most of them, they had the ability to swat this corporal-come-lately like a fly. Talk about second thoughts! How was I to overcome my sudden timidity in the shadow of these six-footers? But I had the fever now, and as the old saying goes, I had made my bed and was determined to lie in it, no matter what.

So it came to pass that I had to get used to the sound of my own voice as I became the one who barked those ridiculous sounding orders and who would show no mercy. Well, hardly any.

Since I couldn't suddenly grow eight inches or take a thirty-day Charles Atlas course, I struggled for answers. I had to offer the squad something more tangible than map reading if they were going to respect me and, ultimately, follow me into battle, whenever that fateful day would come.

Then it hit me. To gain my men's trust and respect, I would lead off with my best skill, which was distance running. Before being drafted, the one thing I could do well was to run, not fast but far. Whenever I felt angry with my stepmother or after a spat with my wife, I'd leave the house and run, block after city block, never bothering to count the distance and, somehow, never running out of breath. I had always been lousy at arguing, so jogging became the psychological outlet that would loosen the knot in my stomach.

"Okay, men. We're going to go a mile this morning." They looked at me strangely, wondering what this was all about, but we ran. First, I started them out with one mile, then graduated to two and more. We did this for months, at least an hour or so every day, our speed and distance depending on the time available in our schedule. I'm sure they must have enjoyed those runs as much as I did, and it felt like one hell of a rush to me when we finally got back to our barracks, heart and lungs pounding. I truly believe that they mutely and unanimously shared that same sense of exultation.

All of us were beginning to feel our oats now, slowly becoming much more hardened and inured to the daily pummelings of Captain Long's basic training schedule. Compared to the sad sacks we once were when first inducted, we became a different crew. Was it only four and a half months ago?

Besides the fact that my chest had begun to expand noticeably and a healthy, ruddy glow replaced my once-ashen pallor, I found that I had gained enormous confidence in my ability to cope with almost any situation, totally unlike the former uncertain klutz I used to be.

From that first plodding mile around the rutty roads of Camp White in February 1943 until the hallowed day of our discharge from active duty two and a half years later, I was never to be challenged, never harassed. Happily, my little section of men had accepted me and even took a kind of quiet, competitive pride in their own ability, ultimately proving themselves to be a strong and dynamic force in the field later, besides being awfully good at map reading.

Becoming somewhat primed for junior command as I was at that time, I'd occasionally take a psychological inventory of the personality of my men, as I now inwardly referred to them. I was extremely fortunate. Handsome hunks that they were, not one of these guys had the temperament to get into trouble during their occasional passes into the nearby town of Medford. Short-arm (penis) inspections to test for gonorrhea were held once a week, and I couldn't care less. I had been lucky enough to inherit a great bunch of upright characters from every corner of the country, which helped my command run as smoothly as anyone could wish.

The battalion's S-2 (intelligence section) officer, young Lieutenant S_____, was the head honcho who took charge of our I and R section. Built like a middleweight boxer, the oafish twenty-eight-year-old back-woodsman would grin like a schoolboy as he did his best to set us up as an example of his own prowess, pushing us as hard as he could in all phases of our training. It seemed to me that the ambitious lieutenant was attempting to emulate some dauntless hero he idolized. One would think that, with all his bravado, he would be certain to win the Congressional Medal of Honor. Although simple, quiet, and innately shy, he was extremely determined to deserve his single, shiny, gold-colored bar. He put my platoon through the hoops without mercy until that very first earth-shattering day of battle in Italy. That turned out to be his last day with us, as will be explained in a later chapter.

It was a paradox how so many of the most obviously gung-ho, give-'em-hell type of young man cracked under real combat conditions, not that I could or would ever blame them. Adjusting to the terror of front-line action in the infantry seemed like the last fiery step before falling into the pits of Hades, as I would soon discover. Oddly, however, the true heroes amongst us usually turned out to be the sweet-natured, simple individuals who, under normal circumstances, wouldn't hurt a fly.

As third in command after Sergeant Sheldon and the lieutenant, I spent much of my time continuing to master the mental discipline I thought would be necessary to better our odds overseas. We even went so far as to learn to get our bearings from the stars during night maneuvers. I made a pest of myself instructing the men further in the arts of observation, more map reading, and directing artillery fire. As it turned out, these were the smartest things I could have done to end the war and do my part to alter its final outcome in the best way I knew how.

On the other hand, per his Fort Benning officer preparation course, Lieutenant S_____ spent most of our section's training time doing motorized reconnaissance maneuvers along the beautiful, pine-forested roads of Oregon. With the three jeeps assigned to us, and in a kind of leap-frog arrangement, the first four-man vehicle would move forward towards an imaginary objective while jeeps two and three would follow at a distance. When the lieutenant determined that some imaginary enemy had been seen or had fired on us, he'd hand signal the others and hop out, taking cover while all the vehicles would disperse off the road and into the woods before we would return fire. At that time, assuming we were still alive, he or we would quickly report to base by radio as much information as possible about the estimated size, strength, and location of the enemy, then wait for further instructions.

We practiced these war games over and over for the distinct pleasure of our young commander, perfecting it to a science, but in combat, it almost never happened that way. Coming into motorized contact with a retreating enemy could and did occur but not often enough to warrant the year we spent in its practice. As we found out later, it was considerably more important to read the map and direct artillery fire at appropriate targets and let the rifle company patrols and armored vehicles do most of the mobile reconnaissance, each pursuing the foe in its own most effective way.

He had learned to play one game well, but to my way of thinking then, much of the combat training these young officers received needed a heck of a lot of revising and updating.

In the end, we all had to learn the hard way.

Chapter 4

Mischief and Maneuvers

S unday! I took advantage of my first half-day pass to visit Medford. It was a small town then, with one movie house and a pretty, tree-lined main street five blocks long, surrounded by acres of barren pear orchards and lush pine forests. The pear trees would leaf out and blossom soon, now that the weather had turned for the better.

As thirty or so furloughed men loaded onto the GI bus, or cattle car as we called it, I felt curiously estranged, and lost long before even arriving at the bus stop downtown. I had known this lonely feeling many times before in my life and had learned how to manage it, how to shake off that orphanage-home sensation of emptiness I had experienced as a child. I worked extra hard at managing it again now but not without dampening much of the enjoyment I anticipated from this escape to the city. Now I knew why the other guys in camp traveled in pairs.

I followed the crowd off the bus for a bit, and when they scattered in different directions, I was alone again, walking down unfamiliar streets for a long, comfortless hour peering absently into store windows. In my cheerless state, the change of scenery offered little excitement, and my only option was to make for the bright neon lights of Medford's lone movie house.

Some Fred Astaire picture followed by a hamburger steak in a café around the corner filled those four long hours before I could reboard the noisy bus back to Camp White. Others had gotten aboard before me, and with limited ventilation, the air reeked offensively of cheap bourbon and scotch. A few had been attempting to harmonize the perennial favorite "Home on the Range" that would be sung on almost every bus trip I ever took returning to camp. At that moment, I felt little need to join in.

I decided I wouldn't be going to town often. It was better to hang around the rec room, listen to good music, or catch up on some letter writing and reading. Television hadn't been invented yet, and the camp movie house changed the rerun flick only once a week, limiting that possibility of escape from reality.

A few weeks later, someone told me about a dance that a church in Medford was sponsoring for the social benefit of the uniformed men at Camp White. Anxious for any change of pace, I decided to go.

To my delight, I found it sparsely attended by my comrades. No more than thirty-five or so fidgety, nervous soldiers were there, along with a similar number of gussied-up young women, milling around the church meeting hall, waiting to be asked to dance. Several couples were already shuffling to the mellow sounds of Tommy Dorsey's trombone playing "Getting Sentimental Over You" as I arrived.

I thought I looked great in my fresh uniform but couldn't shake that suppressed, insecure feeling of appearing boyishly unsophisticated and out of place among these charming, well-dressed ingenues. Never having particularly enjoyed dancing and, aside from partaking of the punch and pastries served by the chaperones, I began to wonder how long it would be before I'd run out of patience just watching the more adept couples on the dance floor. It frustrated me no end that they seemed to know instinctively what to do with their feet. I looked on, feeling like a social outcast.

Having always been known in my teens as the quiet one at school affairs, I had always pruriently reveled in the thought of one day being rescued by a lovely, take-charge type of maiden. Apparently, my idle wish managed to telegraph itself across the dance floor that evening. One particular enchantress was offering me more attention than I'd ever been accustomed to receiving. She kept edging in my direction as I roamed aimlessly around the room. Each time I turned, I could see her looking in my direction and smiling. Helpless, I could only smile back.

Sipping the pinkish punch out of a Dixie cup, I strolled out to the unlit side porch, curious to see if she'd follow, all the while nursing an uneasy guilt. After all, I was supposed to be happily married and had never had the slightest reason to stray; yet, I found it difficult to control an intense inner need for some kind of feminine company.

Suddenly, she was there. I'm sure I must have blushed like mad. I wasn't sure how to act or what to say.

"My name is Alice. What's yours?"

I told her. There it was. She had broken the ice.

"Wouldn't you rather go inside and dance?" she asked, sensing my nervousness.

"Not particularly. It's too nice a night," I responded with false bravado, listening to the recording of "Dipsy Doodle" and trying to imagine myself jitterbugging to it, making a real ass of myself. "I'm a lousy dancer, and anyhow, it's great being out here alone with you," I continued. I was almost sorry that those flirty words had slipped off my tongue. I couldn't take them back at this point and waited to hear her response.

"Then you won't mind dancing out here where no one can see us," she said, tugging at my quivering hand and pulling me up from the stoop.

Fortunately, the tempo of the music had changed. Alice was unusually light on her feet, and as we started to dance, her gracefulness gave me more confidence in my own ability. Together in the dark, we moved to the slow, seductive rhythm of the recording that emanated from inside, humming the haunting melody of "Once in a While."

The combination of my dance partner's perfume and her inviting openness stoked a smoldering fire within me and the need to hold her closer. Slowly but surely, it increasingly provoked the torrent of my raging testosterone further.

"This kind of dancing I could learn to like," I whispered, as our ears poignantly brushed then pressed warmly against each other.

Apparently, I had said and done the right thing because Alice took my hand again and pulled me towards the bottom tier of steps that led down to the garden's fence. Snuggling up with her back to me as we sat there in the dark, nearly out of sight, it would have been virtually impossible for me at that moment to think about rejecting any advances she might choose to make.

Inside, they had begun to dance to the hypnotic beat of a conga, following a leader around the room. Although our feet tapped out the rhythm and we were only a few yards from the boisterous hustle and bustle, I felt as if we were light years away. The smell and texture of her hair as it brushed my face and draped sensually across my cheek was incredible seductive, driving me up the wall.

After a bit more inane conversation, I began to feel relaxed, even adventurous. Amorously, I kissed her neck, and through her light, cashmere sweater, my nervous hands reached for her soft, proffered breasts. The only clue that I had touched a sensitive nerve was the sound of her slight gasp. Alice didn't move away. If anything, she cuddled closer. From then on, our lips and bodies were seldom apart.

It has always been my opinion that, if asked, most sensitive men would admit to heartily enjoying the sensual aggressiveness occasionally displayed by the so-called weaker sex. This feminine forwardness removes most of the formidable guesswork out of how far you can go or if you can even go there. You can have your prim and proper Miss Goodie Two-shoes. I'd take the Alice type anytime.

Time flew. A few lively couples still remained inside dancing, but the moment quickly approached when the social would conclude. With the playing of "Goodnight Sweetheart," I knew it had all to come to an end.

If I didn't look back, if I just kissed her and walked away, I could hold on to this marvelous memory and afterward find it comparatively easy to purge myself of the inherent guilt. But as I would find out later, she hadn't planned the same conclusion. As I left her that night, she was dewy eyed, silent. I felt terribly remorseful. Like a kid caught with his hand in the cookie jar, I realized we had gone too far. I knew as sure as hell that I'd be hearing from her again, and the thought scared me.

Why, after only six months away from home, should I have even dared entertain thoughts and sensations that would create such a scrambled mess of my hormones? As much as I try, I'll never understand these occasional satyric feelings. As much as I thought I loved my wife then, there was very little I could have done to discourage such a sensually delightful suitor.

For whatever reason, I badly needed her affection at that point in time, and maybe Alice, too, hungered for the same elusive emotional thrill. As I wore no ring on my finger, she must have assumed that I was available for much more, and with little thought, I took advantage of that romantic moment but never bedded her.

Now that I'm reminded of her fifty-five years later, I'd like her to know, if she should happen to read this, that I've always wished her a happy life.

A few days after that piquant episode, our division was deployed to Bend, Oregon, for three weeks of serious, warlike maneuvers.

Although I've been told by Oregonians that Bend is now quite a metropolis, I find that almost impossible to believe. When I first saw it in 1943, it was a ten-thousand-square-mile desert of volcanic residue covered by fine ash, very much like how I imagine Pompeii must have appeared after its futile bout with Mount Vesuvius. There we were, thousands of olive-drab intruders amidst a smattering of gray-green, pumice-coated junipers, making tracks in the fine lava soot that covered miles of rarely used trails. By contrast, all this wasteland was wreathed by snow-capped mountains that stretched as far as the eye could see.

It was here that we waited for the Blues to attack the Reds, and vice versa, in this no-man's-land of nature's once hot volcanic excrement. In the midst of our first sham battle, my squad came across a small country store at a crossroads. I called for a ten-minute break to give the men a chance to indulge in cokes and candy. As for me, not having tasted an olive since leaving home, I chose, from all the things on the grocer's shelf, a can of pitted black jumbos and indulged myself. Why, of all the things on the grocer's shelf, did I select a can of olives? Who knows.

Would that combat were as guileless and facile as those maneuvers. For the next several weeks, we played toy soldier for the commanding officers who moved us around like pawns. Hopefully, they gained something more from that disorderly chess match than we foot soldiers did. One of the disadvantages of being an enlisted man in the infantry was being kept in the dark most of the time. Commissioned officers were generally informed about our objectives and what it meant in the big picture. We dogfaces just followed orders.

The joke of the week came when my men and I infiltrated behind enemy lines and captured a truck pulling a 105mm cannon, separating it from the tail end of a column of Blues. This trick couldn't possibly be repeated in a battle with the more proficient Wehrmacht. But our prisoners, the artillery commander and his non-coms in charge of the complement that my platoon had managed to snare that day, had hopefully learned to be more alert for when the real thing would get under way in Italy.

Another unforgettable highlight was when I was ordered to get into a Piper Cub plane to study how camouflage on the ground appears from a few thousand feet up. I had never flown in my life and was horrified. All the officers and two non-coms from each company had to participate in the study. I thought, God, why me?

"Wouldn't you rather show it to one of the other higher-ranking men?" I asked the pilot, quietly wishing to die.

"Get in," he ordered, brooking no further discussion.

Reluctantly, I did. I held my breath and climbed into that two-seater con-traption made like a cloth and wire kite, wondering what in the hell I was doing and why I was doing it, praying for some kind of miracle to save me.

The pilot laughed. "Relax, kid. I'll bring you back alive."

That son-of-a-bitch pilot never even gave me a chance to look at the cam-ouflage on the ground. He did a few inside loops and dives, waiting impatiently for me to heave my guts, but as much as I would have liked to give back my breakfast, I'd never give him the satisfaction.

"This is what we do when we want to get down in a hurry," I heard him yell before he made a beeline straight down towards the tiny, makeshift airport.

I didn't learn a damn thing about camouflage, and I swore to myself that if I ever got out of that thing alive I'd never fly again. But I do fly today and look forward to those occasions immensely because I think I really did learn something up there, especially how not to vomit. So what else could they do me?

As far as I was concerned, those three weeks of gritty maneuvers at Bend were mainly an education in the regimen of sleeping outdoors in slit trenches, using repulsive straddle-trench latrines, and dining alfresco on distastefully cold K rations and C rations.

One cannot adequately describe those canned C rations of cold Vienna sausages, clumpy baked beans, and a few other quite forgettable delicacies that we hardly ever had the time or opportunity to heat up. Strangely enough, one can get used to them, if hungry enough. Within the Cracker-Jack-sized, waxed cardboard box of K rations were some interesting edibles that, unfortunately, needed cooking. I very much looked forward with relish to the can of raw bacon which, of course, was impossible to eat unless I had time and a fire to fry it up. Dessert was either a tin of pudding or a surprisingly delicious fruit bar which appeared to be a tightly compressed brick of prunes, dates, raisins, and who knows what else. All hail the fruit bar! That little miracle got me by then as well as through many days of combat when the real war came along. It should have won a Michelin five-star award for culinary perfection, and it didn't even need cooking.

Almost every day, after the feigned battles had been fought, we'd have to bare most of our bodies, at least the parts we couldn't see, to a so-called tick buddy. Ticks were prevalent in that rural region, and the little buggers, about the size of a very small ladybug, could be extremely hard to find because they'd burrow most of their tiny, blood-sucking bodies beneath your skin. If overlooked, the insidious Rocky Mountain spotted fever they could cause meant extreme illness, even death. Once you discovered one, you'd have to burn the little leech out of your flesh, using the tip of a lit cigarette. Attempting to pull it out with your fingernails wouldn't work because, I was told, it would grow a new body onto the poisonous bloodsucking head that remained under your skin.

To add to the fun, we also had to be very cautious of poisonous rattlesnakes as well as battle pesky mosquitoes that caused us to have to sleep under netting.

During the second week of maneuvers, I received a letter from Alice. She had written a three-page emotional note and mailed it to my company's Army post office address. She wanted me to know that she was feeling badly that I hadn't bothered to get in touch with her since that wonderful night. She wondered if I still felt the same way about her as I seemed to take such pleasure in her nearness when we had been together. If I didn't answer, she said she'd try to understand and vowed never to contact me again.

The truth was that it made me feel lousy. I felt like a bastard for having led her on, even though it was just for that one short interlude. Yes, it was a wonderful night, one I could hardly ever forget, but I just didn't have guts enough to answer her impassioned letter. Hopefully, she'd take the hint, poor kid. She couldn't know what a pusillanimous jerk she had taken up with.

In my way, I still feel something for you, Alice, no matter what you might think of me. The harmless bit of flirtation and petting was unforgettable for me, as I hoped it could have been for you. In retrospect, however, if you and I could move the clock back, if we could do it all over again under the same circumstances, would we?

Later in Italy, whenever I was lonely enough and the opportunity presented itself, there would be other Alices, although their names sounded more like Gina, Maria, or Giulianna, wonderfully musical names that rolled off the tongue like honey.

⊷ ⚌✦⚌ ⊶

Just before returning to camp from maneuvers, I learned that my good friend and superior, Sergeant Sheldon, seeking more action, had arranged for and received his transfer to the paratroopers. I would miss him greatly and thought of him often as I soon assumed not only his staff sergeant stripes but also the heady responsibilities that he had taken so seriously. I hoped that a little of his profound, cool-headed Iowan wisdom had rubbed off on me.

Chapter 5

Get Ready, Set, Go

Shortly after we returned from maneuvers, I was handed printed orders that allowed me to make the leap from corporal to the rank of a rocking-chair staff sergeant. It had been named that because the accompanying insignia was a chevron with three stripes pointed upward and a single arched stripe on the bottom that created the appearance of a rocker. I held this rank until my discharge almost two years later.

With this important advancement to S-2 intelligence sergeant, I became one of the privileged insiders and could almost write my own ticket. The important promotion and the extra few bucks I would earn allowed me to send for my wife and move her from Los Angeles to an inexpensive room of our own not far from camp. I could now spend Sundays and most of my nights with her, even though it meant I had to get up at 4:30 A.M. each frigid morning to catch the bus back to camp in time for reveille. I swore to myself that when and if I ever got back to civilian life, I'd never take a job that got me up before 7:00 in the morning.

For some unknown reason, the division had moved further north to Camp Adair near Albany, Oregon. In looking for our own place, my wife and I discovered Mrs. Evans' attic in the tree-filled suburban township boasting the name Independence, located about a thirty-five-minute drive from camp barracks.

Hands deep in our pockets to keep warm, we shuffled through crimson and gold leaves that covered the rain-wet sidewalks until we found the advertised house. Mrs. Evans greeted us at the door of her home, a two-story plus, white Cape Cod cottage that she and her sister had shared since her husband died a few years before. Widow Evans, who had decided to rent out her decent-sized attic for the supplemental income, thought the best chance of renting it quickly was to someone in the military.

As landladies go, she wasn't bad, but I will never forget that first evening at her home when her curiosity got the better of her. She quizzed us about everything as we sat cozily around the fireplace in her parlor. At some point during the uncomfortable inquisition, she asked our religion.

"We're Jewish."

An embarrassing silence followed until she regained her color, then slowly and politely she said, "Well, you don't look any different."

In all honesty, I don't think she had ever seen a Jew in her small community and was genuinely surprised at our conventional demeanor. We had no horns, no hooked noses, and no skullcaps to set us apart from any other gentile. We had to be quite an eye-opener for these rurally cloistered Evans sisters.

Although they offered us the use of their kitchen, we ate in restaurants most of the time to avoid frightening them with the pungent, spicy aromas of our delicious ethnic food.

Life was simple in Independence in those days before television. I would take Mrs. Evans' skittish old bullterrier for walks in the damp night air, or we would sit around the fireplace and chat, or for a big night out, we would see a movie on Main Street four blocks away.

Our quiet rural existence didn't last very long. Within four months, the long-dreaded alert we had been awaiting was called, and I'd see my wife no more until I returned from overseas a long year and a half later. It wasn't a total surprise as we both knew it would happen this way.

Say your good-byes, soldier, and say them with feeling because there is a hell of a good probability you'll not get to say hello again unless you are one of the lucky ones who come back, and the odds are definitely not stacked in your favor, not when you are in the infantry.

Why should the Army give a hoot that my wife was pregnant? It was time for my outfit to leave, and there could be no appeal during those traumatic times, so that was that.

Where were we headed? East or west? No one would say, not until we took the highly-secret train ride to some unfamiliar embarkation point.

Those last two days in camp readying for the war that was almost upon us can only be described as chaotic. Extraordinary shifts in personnel, too many equipment inspections, and a general attitude of hurry up and wait had the whole camp on edge. No one was permitted to go off base, and the post exchange quickly sold out of its supply of tobacco, candy, and paperback books before we were eventually restricted to barracks.

One day before my company was to get on that train to wherever, word came down from division headquarters that I was to be transferred immediately to Special Service Company, presumably to entertain our men overseas.

Before being drafted, I had been seriously pursuing a singing career. I had studied for several years with singing star Nelson Eddy's teacher in Beverly Hills and had auditioned with the MGM film studio where I was told I could get choral work in one of their famous musicals as soon as I applied for and received my union card. Wouldn't you know that, less than two weeks after that successful audition with the musical directors, Weckstein's Law decreed that I should receive my draft notice.

Following my induction, I did a lot of singing around camp, for local radio programs, and oddly enough, for protestant church services in and outside of our camp. Not surprisingly, there were no synagogues. I must have been asked to sing "The Lord's Prayer" at least fifty times during my year-and-a-half stay in Oregon. Apparently, that is why I was suddenly confronted with a change in plans.

I've never been quite sure who pulled the strings to arrange for that transfer, but whoever it was happened to be about one year too late. I had spent much time, energy, and effort honing my highly important craft as S-2 battalion intelligence sergeant and wasn't the least bit prepared to give it all up now. Although a part of me insisted, "Dummy, go for it. You'll improve your chances of getting home by at least ninety percent," the commanding voice within me still rebelled and refused to accept that radical change.

No matter what my personal wants were, however, one never dared argue with a directive from big brother at division headquarters. Next to God, there was no higher authority. So I schlepped my duffel bag that was already packed for the train ride onto a jeep and reported to Special Service Company located in a different solar system about a mile away. I knew that my wife would be thrilled with the news of my transfer and had begun to convince myself that I really had little choice in the matter.

All my friends in the division band were more than glad to see me, yet they could tell by my attitude that I was one unhappy soldier. I made no secret of the fact that, though nothing personal was intended and although we had worked together on many shows, I didn't belong with them at this time. I tried my best to explain to them that I had become a very efficient killing machine, much to the Army's delight, and so I was eager to do my part to get the damned war over with as soon as possible.

I bitched noisily about this transfer order and did everything except scream that whoever it was who had chosen to change my future at this last minute had to be nuts — well meaning, of course — but completely off his rocker.

"Sergeant, don't unpack."

Apparently, someone in high places had heard me. "Colonel Magill is requesting your transfer back to battalion. He says he needs you more than division." In less than two hours, they had rescinded my transfer. Fifteen minutes later, I was on my way back to my company, breathing a sigh of relief. It was nice to know that I was appreciated, that the battalion needed me that much.

But don't think for a single minute that I didn't have second thoughts after that strange twist of fate, because in every infantryman's mind there must always lurk terrible doubts, a chilling fear for one's own survival.

I wondered, had all this been preordained? Only time would tell.

Chapter 6

Off to War

With duffel bags stuffed to the gills and backpacks ready, we flopped around restlessly on our bunks. Only occasionally did someone interrupt the silence, hardly daring to offer the usual inane conversation that might somehow divert our attention from the queasy feelings we would not openly admit.

"Where do you think we're headed? Two to one it's England."

"Any of you guys see that new Grable flick? Cheez, she's built!"

"Yeah, I'd give a month's pay to get her in the sack for fifteen minutes right now. Anyone got an extra deck of cards?"

And so it went as we waited and waited.

We felt like miserable prisoners of the clock. The dingy, wooden barracks had become all too familiar, and by now we knew every knothole and crack in the stained, wooden floor and slatted ceiling. For what seemed like an eternity until we were to be called, no one felt like kidding around. Every man remained either perched on his bare mattress or foot locker, deep in his own thoughts or silent prayers.

It would do no good to write home because mail was no longer being accepted for fear of a possible breach of security. Ridiculous! We had absolutely no knowledge of where we were going, so what could we divulge? The Army's unwritten motto, hurry up and wait, seemed to be the order of the day, rather than the more common one, loose lips sink ships.

First Sergeant Higdon burst excitedly into the gloomy room.

"Weckstein, Lieutenant R_____ wants your ass down at headquarters on the double."

"What now?" I shot back, wondering what the brass had come up with.

"How the hell should I know? Just do whatever the hell he wants."

Everyone was on edge. I went.

"Sergeant, what the hell kind of code is this?" the lieutenant asked angrily as he waved a paper in front of my face. It was a letter, the last one I had written to my wife a few days ago. In it I had requested that she send me some pipe tobacco called Mixture 79 in her next package to me. That's what he was pointing to.

"Sir, it's a pipe tobacco. I smoke a pipe."

"Who do you think you're kidding, Weckstein? You and I know damn well it's a code."

"Sir, it's only pipe tobacco!" I tried to explain. "Honest! I smoke it in my pipe all the time." I showed him my leatherette tobacco pouch.

"No more of this crap, sergeant. We don't want our destination leaked." He handed me back the letter to remail, with the part about Mixture 79 cut out.

I saluted, turned, and left, seriously doubting if that ridiculous lieutenant had the slightest idea of where we were headed any more than I did. Even if I had known, I would never for one second take the chance of not getting there in one piece. Most officers seemed to have a grip on things, but not this cretin. Fortunately, I had little to do with his anti-tank platoon and didn't see much of him overseas.

Our commanding general had notified the big brass at the War Department that his 19,000 men were ready for action, and by the next morning, most of our 91st Infantry Division had departed camp. However, just before we boarded the trucks, our assertive new company commander, Captain C_____, called for yet another equipment inspection. In retrospect, I'm sure that all those redundant inspections had been called just to keep us busy and occupied at a feverish pitch.

Our previous company commander, Captain Glen C. Long, hard-driving taskmaster of the last year and a half, had been promoted to commander of the 363rd Infantry's 3rd Battalion. All through the Italian campaign, he deservedly filled that important post as a fiery and fearless lieutenant colonel, who retained his respected, superman image by one and all because he continuously displayed unflinching courage and superb leadership. Although I did not follow his career after I was discharged, I would bet that the man ultimately made general.

The strange thing about our regiment's three battalion commanders was that all of these men showed themselves to be superbly brave and highly intelligent professional fighting men. Of the two I worked most closely with, each was a perfect example of a leader that I would have followed anywhere, but interestingly enough, they were oceans apart in outward personality. While the rambunctious Colonel Long was noisily dynamic and dogmatically belligerent, my own revered 1st Battalion colonel, Ralph N. Woods, was completely the opposite. Invariably soft-spoken, he was a man of few but essential words. His graying hair and sober pensive face reminded me of how General George Washington might have appeared during the Revolutionary War. The lanky, middle-aged West Pointer was always surprisingly restrained in his manner of addressing the men and unbelievably calm in the face of battle. I hardly ever saw him flinch, even when we were at the wrong end of an artillery barrage.

Once you earned his respect, he was as malleable as putty in your hands, but that certainly was no easy task. I quickly learned to respect his modest composure after he reported in, just before we left for overseas.

When I heard that he had been a map reading teacher at West Point, I was a bit apprehensive. I hoped our joint effort would be a union made in heaven, one bound to succeed, but I knew this wouldn't be a simple walk in the park. No question, I would have to stay on my toes. Colonel Woods was destined to make good use of me, a lot more than either of us anticipated at the time. At last we heard the rumble of the big trucks coming to get us. Where we were headed was still anybody's guess, in spite of Lieutenant R_____'s insinuations. Would it be the east coast or west? Hopefully, it wouldn't be the Pacific, the dreaded Japanese theater of war, which the media had portrayed as a hellhole of disaster-ridden battlegrounds, each one viciously fought over in bloody combat on insignificant little palm-covered atolls, the names of which were impossible to remember.

In order to cover my behind and prepare for any eventuality, I had held classes for my section in basic Japanese, including martial terminology, military markings, and descriptions of their war equipment, hoping against hope that we'd never have to use that information. That terror-ridden area of the world beyond Hawaii, the mysterious Orient, seemed so alien, so foreboding to me. In no way did I envy our U.S. Marines who seemed to be taking the brunt of the action in that perilous sector.

The engine of the long train we loaded onto was pointed northeast, a good omen, but we all held our breath because the thing could be pushing instead of pulling, and one never knew for certain where we'd ultimately end up. For a while the men were quiet. Then a uniform sigh of relief emanated from every compartment of that train a short time later when we passed a railroad station sign marked "Welcome to Boise."

All at once the emotionally drained men grew boisterous and playfully rowdy again, obviously relieved to know our general destination. A ship would be waiting for us somewhere on the east coast.

Almost everyone used cigarettes in those days, and the train became absolutely filled with smoke. After being made prisoner to that tobacco-reeking train night and day, the overused toilets stinking of half-smoked cigarette butts and human waste, we finally arrived at Camp Patrick Henry, near Hampton Roads, Virginia. Everyone was glad to get their sore rear ends up and out into the brisk, clean, early-April air of the Atlantic seacoast.

Smelling most agreeably of the nearby Atlantic Ocean, the rickety old wooden barracks that awaited us appeared to be Civil War relics. I had never before seen a potbellied stove and watched fascinated as a tall man wearing a jacket with a huge, white PW, for prisoner of war, embossed on the back of it, brought wood to feed the huge metal contraption.

We were all amazed at how prisoners of war seemed to roam freely in and around our barracks at these camps, toiling happily at one thing or another. Only then did I realize that they probably preferred to be imprisoned here than be back in their miserable, war-torn homelands. At least for them, the war was over.

Two days later we boarded the massive, camouflaged liberty troop ship that would brave the waters of the submarine-infested Atlantic to transport us to our destiny with Hitler, somewhere in the European theater of operations, or so we assumed.

My regiment of well over three thousand men had been hastily loaded onto eight of these ships, each hulking vessel crammed to the rafters with supplies and troops. That valuable cargo of dazed and anxious young fighting men hadn't the slightest idea yet what port we were headed for on that chilly spring day in April of 1944, nor would we know until we got there.

The hammock bunks that were assigned to us were in triple tiers to preserve space. That entire lower deck in the belly of the ship looked as thought we were being stacked like sardines in a can, and I ventured to make that obvious comparison out loud. One of the Naval officers who was directing the boarding operation overheard my comment, and despite the oppressive darkness down there, I could see him stare through me with a venomous look in his eyes and sense his hostility born of weary concern.

"Sergeant, you'll take the damn top bunk," he said.

I wouldn't ever complain again, at least not out loud, from then on.

All duffel bags, backpacks, and rifles were stowed underneath the bottom-tiered hammock. Mess times and showers were made available to us on a tightly scheduled, company-by-company basis. The heads (latrines) were catch-as-catch-can.

Once we left the harbor and hit the rough Atlantic, I remember all too clearly getting desperately seasick, spending most of my time snuggling deep into my canvas berth, and attempting to find some relief in the fetal position. With no deliverance from that yellow-green nausea for five miserable days and nights, I recall seriously wishing I were dead.

Occasionally, I managed to struggle up to the top deck three landings above for some fresh air. There were a lot of poker games going on there, as well as games I'd never heard of, such as Acey-Deucy, which was the most popular. I never quite got the hang of that game, but I watched enthralled as a great deal of cash changed hands. I couldn't help feeling sorry for those poor, naïve pigeons who were literally losing the farm to the pros in the group who knew exactly what they were doing. With the bleak future that lay ahead, I could almost understand the feeling of tense futility among the losers and their tendency to go for broke.

The ship's mess below deck served up adequate and decent chow as I recall, but I had a hell of a time keeping it down and was never quite sure whether food was good or bad for this kind of prolonged, repugnant sickness. After eating as little as possible, I'd generally rush up to the main deck, gasp frantically at the fresh ocean air, and try to keep my knees from buckling. Then I'd talk soothingly to the contents of my stomach to persuade what still remained there to stay put.

Eventually, my digestive tract had reason to celebrate. After what seemed like an eternity of misery, my situation would soon take a turn for the better. I was ordered to report to our command post on the main deck where Colonel Woods stood, planning to request his sickly, haggard intelligence sergeant to handle a special assignment.

"Sergeant, you look like death warmed over." He looked at and through me with honest concern. The breeze had turned cold, and he turned up my collar. "Do you think you're up to creating a simple, hand-out newsletter for the men? It could be something with current events and entertaining banter, a sort of morale builder."

How could I say no?

"Move your gear to cabin A106 on the main deck," he continued. "It has a radio, mimeograph machine, and typing equipment ready to go. Try to get something out about every other day. Use an assistant if you need one, but get some damn rest first."

"Yes, sir! Thank you, sir!" I shouted into the wind.

I was saved! If I needed any further proof of my standing with this new battalion commander or, for that matter, heaven on high, this had to be it.

One of my men served as a gofer to bring coffee, print and distribute the copies, and generally just hang around to keep me company. Then every other day for the next few weeks, I listened to and reported all sorts of radio broadcasts, American, BBC, and others. I'd type and pass out the reams of mimeographed copies of my "1st Battalion News" to the men, meanwhile luxuriating as best I could in my pleasant, comfortable stateroom like a senior executive officer.

Now that I was working by day and sleeping comfortably at night on a comparatively plush mattress rather than the canvas hammock below, my skittish stomach soon settled down, much to my relief.

Then I chose to tempt fate. For whatever reason, some innate, danger-seeking quirk of mine tends to rear its ugly head when everything is going too well, and I manage to screw things up. That last week we were at sea, I became so good-humoredly complacent and drunk with my own power that I decided to manufacture my own news as a prank. I planned to do a limited production of this "1st Battalion News" bulletin of about thirty copies for distribution to a few of my comrades, guys in my company who I thought would be gullible, good-natured suckers.

I suppose at that time I had been wishfully hoping that a European invasion would occur before we got to wherever we were headed. Anyway, I sophomorically described General Eisenhower's armies deployed in an amphibious attack across the English Channel. I opted for the landings to take place along the French coast and even named points of infiltration, cities and towns I picked from the map, just as though I knew what I was doing. On paper I fiendishly attacked St. Lo and Cherbourg with airborne divisions, Holland with the British 8th Army, and Caen with two American infantry divisions. Then I had my innocent assistant pass out the limited number of copies of this phony twaddle to certain specified men on the gambling deck to see what would happen.

I really should have known better. It didn't take long before I was summarily called on the carpet.

"Where did you get this crap?" Colonel Woods asked angrily, handing me a copy. "What in the hell do you think you are doing?"

I could see that he was boiling mad and ready to chew my ass. Didn't he know he wasn't supposed to read the thing?

With sincere apologies, proper humility, and a cowering salute I left him, hoping it wouldn't mean the end of my cherished stateroom, let alone my stripes. Fortunately, it didn't, but I chided myself over and over again for stupidly gambling on the chance that my little joke wouldn't go very far. Dumb!

Two months after I produced this bit of fluff and nonsense, the announcement came that our forces really did attack the French coast, much to my astonishment, not much differently than I had described it in that never-to-be-forgotten "1st Battalion News" bulletin.

So, poor General Eisenhower could have consulted with me first before instigating his tactical invasion plans. Why wasn't he told that I was available to assist him no end with my own successful imaginary landing assaults? Most likely he would have seen to it that I was immediately promoted to full colonel and given the Congressional Medal of Honor. Of course!

The Navy battleships and destroyers that accompanied our convoy had to constantly drill and practice firing their weapons daily to stay in readiness for the probability of both air and submarine attacks. We and our own naval crew also had to train for similar misadventures as well as for the possibility of fire aboard ship. These practice alerts were standard, done on a regular basis, but as tyros, we never knew for sure if they were the real thing or not.

Toward the end of our second week at sea, a rare and improbable accident occurred on board. One afternoon the ship's frightening alarm sounded, a whooping and undulating siren that must have been the size of Manhattan, signaling all crewmen and Army personnel below to double-time it up for action on the main deck. At this same time, one of our convoy, a naval destroyer in the vicinity happened to be doing anti-aircraft practice with live ammunition. We watched the impressive aerial show for a while. Suddenly, one of their small explosive rounds accidentally smashed into our deck about twenty-five yards from where I had been standing in company formation. The splintering shell fragments hit three men, taking away a part of a lieutenant's stomach, but magically the other two men were only slightly wounded.

Later, after our crew had a chance to regain their composure, I watched with fascination as they transferred the lieutenant by a cable and portable sling cot to a more medically equipped destroyer that came almost alongside. Word came the next day that, fortunately, he hadn't lost too much blood and was very likely going to make it. He was our battalion's first casualty. I couldn't help wondering about our survival odds, even now, even before we got close to the real hostilities.

We had been either extremely lucky or very well protected because, to my knowledge, no enemy submarines or aircraft had chosen to attack our part of the convoy during those last two and a half weeks at sea.

Word spread from the ship's deckhands that we were getting very close to Gibraltar, the renowned entrance to the Mediterranean Sea, then from there most likely we'd head for some as yet unidentified landing point in Italy or Sicily.

I had expected the famous rock of Gibraltar to loom clearly on the horizon like the logo on the Prudential Insurance Company's promotional material, very much like Diamond Head in Hawaii. When it finally appeared mistily on the horizon, it didn't seem at all prominent but looked much like any other cliff-lined shores I'd seen.

My compass reading didn't change drastically as we spied the Moroccan coast a few miles to starboard. As we drew closer, the mysterious, fairy-tale city of Tangier arose from the African shoreline with its all white stucco and stone buildings shimmering majestically in the tropical rays of the bright Mediterranean sun. It hit me then that this was the fabled land of genies and sultans, and I would very much have loved to visit its beckoning shores, especially after those last three weeks aboard our transport that by now stank badly of its sweaty, human cargo.

As we sailed tranquilly along the Strait of Gibraltar, I delighted in the change that this more peaceful sea had brought. But where would we debark? Naples? Palermo? Maybe Greece? I had read and heard much about Winston Churchill's inclination for the Allied forces to attack the so-called soft under-belly of Europe and wondered if we were it and just how soft it really was. Once past Gibraltar and the city of Tangier, we seemed to be taking a southeasterly course, slowly swerving away from the disappearing Spanish coastline and stay-ing even with the Moroccan coastal strand and North Africa.

The war in Africa had already ended some months ago with the defeat of Field Marshal Rommel's forces and no longer required our assistance. Unless we made a radical swing toward the northeast, we'd certainly miss the Italian penin-sula and Sicily by many miles. But our sea-going convoy continued onward, keeping within sight of the misty North African coast. Rumors were rampant. Malta? Sardinia?

Very early the next morning, the ship slowed noticeably. As we sluggishly arose to see why, another brilliantly glowing city that reflected the early light of the hot North African dawn greeted our eyes. Whispering voices favored the guess that it was Oran, Algeria, appearing much as its sister city of Tangier had from about three miles off shore.

We had anchored, and it became obvious that preparations were being made by the crew to rid themselves of us. We were ordered to strap on our back-packs, take our rifles, and prepare to disembark, leaving behind our clumsy duf-fel bags for some other slower form of transportation to get them to us later.

Coarse, web-like nets of bulky sisal rope were quickly cast over the sides of the ship, and it looked as though we'd have to climb down that shaky, makeshift ladder with full packs and rifle to the water transportation waiting below. Before long, the churning, white-capped sea around us was afloat with variegated landing craft of all types as we waited for our company's turn to descend the rope netting and enter the nearest floating vehicle that would take us ashore.

Never before have I experienced anything like shinnying down that stretchy, mountain-high ladder that bounced perilously underfoot with each step I took. I will never forget it. During the previous year and a half, I had learned very well to be disciplined in the ways of the Army, but my unexpected descent down that skyscraper of a ship, loaded down as I was with pack and rifle, had to be near the top of my list of never agains. It was an experience I could very happily do without forever, thank you.

Disembarking from the undulating, amphibious "duck" that carried us almost to shore was another tricky matter. It seemed that one of the generals had gotten the bright idea of converting our debarkation into a tactical training maneuver, leaving us to wade to the beach through chest high waves, rifles carried high over our heads. I cannot say that it was the greatest idea in the world because my battalion was never put in the position of invading from the sea. But in retrospect, I figured what could it hurt, especially as the strangely warm sea was a welcome change from those regimented cold showers aboard ship, ridding us and our clothes of the stinking body odors we must have accumulated during the last three weeks.

Landing in Oran with its apparently white shimmering edifices, I discovered to my dismay that what had appeared from the stern of the ship to be pristine, glistening buildings were anything but that. Every dingy one of them could have used a decent paint job. Everything in this commercial city of Oran was permeated with an intense smell of pressed olives that hung heavily in the sultry, saturated air to an unbelievable extent. Even though I love olives, this stink was nothing you'd ever care to live with for more than ten minutes at a time. I suppose one can get used to anything, especially if you live and breathe it every day of your life as the Arabs here did. Thankfully, that wasn't me.

The next annoying surprise came quickly with the onslaught of hordes of eleven- and twelve-year-old Algerian boys with wooden shoe-shine boxes casually slung over their shoulders. No sooner had we arrived ashore than they smeared our combat boots with a brown, sticky mess resembling fresh cow dung and shouted "Shine, Joe?" Of course, shine! How else could we get that damned crap off our shoes? They made a game out of our attempts to avoid their aggression, but the soft-natured Americans almost always lost out.

While they removed the gooey stuff with their American-made daubers and brushes, their next question thoroughly jolted my guileless sensibilities.

"You want my seester, Joe? Only sixteen! Nice teets, nice ass. Good blow job. Only five dollars, Joe."

The blasphemous idea of these children selling their sisters, of selling anybody, was just the beginning stage of my indoctrination to a degrading lifestyle extant in this war-torn continent. This kind of unabashed pimping totally disrupted my previously cloistered way of life and called it into question. I was suddenly forced to recognize the fact that there was a strident commerce of sex for sale, indelicately foisted on me as it was by this tragically impoverished part of the world.

Could this be the wonderful Old World I had just been transported to, a world I would never have suspected as being so uncouth, so noxiously uncivilized? Was Europe also as depraved as this? These and other philosophical questions rattled me but only momentarily. Anything seemed possible now, and I knew I'd find or be given the answers soon enough. I'd just chalk it up to experience.

⋯ ▰◆▰ ⋯

With our headquarters now set up in the arid Sahara desert region of Algeria's Port aux Poules, we spent the next two months in amphibious invasion training and practicing attacks against real, concrete pillbox fortresses and rusty barbed-wire anti-tank traps that made a tangled mess in the sand. Some once-beleaguered army had previously erected these fortifications along the rocky strand not realizing that, months after they had collected their dead and wounded, we'd make additional use of them. Our training included our first use of deadly flame throwers and bangalore torpedoes, leaving us little doubt as to what the brass planned for us later.

In retrospect, I don't believe even the generals knew what to expect at that time. I suspected that my original guess might be correct, that we might be part of a task force meant to attack the heavily fortified Adriatic coast, maybe Greece or Albania.

The costly Sicilian offensive was over, and the bloody battle up the boot of Italy had already been under way for a few months. We were aware that our Allied forces had been meeting extremely stiff resistance, especially just north of Rome, in the vicinity of Cassino, an enormous mountaintop abbey and enclave held by the Germans. That strategically positioned monastery was a defender's dream because it commanded a totally panoramic view of approaching infantry as well as offering extremely effective protection against any Allied air or ground attacks. Vast tons of rubble left by our heavy artillery shelling as well as around-the-clock bombing raids by air had been cleverly utilized by the enemy to their advantage to form additional concrete barriers and protective cover.

Perhaps the generals wanted our battle-ready 91st Division to relieve those war-weary troops who had been taking an awful beating from enemy artillery and mortars located just beyond the crest. Their barrages were undoubtedly being directed from concealed observation posts in and around the abbey. But in time, even the well entrenched Germans could not hold out forever against the perpetual Allied onslaught without receiving fresh supplies. Sooner or later they'd have to retreat but not until they had earned the grudging respect of our

36

generals and had let it be known how costly it was going to be to continue to chase them.

We waited in Algeria for a clue to when and where we'd be committed, but nothing was forthcoming. Unknown to us at the time, it would be only three weeks later that our own fledgling troops would literally get their feet wet crossing the Cecina River in Italy as the 363rd Infantry Regiment continued to push the stubborn Wehrmacht from there all the way to the Alps.

But as yet, we were still in North Africa. After our daily training maneuvers, we were occasionally allowed the privilege of plunging into the pleasantly warm, pebbly Mediterranean. It was a treat we looked forward to with great relish because we could rid ourselves of the ever-present, superfine dust of the Sahara that threatened to clog not only every pore in our bodies but also our precious equipment as well. Rifle barrels were especially prone both to rust and to getting filled with that sandy grit, making daily reaming and oiling a must.

Even though we posted twenty-four-hour guards, almost every evening rogue Arabs would raid our pup tents attempting to filch such things as bars of soap and bed sheets, which sold in Oran at a premium. GI cotton sheets would bring an unbelievable sixty dollars in the black market — more money than most of us made in a month — because they could be used for clothing. There was also talk that these poor nomads accumulated human feces to sell or use for fertilizing their small vineyards, which seemed plausible once one saw these peoples' miserable living conditions.

I have so far neglected to mention our toilet facilities. This is because I can honestly state that, throughout my three-year hitch, I have never suffered any greater indignity and never felt more diminution of the human spirit than in my dreaded treks to those infernal outhouses. Wherever we camped, those hideous wooden holes replaced the glorious white porcelain receptacles we once had taken for granted. These outhouses were teeming with huge, droning flies and filled with the acrid stench of antiseptic creosote powder sickeningly intermingled with excrement. Later on, in times of open field combat that often lasted several weeks at a time, we simply let nature take its course, making the best of it without those unholy shrines to humiliation.

During the last few weeks spent in the searing Algerian sun, we were invaded by a storm of insects, locusts I think they were. They ate everything in sight, right down to the few blades of desert grass and dry, scrubby shrubs that had been all around us. Without exaggeration, billions of them appeared one day in a noisy, dark cloud of swarming insects that must have resembled Moses' plague visited on Pharaoh three thousand years ago. Even in the midst of this endless desert, you couldn't take a step without scrunching at least four or five locusts underfoot. Although basically harmless, they even infiltrated our pup tents. We learned later that this natural phenomenon occurred only about once in a decade and that we had just happened to be at their feeding grounds at the same time. It was another bit of wonderful news to write home about.

Two weeks before our departure from Algeria, a somber Red Cross official visited me and, after putting his arm around me solicitously, told me that my wife had had a miscarriage. It had something to do with a negative RH blood factor I couldn't quite understand at the time.

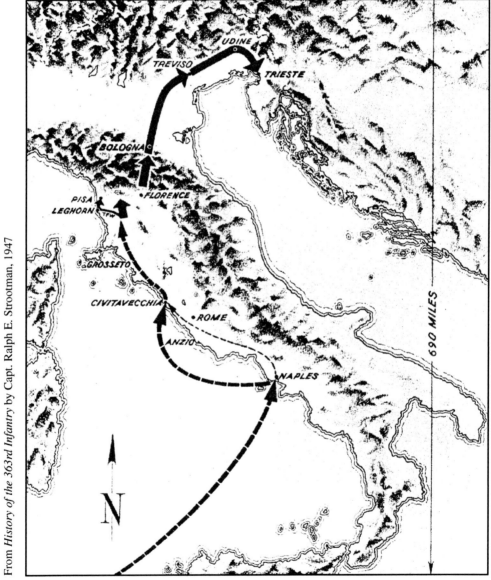

From *History of the 363rd Infantry* by Capt. Ralph E. Strootman, 1947

Route of the 363rd Infantry Regiment

"She's doing fine, though," he offered. "Is there anything we can do for you, such as send her a message?"

I tried to comprehend what she might be going through, but what could I do or say? What message could I send through him that I couldn't better express myself? I took the next day off so that I could write her a letter expressing my sadness and concern, saying I wished I were there, and offering vague hope that we'd have plenty of kids when I got back. All the while I reflected, wondering if it hadn't been for the best. She just might be better off without my baby since the possibility seemed pretty damn good that I wouldn't make it back at all. Of course, neither of us could know at that time that, after my return in 1945, we would ultimately have the good fortune to birth and rear two healthy, wonderful kids who would, at least, have the opportunity to live in a much safer but ever-more changed world.

Except for our almost daily war games, the idea of our engaging in combat somehow seemed to grow more distant and had almost ceased to be a threat until one fateful morning.

"OK, men, we're pulling out." The long-expected order echoed through the camp. "Take down your tents and get ready to police the area. We haul ass right after breakfast."

By 1:00 P.M. we had rejoined our duffel bags aboard the ship and were headed out to sea, with no secrets this time. We were going to Naples.

Chapter 7

Italy, at Last

"Take everything" was the command over the bullhorn from the ship's bridge. "You guys are going to need all your crap now. Good luck!"

We crowded down the gangplank of the ship at the port of Bagnoli, a few miles from Naples, Italy, sweating profusely in the heat of a brilliant, cloudless sky, wearing our heavy helmets, and toting duffel bags and rifles while the ever present backpacks pushed oppressively against our spinal columns.

I stepped onto the Neapolitan dockside in a kind of mental fog, glad to be in mystically romantic Italy, yet feeling my sweat turn chilly with the fear of getting so near to where the battle was raging, where men were actually getting killed. I wondered if the others felt the same way.

After Red Cross personnel handed us cigarettes, some toilet articles, and a doughnut, we were quickly trucked off to a nearby concrete and marble building at the edge of the Bay of Naples. Someone said the place had once belonged to Count Cianni, Mussolini's former son-in-law who had been assassinated last year by Il Duce for daring to plot against him.

"Pick a spot on the ballroom floor for your fart-sack," a voice announced, using the unofficial GI term for sleeping bag. "Your ass is going to be here for a few days, so take a lease on a comfortable neighborhood."

A few days, did he say? I had become used to sleeping on the ground by now, but this cold, hard marble seemed like no bedding accommodation I'd ever pick for myself. Nevertheless, I chose a spot about five feet from a grubby private to my left, dropped everything onto my imaginary space, and wondered about the likelihood of doing damage to my back. If I got lucky, it just might do enough temporary damage to my sacroiliac to postpone the dreaded day I knew would be coming too soon. No such luck. I managed to make it through the ordeal, relearning the captain's lesson that, if you're tired enough, your body is capable of resting damned near anywhere.

⋯ ▰◆▰ ⋯

"Anyone wanna go into Naples tomorrow?" Sergeant Higdon asked, smirking broadly as he waved the passes in the air. "Four-hour passes, ten bucks each." Of course, he was teasing about the money, but even if he wasn't, he would have had plenty of takers. Everyone wanted to go.

I can't describe the exhilaration, the exquisite feeling of adventure I had, taking my first step into that wondrous world of Italy that I'd only heard about or seen in movies. I immediately marveled at the sight of the spectacularly blue Bay of Naples that I saw from the lush, bougainvillea-covered portico that surrounded my temporary dormitory. Partially shrouded in the distant haze, the fabulous Isle of Capri seemed to float above the water, and startling Mount Vesuvius, still threatening, was a smoky-colored silhouette off to the southeast. I could hardly wait to board the GI truck to downtown Naples the next morning.

It would be impossible to forget the turbulent drive through that vibrant city full of jaywalking pedestrians and oceans of peddling and weaving bicyclists of all sizes and shapes, people bustling about like bees in a hive to earn their living or perhaps simply out to shop for food. Most ignored the GI traffic, but they always had time to wave and shout a loud, friendly greeting when we waved at them. "Allo, Joe! Buona fortuna, Joe!" Somehow each of us had acquired this new surname, and we accepted its friendly agreeableness. Anything in a skirt produced a chorus of whistles from our truck and, more often than not, a pleasant, taunting smile from the recipient.

For these seemingly carefree Neapolitans, except for the short supplies of flour, meat, and sugar, the war had ended some nine months before. It quickly became apparent that these people genuinely liked us and didn't mind that we were occupying much of their real estate. Now I felt more confident and eager to get off the truck, to mix with the scurrying crowd, and to experience firsthand their exuberance and warm hospitality.

My fellow passengers scattered in different directions, and I took off alone toward what I felt was the center of town. Pots of geraniums overflowed from almost every windowsill, but the sight of laundry hanging from their wrought-iron balconies would always remain among my most indelible memories of the inner city of Naples. And I'd be willing to bet that it hasn't changed since I last visited it.

I hadn't yet had the opportunity to learn to speak Italian, but I vowed it would be one of my priorities. Why not start now? First, I needed to trade in most of my American dollars for Italian lira. That could be a start.

A nearby outdoor café seemed made to order for my plan. Alone and feeling a sense of bravado in my uniform, I sat down at a tiny, round, travertine table, asked for a cup of coffee, lit my pipe, and enjoyed the street scene. Fortunately, I had a waiter who was gregarious and especially happy to see anyone, let alone an American soldier, at 10:40 in the morning. The Italian lessons began.

Having learned to drink my java straight up during the cold nights while on maneuvers in Oregon, I asked the waiter for "black coffee, please." He smiled and brought a half cup of thick, very black liquid.

"Caffè nero Americano, Joe," he said as he placed the cup and a ceramic pitcher of hot water in front of me. He explained in charming, broken English that anytime I wanted black coffee I should request it that way, and it would most likely come with a side of hot water, "acqua calda," he stressed, to dilute it. Otherwise, it would probably appear with milk and sugar already in it.

That was my very first lesson, nothing earthshaking but a start, from Roberto, the waiter. "You speak good English," I said, hopefully encouraging him to continue.

"Si, signore. Alamost alla the peopla in Napoli speak a littla Inglese," Roberto offered with a proud grin and effusive hand gestures.

I took advantage of his apparent friendliness and learned a few more basic words and phrases, enough to satisfy me for the moment. Of course, I gave him a tip in the only kind of money I had with me, an American dollar, an exorbitant amount I learned later. He offered to exchange all my dollars for lira, a common practice for shopkeepers and black marketers then as well as now. I learned later that his rate of exchange wasn't unfair, the benefit to him being for how much more he could trade in those highly sought-after paper bills.

"Mille grazie (a thousand thanks)," I said when I left, feeling proud of myself for beginning to learn and use his language.

"Grazie a lei!" Roberto responded, bowing politely. I now added that phrase that meant "you're welcome" to my vocabulary, repeating it to myself as I walked down the busy street with my money belt full of confusing, multicolored Italian notes.

Almost immediately, I was accosted from a side street by a well-dressed young man of about twenty-five, who insisted on walking alongside and keeping pace with me.

"Hey, Joe. Like a nice, clean virgin?"

Here we go again, I thought. Just like Algeria. How disappointing!

"No! No virgin. Beat it!" I said, feeling angry and let down.

"Any kind, Joe. Beautiful, seventeen years old. Only five bucks, Joe. Best blow job. Maybe you got cigarettes. Two packs, Joe. Lucky Strikes, maybe?" the man persisted. As I kept walking, he pleaded and cajoled, suggesting and offering me all the detailed tricks his "virgin" would be happy to share with me.

"Leave me alone! No money, no cigarettes, capish? Get the hell away from me!"

Sensing my disdain, he finally left, looking for greener pastures among the myriad other roaming Joes spending the day in Naples. I do not know how many times this guy managed to foist off his supposed virgin, but he was wearing a beautiful pair of perfectly tailored gabardine slacks and an open-collared silk shirt, obviously doing very well for himself. I could be sure he wasn't the only pimp in this town of a million people.

I considered how to write home about this. My wife would enjoy the story. I decided to save it, though, and wait for the time I might be lucky enough to get home so that I could recall and tell all I'd seen but couldn't take the time to put down on paper right then.

Later, I spotted a few familiar faces, men from my company who were sitting outdoors at a bar and noisily enjoying bottles of unlabeled wine. It's funny how boisterous and rowdy guys can become when at least two or three of them get together. I decided that I needed to join them and add to the ruckus.

I had always thought of myself as a loner, enjoying my own thoughts and reveries most of the time, but not that day. The babble of their animated company, inane as it probably was on this occasion, was something I needed then and would require even more of in the near future.

"Hey, sarge, you get laid yet?"

"Sure. Didn't you?" I lied.

"Yeah! How about those Eyetye broads!"

There was no way of knowing if he was for real or not, but I didn't want to seem disagreeable. "We'd better get to the pro station when we get back," I suggested, just in case he happened to be telling the truth. The pro station was a term used by the military for prophylactic first-aid station, and I couldn't easily forget those venereal disease movies the Army had insisted on showing all through our training days.

It would be hard to deny the all-important part sex played in the lives of our young men before and after battle. But who just talked and who really acted on his fantasies is anybody's guess. Most likely it depended upon the individual because opportunities certainly abounded in this strange new world. Wartime created situations that most probably would never again occur in civilian life, and this fact of life was brought home to me very clearly, affording me an advanced education that would have been denied me in the cloistered surroundings of my own former Caspar Milquetoast life.

Thousands of miles from home, I could easily empathize with their need for the soft sweetness of a woman, the need to relate to some feminine reminder of life as it once was and could be again, and ultimately, the overwhelming need for even a momentary fulfillment of nature's primal urge. Combined with the nostalgia of separation and the constant but always shrouded fear of death, being with a woman who could bring you to the heights of remembered passion was an easily understandable need for many.

A few hours later back at the staging area after we had all sobered up, we did a cursory inventory of our equipment and waited in the chow line on the crusty courtyard soil of Count Cianni's palace for our next supper. No, it wasn't pasta but Spam again.

This time, however, something was different. Lean-faced, barefooted, and ragged-looking kids from about six to twelve years of age were timidly standing in line at our garbage pails, waiting patiently for the scrapings from our mess kits after we had had our fill. Disconsolate as it made me feel at the time, it was a scene that was repeated throughout the entire Italian campaign at every rear echelon chow line. But I never did get used to it.

We got word that the famous violinist Jascha Heifetz would be performing for us the next day. I had the choice of attending his concert or heading for downtown again. I chose the concert. Maybe I lost out on an experience or two in Naples that afternoon, but no matter what I had given up, I'd never miss that as much as having stood in the presence of the dour-faced, great maestro and heard him play.

I don't remember now what he played or, for that matter, how he played it, but this was the great Heifetz, and what could it matter? Afterward, I rushed to his side and asked for his autograph. I had no paper handy except my Italian money. He signed my two-thousand-lira note, worth about two American dollars, and gave me the oddest look. I'm sure he was wondering what kind of nut I was, using money this way. Carelessly, I later misplaced or spent the money and never again found his cherished signature.

Another day in Naples found me sharing the company of a delightful American fellow soldier I had begun to like for many reasons, Sergeant Paul Brown of Fairmont, Virginia. This was probably to be our last memory of that bustling city before we would be sent to the front, and as much as we tried, we found no signs of another Sophia Loren hiding in the crowd.

Brown, I'm happy to say, would remain a great pal of mine right up to the day of discharge, a calming influence in the often stormy times ahead. His quiet, back-woodsish demeanor and sense of humor contrasted with and complemented my edgy, city-boy persona.

During the tumultuous year and a half that followed, I can't say I ever saw him ruffled or thrown. He reminded me of a cool-headed, saddle-hardened cowhand, someone in whose company I could always find solace, especially as a drinking buddy when I needed one.

It was funny that, no matter how friendly you'd get with your Army buddies, you would only address them by their last name. I found this to be true except in the case of my big Irish cohort, Jess P. Dunnagen, from Berkeley, California. I simply called him J.P., while he delighted in calling me Weck or Weckershimmer.

The military transport bus from Naples dropped Brown and me back at the staging area late that afternoon, and no sooner had we gotten off the tailgate of that dust-covered taxi than we were advised that we'd be moving out first thing in the morning. I immediately had butterflies in my stomach. I think I saw Brown pale a bit, too.

An hour or so later, after we had chowed down, we were much too edgy to hit the sack.

"Remember that bar we passed about a quarter mile up the road?" Brown asked, as if testing my ability to read his mind.

I too, had thought of its possibilities. "What are we waiting for? Let's go," I answered. "I'll tell Higdon so he'll know where we are if there's a sudden change in plans."

Sergeant Higdon's irritation showed on his leathery face when I told him "If your asses ain't back here by 2300, I'll send the MPs to get you, and the colonel ain't going to like that one friggin' bit."

I reassured him, and we took off on foot at a fast pace. When we got there, we walked down two steps and entered through the beaded curtain, then let our eyes adjust to the semi-darkness of the saloon. Surprised that other GIs with unfamiliar shoulder insignia were already there and seated around tables, we picked a section of the room near a talkative group, wondering what they were doing this far off the beaten path.

No doubt at the request of the neighbors living above the bar, the juke box was turned down to about half its regular decibel level; otherwise, the raucous sound of "The Beer Barrel Polka" could have been awfully nerve-racking on this portentous night. Soon we didn't pay any attention to it. We ordered cognac from the gruff, portly woman who seemed to be the owner of the place. Most of the other men in the bar were drinking beer, appearing fatigued, listless.

"What outfit do you think these guys are attached to?" I asked Brown.

"Beats me. We'll find out sooner or later. They sure as hell look like they've been through the mill."

Two men at a nearby table spotted the fir tree insignia on our uniforms and out of curiosity asked the name of our division.

"Ninety-first Infantry," I answered.

"We're 1st Armored, just got released from the medics. You guys look like you ain't seen much action. No infantry badge," said one of the men. They both rose and came over to our table, staggering clumsily, partially anesthetized from the effects of the beer and partially from their apparent battle wounds. They said they had been wounded in the battle for Sicily and would soon be going stateside for further treatment.

"We just got here," Brown told them. "We're headed for our baptism by fire first thing tomorrow."

"Lucky bastards. Where the hell were you guys when we needed you a year ago?" said one.

We assumed he was referring to the fiasco in North Africa that we had heard so much about. Considering his sudden sullen mood, we picked this time to change the subject and introduce ourselves. They did the same.

Sitting opposite us and sporting a GI cane was Tech Sergeant Bob Anderson with a large bandage covering what used to be part of his right calf. Tech Sergeant Ron Rosen had a surgical compress covering most of his left hand, concealing burns that would probably handicap him forever.

"You guys don't know what fun you missed," Rosen snorted. "You should have been with us in Tunisia at the friggin' Kassarine Pass."

Bob Anderson appeared to be the worse off for drink and seemed a hair away from passing out. They must have been indulging themselves all afternoon. The two of them looked amazingly like Bill Mauldin's cartoon characters, infantrymen Willie and Joe, except that these guys happened to be tankers.

"Here's to Patton and Monty, friggin' almighty cocks of the walk," Anderson toasted with a sneer. "Long may they shee-it!" He slurred out the last words in as loud a voice as he could manage in his condition. A few other 1st Armored men at nearby tables joined in Anderson's derisive toast, raising their mugs.

Reprinted by permission of Bill Mauldin and the Watkins/Loomis Agency

"We just landed. Do you know any good war stories?"

"What the hell happened?" I asked, seeing the disdain these war-weary men had for their generals as well as for their own self-esteem.

At this point Anderson laid his head across his forearm, fingers gripping his beer mug that rested on the table. We watched with concealed dismay as he started to shudder and weep silently, uncontrollably. With his good hand, Rosen patted Anderson's back, attempting futilely to offer solace.

"Cheez, Bob, this ain't Tunisia. You want to let it out, OK, let it out. But for crissake get used to it. Those guys ain't never comin' back. Forget it already. At least *we're* goin' home."

Brown and I looked at Anderson and then at each other, feeling utterly helpless.

"You wanna know why this poor guy is sufferin', why he's so damned spooked out?" Sergeant Rosen asked, anxious to tell us.

His distressful tale began in Africa and nearly ended there with the beating they took from Rommel's well trained, battle-indoctrinated desert forces in a blitz that had targeted this poorly led American tank corps as its hapless victim, reducing it to a semblance of the fighting force it could have been under more expert leadership. They had suffered tremendous casualties until George S. Patton, Jr. came on the scene to replace their inept commander. With time to lick their wounds and this new blustery general's driving aggressiveness, they pulled together and proved themselves to be much more than capable, valiantly fighting their hearts out in the Sicilian campaign.

"Monty figured all Americans had to be chicken," Rosen went on, referring to British Field Marshal Bernard Montgomery. "Yeah, we had the shit kicked out of us for a while, until that crazy, sonovabitch Patton took over."

"I heard he was one hell of a general," I said.

"Yeah, but the guy was nuts! He used us and used our division to show Monty that Americans could outfight the Brits anytime and drove us through Sicily like a herd of friggin' wild elephants. The bastard knew how to fight, alright, but he made us all wacko, cursing and waving his damned pearl-handled .45 around like a goddamned idiot. Buster, you'd get your ass in a sling if he ever caught you without your helmet or missing a lousy loose button off your uniform. The man was nuts, I tell you."

Rosen's agitated voice trailed off as if to catch his breath. He pointed at Sergeant Anderson, speaking in a half whisper so as not to disturb his friend's semiconscious stupor. "To top it off, this poor bastard's kid brother was a paratrooper, killed during the invasion of Sicily after the friggin' brass screwed up the drop zone."

"Sounds to me like the whole thing was pretty bad, a real snafu," Brown said. Snafu stood for "situation normal, all fouled up."

"Bad? You'll never know the half of it. What with friggin' Montgomery and Eisenhower having a personal ego battle of their own, who'd give the shaft to who, it's a wonder any of us got through."

Someone had put a coin in the juke box, and the sweet, mellow voice of Ella Fitzgerald was trilling Gershwin's "Foggy Day." I ordered another cognac. Rosen, as garrulous as before, was anxious to tell us everything he thought we had missed in his private war.

"Did you guys know that the sonovabitch Patton saved our butts in Sicily?"

Of course, at that stage we had very little information of who the real Patton was or how he saved Rosen's behind. Biographies of his exploits tell us now that, although often chastised by Eisenhower, he had turned out to be one hell of a general, as well as a premier nut case.

"Yeah, he took what was left of our outfit and we wound up beating the crap out of the Krauts and eyetyes." Rosen's bleary eyes lit up, shining a bit brighter in the dim light of the bistro, staring at nothing in particular, remembering.

Brown and I were almost feeling guilty for not having seen action in the African and Sicilian campaigns, but the second drink soon began to take effect, dulling our senses and the sincere empathy we had been suffering for Sergeant Bob Anderson. We got up to leave and wish them luck when Anderson raised his head and glared after us with glazed, blank eyes. We waited.

"You poor slobs are startin' tomorrow." He waved feebly. "Good luck. It's gonna be shitty at best, but do me a favor and get a few Krauts for me. I wish . . . ." At that point he choked up and began to sob again. Embarrassed, he grabbed for his cane and left the table, dragging his wounded leg.

We left them a minute later and walked back to camp, sharing an awkward, thoughtful silence.

⋆ ⋆ ⋆

The 361st Regimental Combat Team had preceded my own regiment to Italy and had been first among the men of our 91st Division to taste the bitter sting of war. Landing at Anzio Beach, they had relieved part of the veteran 34th Infantry Division near the city of Civitavecchia, just north of Rome. It was now nearly nine months since the furiously contended invasion of Sicily and the 5th Army's savagely fought Salerno beach landings, and our forced vacation was at an end. Our turn in the field had arrived. My own 363rd Infantry Regiment had been attached to the combat-indoctrinated 34th Division so that we could gain battle experience as quickly as possible.

The surprisingly mountainous area the brass had chosen for our initiation had waterways galore. Rivers most Americans had never heard of, the Ombrone, the Cecina, and others, were each a defensive waterblock seemingly custom-designed for the benefit of the Germans. It was obviously easier for them to create havoc from behind such geographic dividers, and you can bet the cagey German Field Marshal Kesselring took full advantage of it to make our lives hell.

My battalion received its baptism by fire on July 4, 1944, near the farming village of Chianni approximately sixty-five miles from Rome. Our men had to fight their hearts out from this point northward, proceeding inch by inch, hill by hill, to reach our first set of main objectives to the north, Leghorn, Pisa, and the Arno River.

Giving you a blow-by-blow account, naming each and every hilltop village and numbered gully we fought for, would be tedious and not serve the real purpose of this book. Instead, I will simplify the geographics and other details for an inside glimpse of the soul-shattering, bloody hostilities as I saw them through my eyes.

Dazed and scared, we left the trucks near the foothills below Chianni. My company, Headquarters Company, spread out and proceeded single file up the already battle-scarred slope behind two of our rifle companies. We were to set up our battalion command post (C.P.) near the unoccupied crest about two-hundred yards up the slope. The initial command post would have to be dug out of the exposed, practically barren ground somewhere along the south side of hill number something or another. No brush nor trees stood on our side of a hill that was once part of a pleasant terraced vineyard.

As our trucks drove off and we timorously started up the rough path, we could hear but not see the terrible battle being waged not too many yards away just over the crest. It sounded as if we were getting awfully close to the crunching, brain-jarring noises of bursting shells and automatic weapon fire. Along the snaky gulch that was our dirt trail to the top, khaki-clad, bloodsoaked broken bodies lay scattered, some hurriedly covered by blankets, some not, in grim and final repose as a result of some costly assault earlier that day.

Holy crap! These were dead Americans! Hardly a single enemy uniform to be seen. I paled at the sight of those bloodstained blankets and grotesquely twisted, lifeless bodies. Shaken to the core and rattled as I was with that gory scene, I had to keep in mind the reason for being there, only momentarily dissuaded from facing the music if I must. Hate and blind rage soon followed as I scampered and stumbled along with the lead group.

Our destination was just twenty or thirty yards, that seemed like inches, from the very top of the ridge. This was considered to be the safe side as all the shooting came from somewhere just over the crest. Lieutenant Colonel Woods had led the uphill column and was waiting for me in a broad, shell hole within the gully as I approached. The meeting was short. His words were terse. I listened, just plain scared.

"Sergeant, stay here and have your men dig in. Lieutenant S_____ and I are going ahead to check out the situation. Set up this spot as battalion command post. We'll try to stay in contact by radio." With that, the colonel and my platoon leader, Lieutenant S_____, the mighty one of our previously rough and tumble training days, took off and disappeared over the hill. They quickly melted out of sight into the deep brush on the far side and slithered down the slope that separated us from the next enemy-occupied hill into the valley that had been reverberating with never to be forgotten sounds of automatic gun fire and brain-splitting artillery blasts.

Recalling those torn cadavers I had seen as I came up the hill just a few minutes before, I was one very frightened soldier, thankful I was told to remain behind during the opening act of this raging battle. With my pale and frightened radioman nearby, I waited in kind of a stupor with my pale-faced radioman standing by along with the rest of my quaking men in that open, shell-pocked gulch that the Colonel had designated to be the battalion CP.

About half an hour later, an unbelievable procession of seventeen soldiers wearing swastikas emerged out of the smoke-filled mist from the hill on our left flank and moved single file toward us with their fingers tightly interlocked behind their heads. One, apparently the leader, was carrying a small white flag. Like a mirage they came forward, appearing subdued and more frightened than we were but more than happy to be giving themselves up. For a moment I thought that they might be Japanese but then realized that their almond shaped eyes marked them as probable Turkestani conscripts.

They had already dropped their weapons, and I instructed two of my men to take them back down the hill to our rear echelon at regimental headquarters for questioning. They were to keep within the path we had taken coming up the hill, because mines could be anywhere.

I couldn't help wondering what these people were doing here in Italy fighting on the German side. Like any raw recruit, I had a lot to learn that first day. It seemed that Hitler was prepared to use almost anyone of any nationality or age group in his mad attempt to defeat us. Unfortunately for us, however, he also made excellent use of his well-trained, elite-guard Nazi storm troopers in critical situations much more often than people like these simple, innocent conscripts who really had no intention of raining on our parade.

After that episode, I began to relax. If this was war and I would merely be assigned as caretaker for the battalion command post and to wait for enemy squads to surrender, what could be bad?

It was only wishful thinking, of course. It wasn't long before a barrage of artillery rounds smashed the comparative quiet on our side of the hill, a few rounds landing much too close for comfort. Quickly, the sound and fury converted my men and I back into quivering mortals once again. Snail-like, we all receded tightly into our protective trenches. Digging these slit trenches wherever we were likely to remain for more than twenty minutes would be my firm modus operandi from that first day on, proving to be a life-saver on many occasions.

It is impossible to fully describe the blood-curdling experience of an artillery barrage. If you aren't violently finished off by concussion from the terrible, brain-crushing noise of the explosion, with blood emanating from your ears and eyes, there is always a good chance that a half-inch splinter of wildly spinning, screaming, white-hot shrapnel would tear your flesh to ribbons. No matter what the movies show, very few survive an encounter with a shell exploding within thirty feet, unless you're lucky enough to be in a foxhole or slit trench. I concentrated on keeping my body as close to earth's center as possible during those intermittent shellings. As nerve-shattering as these hit-and-miss barrages were, I'd discover later these random barrages were only a very disagreeable annoyance compared to those hellish times when it became my turn to be the designated target, the center of their bull's eye.

The radio remained strangely silent in the endlessly long hour and a half that passed. Suddenly, Colonel Woods and Lieutenant S_____ reappeared on the run from over the hill.

"God, am I glad to see you, sergeant," said the obviously shaken, breathless lieutenant. Those were the last words I'd ever hear him utter. He immediately took off like a bat out of hell, running back down the hill in the direction from which we had originally started, and we would never see him again.

This was the heroic officer who had taught us all we knew, the mighty one of previously rough-and-tumble training days, who had demonstrated all his macho bravado back in the training fields of Oregon. Thank you very much! So where did you go when we needed you, and where are you now, Prince Valiant? Didn't you know that I would have be your stand-in?

From that day until almost the end of the war, Colonel Woods made full use of me as the departed lieutenant's replacement, without benefit of his gold bars and salary. I can't help thinking that the colonel's unusual confidence in me might have been partially due to my silent acceptance of the realities of war or of my being ashamed to appear scared when he was near. Then again maybe it was the result of my actions in our very next encounter with Germany's stubborn elitists, those extremely proficient SS troops of the Wehrmacht, Hitler's talented killing machine. It seemed they would choose to die before giving up a single inch of that rugged Italian terrain.

After this first introduction to battle near Chianni, something mystical occurred deep within my psyche. As scared as I truly was, I had to face the fact that this was really going to be a very precarious, life-or-death business and that I'd have to destroy this hated enemy wherever, whenever, and however I could before he destroyed me. I would try my damnedest always to be at least one neuron cleverer than he was — to outkill him!

I made this a personal war. Fortunately, destiny provided that I'd succeed, more often than not, by making the best use of my innate ability to read a map and my latent optical ability to spot and pinpoint the enemy's key positions at any hour of the day or night. Once I had located them, I'd be hidebound to destroy them, directing deadly artillery or mortar fire, finding myself entranced and exhilarated with each new target, like a kid with a new computer game. If only the guys who had turned me down in the Navy and Coast Guard could have seen me then!

This game wasn't one-sided, of course, but the end result indicated that somehow I turned out to be better at it than the enemy was.

Chapter 8

The Observation Post

A fter Chianni there was Bagni, another once picturesque tiny hill-top town and another hill to conquer rock by rock and gully by gully along Highway 65, the main road that sliced through the center of Italy. If we managed to take enough of these quaint, scenic towns and all the mountains, valleys, and rivulets in between, it would bring us to the 5th Army's next main objective, the undulating east to west Arno River about twenty-five long, trauma-filled miles to the north.

Along the way there were villages with wonderful sounding names like Terriciola, Peccoli, Capannoli, Ponsacco, La Serra, Casaglia, Montalone, and Pgio Castagnolo. But, believe it, each and every one was occupied by obstinate German defenders fully prepared to inflict death and destruction in their wake as they made a super-human effort to hold us off.

Our casualties had to be heavy because the Wehrmacht nearly always had the military advantages of the protective house and the optimum use of high ground or slippery river bank. From day one, our foot soldiers had to dislodge them piecemeal from those simple, stone-framed casas, innocent-looking churches, and well-dug-in fortifications on the southern side of each hill that faced us, hills all carefully seeded with devastating mines and under cover of machine-gun fire.

At our field headquarters one morning, I was busy assembling the next day's battle maps for the officers, getting ready as usual for Colonel Woods' orientation and attack-route plans for the next assault. It had become routine for me to sculpt a six-foot-square area of dirt to show the three-dimensional details of the local terrain as I interpreted them from the aerial photographs forwarded to us from division's G-2 intelligence section.

The use of this modeling technique in the field cannot be over-estimated. Each of the platoon commanders could see in advance what three-dimensional topographical features his troops were facing and where the enemy might be positioned to create the biggest headache. From this information, the officer could formulate a clear battle plan to pass on to his squad leaders.

That morning we had a sudden interruption. "Mine! Mine!" The elderly peasant pronounced it "meenay" as he waved his hands, frantically scurrying toward us. The old man was insistent. "Mine! Mine!"

"Send some men with him to mark off the damn minefield, sergeant," Colonel Woods ordered tersely, but he wanted me to stay and finish the important model preparations.

Marking a minefield was normally a job given to the engineers. Although my men had had some verbal instruction about mines when we were back in Oregon, they had no real experience in this sort of thing. Impatient to finish the planning for the next assault, however, I'm sure the colonel didn't realize that our intelligence section had little knowledge of what to do should they come upon a minefield except, of course, not to enter it. All that seemed necessary was to mark the area with yellow tape, which my men were prepared to do after obtaining the markers from the nearby quartermaster sergeant.

"Be careful," I warned them. "Be sure you follow and stay behind the old man." In that way, he would be the first to feel the effects in case of a trick or to become a victim of his own carelessness, or so I thought.

About an hour after they left, my stomach tightened in fear as I saw a telltale puff of black smoke appear above the wooded area. A second later I heard the ominous crunch of a sizeable detonation about three-quarters of a mile distant.

I should never have let them go without firmly reminding them to space themselves apart as we all had constantly been told to do during basic training. I fervently hoped they would know enough to handle that much without me. They didn't.

At first, I saw only the old man shuffle out of the woods in our direction. His glazed eyes avoided mine as he plodded past me, staring strangely straight ahead. Needless to say, that gave me no peace of mind. A few minutes later, three of the six men I had sent off reappeared, badly shaken and spattered with blood.

"What the hell happened?" I asked, anticipating the worst.

"Cheatham and Nelson got it!" Private Lott informed me. "Phillips looked pretty bad too. I already sent the medics to check on him."

That deplorable calamity was the result of a single Bouncing Betty, Germany's diabolical spring-activated anti-personnel mine. It activates when stepped on and vaults about six feet into the air where it explodes again, disbursing a multitude of metal shrapnel particles. Apparently, the old man had unknowingly stepped over or around its three-pronged trigger mechanism as my unmindful men followed, spaced too closely together.

My first reaction was to hurl my helmet to the ground in a fit of anger and disgust, then I retched, vomited, and grew sick.

Edwin Nelson and Ermy Cheatham were dead. The other man, Lee Phillips, had been terribly wounded, and I'd never see him again either. They were wonderful, sweet-natured young men, all of them. I had seen others die, but these were different. They were my men. What a damn waste! Even today, the memory of it still continues to turn my stomach, and I cringe as I recall this bitter event of more than fifty years ago.

I kept feeling that I was to blame for permitting this to happen, and it took one hell of a long time before I could allow myself some meager absolution. The only thing that helped alleviate my personal torment during the next few months was the fact that many men were dying all around me, good men I had come to know and respect. It happened to be a particularly bloody time for everyone, but it was a hell of a way to ease one's guilt.

By the time the war ended in 1945, I had lamentably lost the full complement of my section of men several times over, and every day I wondered uneasily if my turn would come soon.

Beyond their devastating mines, this enemy that I grew to hate more each day had in its arsenal a most monstrous weapon that they had learned to use extremely well. Known by one and all simply as the "damned 88," this infamous self-propelled, 88mm, high-velocity cannon became the infantryman's nightmare. Unlike the slower howitzer shell, its missile came at you like a rifle bullet. Its explosive power was on you before you even heard the telltale blast of its cannon. At other times, depending on the atmosphere, you might hear only the crack of the shell's spinning, supersonic velocity as it left the barrel, hissing rather than whistling for only a fraction of a second before you heard the frightfully sharp explosion. If you were lucky enough not to have been its victim, by the time you could pick yourself up off the ground, the motorized cannon would have moved behind the hill to another location so that you couldn't easily locate it to destroy it.

My private war with these killing machines occurred on an almost daily basis because I spent all of the daylight hours from predawn to after dusk at the battalion observation post. Colonel Woods would select a craggy hilltop, a stone farmhouse, or on occasion just a ditch as an observation post (O.P.) from which it was my sordid business to search for any enemy movement and direct artillery or mortar fire on all suspicious targets. First I'd study my map and orient myself, that is, locate my position in relationship to the terrain before me, then I'd stealthily set up my telescope and stay glued to that spot until after the sky grew too dark to see anything more. I rarely left the telescope, contrary to what the manual proscribed. Sure, I knew full well that the book said: "The observer must be spelled often to rest his eyes." But I just couldn't pull myself away.

I discovered I had an uncanny gift for observation. This I used constantly and most effectively to create havoc with any and all enemy targets, moving or not, that had been unfortunate enough to be caught in the lenses of my scope. Stationary enemy positions such as machine-gun nests, camouflaged tanks, and dug-in ground troops were comparatively easy targets for me to spot. A little harder to find and eliminate were camouflaged motorized transports that moved at twilight or under cover of darkness, targets that I'd been barely able to observe miles off as they drove away from or towards the front. Then I would look for other signs that helped give their positions away, such as a dust trail or a reflection from a momentary glint of light just before the sun set.

It was easiest for me to find the Germans' well-hidden heavy artillery at night when the flashing blast I'd seen could be timed with how long it took for the explosive sound of the cannon to reach us. The speed of light and sound came into play, and I could use a set of pre-established statistical formulas to mathematically determine the distance to the probable location of those big guns. But, of course, the enemy would be clever enough to change their location the next day and often did.

The enemy would attempt to fool me by using variegated, earth-toned paint that blended with nature on their Tiger or Panzer tanks and conceal them behind dense shrubbery. I loved to make a game of it and always had a ball trying to pick off those steel jalopies with our 105s. But in general, directing artillery fire at such an armored vehicle was almost always fruitless. When my carefully calculated and adjusted bursts of firepower got too near to their intended target, I'd watch helplessly as the tank crews scrambled back into their turrets and hurriedly took off to relocate elsewhere. Even then, however, I considered it a success, my mission having been accomplished in disrupting the enemy's firepower along our line of advance.

One day I used at least 300 rounds trying to hit a lone Panzer parked 200 yards from my O.P. behind the far wall of a partially destroyed farmhouse. For camouflage they had used wood scraps, plaster chunks, and rough, broken beams to make it look like it was a portion of the house that had been knocked down. They had done an exceptionally good job of creating an inconspicuous panorama of farmyard junk loosely scattered around, making it extremely difficult to pick out the hidden quarry.

One of the secrets of my success was always to look for any tell-tale evidence of tampering with the natural surroundings, such as a sightly off-color piece of shrubbery or a pile of leaves that shouldn't have been there. The real target would always be well concealed.

In the case of this tank, I sensed, more than saw, something different about the way the rubbish was piled and I tested my judgment with a couple of salvos of 105s to see what would happen. The explosive air pressure caused by the last burst of shells displaced two or three boards, exposing a fraction of the gun turret. I licked the soft part of my thumb and rubbed it across my chest for luck, and from that point on, it was only a matter of trying for a direct hit as I called in fire directions to all batteries of 105s at my disposal.

The next half hour tended to prove the needle-in-the-haystack theory as I had finally used up our quota of shells for that target. In the lull that followed, all I could do was watch in helpless frustration while three German tankers scampered from their protection within the ruins of the farmhouse, jumped into their Panzer, started the engine. Without bothering to remove the rubbish that still covered their bulky steel shell, they took off with gears grinding noisily, leaving me to watch their metal ass slink contemptuously off towards the north. As if thumbing their noses at me, they finally disappeared around a bend of the nearest hill. All I had managed to do was scare them off.

Our battalion anti-tank crews would have found it impossible in most instances to handle this kind of situation because my observation post was generally located as near to the front lines as possible, too close to the action for them to haul up those clumsy little cannons without being quickly annihilated. The distance of 200 yards was also much too far for bazookas to make a direct hit, and our Sherman tanks were not always in the neighborhood to do battle. With today's infrared and electronically controlled infantry weapons, I'm sure that tank would have been a goner, but those were different times.

On that same day, I reported two other enemy tanks, both hidden in the trees 300 yards to my front, but the artillery officers at the other end of my radio wanted to conserve their ammunition for a planned attack the next day. At least it was good to know where those Panzers were hidden once our next attack started.

The enemy also had their observers. Too often they would spot my observation post and try their best to eliminate me in this deadly game they were so good at. Don't think for a moment that I didn't greatly fear the precision of those terrifying 88s and their ability to make hamburger out of me. Day after day, we'd play a kind of cat-and-mouse game with each other, attempting to savor the questionable achievement of who could kill whom, but they definitely had the advantage. I can report with all humility that I hardly ever won the risky match I played against the marksmen in charge of those damned 88s, but thankfully, I didn't lose either.

During the rare times when the 88s weren't firing, I had to deal with the shelling of their bigger guns, their 105s and 155s. Occasionally, when they tried extra hard to make a point, they'd even call into play their Big Bertha railroad guns, which were heavy, heavy artillery, to say the least. Fortunately, these weren't pinpoint accurate, but just the sound of those incoming rounds and subsequent detonations were enough to create a local earthquake.

It is nearly impossible to describe the high-pitched roar of those incoming missiles. Those barrages sounded to me much like a high-speed freight train would sound if you stood in front of it until the very last second. This was followed immediately by ear-splitting, skull-crushing, thunderous explosions that, by themselves, were often enough to kill or give one a lifelong brain concussion.

Too often those missiles were directed at me as their target. Much of my day was spent attempting to dodge some wily enemy observer's retaliation. During his cooling-off and reloading time, I'd attempt to get in as much of our own artillery fire as possible. Always on the lookout to pinpoint the enemy's defensive ground positions, I'd stay at the telescope until it became much too dark to see. Attempting to make life a little easier for our rifle companies, I'd strive to let each of them know by radio precisely where they'd run into automatic gunfire, dug-in infantry, or defensive traps. Also, I often let headquarters know the flank extension of our men who might have disoriented themselves during those viciously fought battles.

Around 11:00 P.M., the mules would arrive with supplies and, at rare times, with hot food for the men who were in untenable mountain positions a hundred yards or so to the front.

"Sergeant, show them the way to the companies," came the order, usually for me. I was the most likely one to know where our troops were dispersed and how to get there in the dark without falling off a cliff or into a ravine. It was remarkable to see those poor mules, their intelligence newly respected by me, inch their way up narrow mountain paths they had never been on before, delivering morale-building sustenance to where it was most needed.

Directing the mule traffic, my squad or I would sometimes lead them there before returning to our command post an hour or so later, often dodging mortar fire if the noise of the animals gave our position away. Arriving back, I'd prepare the officers' maps for the next day's assault. Maybe I'd get three hours of sleep.

Reprinted by permission of Bill Mauldin and the Watkins/Loomis Agency

"I'll let ya know if I find th' one wot invented th' 88."

Except for my flimsy sleeping bag, my bed was usually the straw-littered dirt floor of a flea-infested barn or deserted farmhouse. At other times, a slit trench hastily dug into the hard earth would have to do. If it rained that night and I had chosen the wrong spot, my bed became an ugly, warm brown river.

Without a bath for weeks at a time, I must have stunk to high heaven. My legs had been chewed up by fleas, and the only salvation for that problem was some kind of talcum-like powder the Army gave us, probably a form of DDT that didn't work very well with Italian bugs. I hoped if I ignored the little suckers, they'd go away, but they never did. To this day I still bear the scars around my shins left by those saber-toothed little devils.

By now we had been on the line for the better part of two weeks. Almost to Pisa, we had gained only about twenty miles as the crow flies, but up and around the interminable bloody trails from where we started our first attack, the distance seemed more like a hundred miles. Conquer those last few lousy miles and we could rest our tails in Pisa and Pontedera, on the other side of the Arno River. Once again, however, our rifle companies found themselves stymied by stronger than usual defensive action. Although daytime was still busy time, observation post time, the lull allowed me to take a breather for a couple nights while the brass decided on the next move.

A farmhouse nearby looked particularly appealing. I was hoping for some kind of change of pace, a moment's refuge from war and gore. I knew I could depend on Sergeant Brown at the command post to let me know if I was suddenly needed, and I told him where I was going.

Perhaps this padrone or his paesano tenant farmer would manage to find a chicken or a remnant of head cheese that the Germans hadn't already confiscated. Maybe I'd get lucky and he'd open his hidden cache of cognac. I had been introduced by now to the tranquilizing pleasures of drinking. The stock answer wherever we had been was, "*Tedeschi tutta porta via* (the Germans took it all)." Probably so, but nothing was etched in stone, as I discovered that night.

It was then that I first met my long-term Army buddy, big clutzy Irish Corporal Jess P. Dunnagen who, like myself, enjoyed exploring and also sought the respite and change of scenery that this simple, handmade stone cabin might offer. A wispy trail of white smoke floated up into the dark sky from its battle-scarred chimney.

"Feel like checking it out?" I asked, pointing to the house.

"That's what I was thinking," J.P. responded as we walked the 200 or so yards together.

We greeted the middle-aged peasant sitting outside his front door. J.P., with his crow-footed smiling eyes and pleasant "*buonasera*," cleverly offered the man a cigarette and told him to keep the whole pack before chancing to ask about the possibility of buying a bottle of something alcoholic.

The farmer's face lit up with the presentation of the smokes. Still grinning, he left us for a moment then reappeared from somewhere behind the dark barnyard carrying two grit-covered, unmarked bottles. He wiped the necks and uncorked both bottles of apparently homemade, blackish-red wine. Handing them to us, he jubilantly announced in his language, "To celebrate my liberty from the Germans." We understood and made it apparent that we'd share his toast and tilted the bottles to our lips. It could have tasted like vintage Chateau Rothschild for all I knew about wine, but the two of us drank like it was.

I soon learned that J.P. was a staunch Republican. I was a liberal, almost left-wing Democrat, so needless to say, we had a lot to yak about. It's interesting what may draw one person to another among the hordes of possibilities available, who we choose to become close to on the battlefield. From the very start I liked his ability to listen when I argued my salient points and especially the way his Celtic blue eyes laughed.

About an hour later, a voluptuous kind of drowsiness overtook me. This was the first time in my life I had ever finished a whole bottle of wine by myself, something I had never attempted to do before. When I yawned, trying vainly to keep my eyes open, J.P. noticed and smiled.

"Come on, Weck. Let's leave a couple hundred lira and get you back before you fall on your keister."

J.P. had a terrible time pronouncing my name. To this day he still calls me Weck or Weckershimmer. Why he chose to appreciate my company throughout the war remains his secret, but opposites often attract, and whenever we could, we'd spend our rest time together.

Too soon, though, our push had to continue. The generals made it known that they badly needed Pisa, Leghorn, and the Arno, and we, of course, had to deliver.

Chapter 9

Pisa

In the heat of a steamy July morning, I once again carefully molded the sandbox miniature image of the Arno River terrain our troops would have to do costly battle for, die for, during the next few days. My fingers felt strange, more sensitive than usual for some intangible reason, as I gingerly pressed in the crease lines of the impeding gullies, streams, and ridges that waited threateningly ahead of our advance.

I vaguely remember a feeling of uncertainty, couldn't be sure, but I could have sworn something unusual was about to happen, something big, not the usual fear that we normally felt with most of these new assaults.

This time the aerial photos showed a vast diversification of natural features, from the kind of rough mountainous area we were now attempting to break out of to a hodgepodge of soggy canals in and around our western flank, uncommonly known by it's geographically descriptive name as Marina di Pisa.

In an air of unusual somberness, all platoon leaders made notes and listened carefully as they were given their attack plans by Colonel Woods, who used an olive tree branch as a pointer to designate each group's particular assignment.

"Company B's 1st Platoon should be watching out for Charlie Company's left flank at *this* point after passing *this* knoll we'll call point G; Able Company will remain in reserve behind *this* ravine in front of Dog Company mortars ready to hit in either direction. Charlie Company has to avoid the streambed *here*; G-2 suspects that it's laced with booby traps or S-mines. Keep to the east of it."

And so it went, hopefully to proceed as smoothly as planned from the mounds of earth I had sculpted, interpreted from those all-important, black-and-white aerial photographs.

Each silently studied my pile of reshaped dirt then synchronized their watches as the officers of our battalion readied themselves for this next deadly agenda. I silently wondered if the other men felt the same nauseating churning in the pit of their stomachs that I did every time we approached one of these new attacks.

It was at this critical point in time that I first began to sense something new, an unusual attitude of respect that officers and enlisted men alike were extending to me. Considering the living hell I had watched each of them go through, that feeling of respect was most certainly mutual. I gained a tremendous amount of personal satisfaction from their mute but obvious regard, occurring as it did only a couple of weeks after we first entered combat. It did a great deal to buoy my previously shaky self-esteem.

Of course, I allowed for the fact that all of us in the infantry had learned to give silent praise, acknowledging one another's proven ability to take the mental and physical punishment dished out to them on a daily basis. Anyone who had made it this far was surely to be respected as a comrade-in-arms to the very end.

To my apprehensive, approval-seeking eyes, it seemed this kid from Brooklyn Avenue in east Los Angeles had made it. Halleluya! It felt great to think that I had been accepted. I was more than proud now to freely display my dog-tag chain from which also dangled a miniature mezuzah, the little metal tube that encased a parchment scroll inscribed in Hebrew with biblical passages and the word referring to God. This unqualified respect gave me reason to try harder still and vow to live up to their expectations. Ever more diligently I'd finish what I was sent here to do and bust my butt to get the damned war over with.

I was certainly more determined now, but was I braver? No way! I was just less intimidated by the thought of being judged harshly by my own peers. I had already made the discovery that, almost to a man, everyone doing duty on the front lines was either as scared as I was or was just plain crazy.

This point came home to me more clearly one day when I found myself working closely with a captain from the 347th Field Artillery Battalion. Both of us were busily viewing a panorama of potential targets from my forward observation post. We had tried to conceal ourselves behind the partially bombed-out basement wall of an old farmhouse when we suddenly came under extremely heavy, concentrated howitzer fire. We realized that they were aiming at us in particular when salvos of four shells at a time pounded what was left of the once sturdy building and the grounds surrounding it. Simultaneously, we dived for the nearest protective cover, a single narrow slit trench my men had dug for us in the cellar for just this kind of emergency. Foxholes would have taken days to dig in that clay.

Once spotted, if we had attempted to escape the building, their deadly 88s would have been ready to send us home in body bags. So there we stayed. Chunks of masonry and lumber kept falling with each explosive hit, adding little to our sense of well-being. After ten endless minutes of being on the receiving end of some Kraut's binoculars and taking the worst pounding either of us had had to that time, our legs began to shake uncontrollably. As we faced one another in the narrow, twenty-eight-inch trench, the captain's knees and mine knocked convulsively against each other like flamenco castanets. We both laughed moronically, mortally frightened.

It was reassuring to know that just about everyone identified with the kind of mutual terror that ran rampant on the battlefield. The only difference was that some of us displayed it more openly than others and acted on it in disparate ways.

One day I came upon an unusual old telescope in a vacated, bombed-out house. It must have been about a twenty power, almost twice as strong as the sleeker, more compact GI scope the Army had supplied me with.

The better to see them and kill them with, I thought, as I remembered the old nursery rhyme. I'd make good use of that collapsible contraption despite its one major drawback. It lacked the few inches of overhanging lens protection that would shield it from the telltale flash of light produced by the sun's glare against the glass. Except for cloudy days, it could leave me vulnerable, exposing my position to enemy spotters if I couldn't find a well-shaded area to work from. What it lacked in protection it more than made up for in its perceptive accuracy. That was of greater importance to me. The choice was clear.

It was around July 20, 1944. Taking the important seaport of Leghorn (Livorno on the European maps) became an urgent priority because it would mean that our support troops would no longer have to transport supplies to us over the 250 miles of dusty mountainous road from the supply port in Naples. Word had come down from the high command: "Bypass any large resistance. Push on rapidly. Get Leghorn."

To accomplish this, numerous little towns and rocky hillsides that were numerically noted on our map would have to be fiercely wrestled away from an obstinate Wehrmacht. Almost every bend of road and each farmhouse and stony escarpment invariably held a small group of defiant and stubborn defenders who had to be killed or routed out. Left alive, they would then retrench on the next hill and delay us further.

Without a doubt, these had been the longest few weeks of my life, but we were finally and most gratefully ordered to stop. Our battalion had orders to go into reserve for our first blessed short rest near a village called Bagni di Casciana, eight, very long, miles east of Leghorn and less than a mile from the front.

Feeling extremely fatigued and battle weary, we relaxed blissfully in the shade of a quiet olive grove, later taking full advantage of most welcome field showers arranged for us by the service company engineers. I took that opportunity to write to the parents of my men, my revered comrades who had been slaughtered in the mine field — was it only a week ago? — and to assure my wife that I was still among the living.

More than ever, I thoroughly enjoyed that often-ridiculed hot mutton stew served al fresco and gladly took seconds, ladled out as it was into my mess kit from the tail end of a camouflaged truck parked in the comparatively quiet field.

J.P. and I spent most of our free time catching up on sleep and occasionally just idly chatting while other very exhausted regiments fought for those eight tortuous miles. Our turn would come soon enough when we'd have to go back to the front.

Much to my astonishment, during this short rest time a number of unattached Italian partisans joined us. These were courageous young anti-Fascists, Mussolini haters who, besides doing undercover work, annexed themselves to any company of Allied troops they took a liking to. Apparently, our leaders did not mind because they ate and slept with us without any interference from the high command.

Alberto Sechi was one of those unsung heroes, a member of the partisani whose company I thoroughly enjoyed, lasting as it did for the duration of the war. He was disarmingly sociable and gregarious, and I ultimately learned much from him about his country's language and customs. Unfortunately, I later lost track of him in the confusion of being shipped home after the war and since then have tried to locate him on numerous trips I've taken back to his home town of Florence. I looked up any name in the phone book that sounded like Sechi. There were names like Cechi, Secci, Secchi, but when I phoned them, each was a wrong number. Sadly, too much time had elapsed for me to recall even the approximate location of his home. Without success I've finally given up. He could very likely be living in New York, for all I know.

At twilight on the second night of our relief, German Field Marshal Kesselring chose to introduce us to a new weapon known as the Nebelwerfer. Screaming Mimi, we called it, and it lived up to its frightening nickname. It was a multi-barreled rocket launcher that hurled twenty or more deadly rockets in quick succession from its special mobile truck. The sound of these rockets wailing hideously through the air assaulted our ears before exploding violently in and around our present reserve position. Didn't those shmucks know we were resting? And exactly what were they using for their observation post to be able to direct those missiles at us? This area was fairly flat, not conducive for observing our movements or we theirs.

As was my usual practice, I had prepared a slit trench for myself, and I was awfully glad I had avoided the tendency to be lazy in the intense heat of that Italian summer. We all knew, of course, that being this close to the front meant there was always the chance of being on the receiving end of scattered nuisance artillery fire or of Bed-check Charlie's occasional nightly foray.

Bed-check Charlie was our name for a single-engine German airplane of the Piper Cub type. Heard but unseen, this mosquitolike pest would regularly arrive only after dark, when it would drop a small bomb or two or sometimes leaflets depicting nude women or anti-Semitic propaganda in an attempt to fray our nerves. Often while we were in the midst of watching a movie miles behind the lines, the projector had to be shut down and all the lights in our encampment turned off as the plane skittered away untouched. I never saw anyone take a shot at the tiny plane because we knew the flash could give away our position and invite more unwanted retaliation.

The Girl You Left Behind

THE WAY OF ALL FLESH

When pretty Joan Hopkins was still standing behind the ribbon counter of a 5 & 10 cts. store on 3rd Avenue in New York City, she never dreamed of ever seeing the interior of a duplex Park Avenue apartment. Neither did young Bob Harrison, the man she loves. Bob was drafted and sent to the battlefields in Europe thousands of miles away from her. Through Lazare's Employment Agency Joan got a job as private secretary with wily Sam Levy. Sam is piling up big money on war contracts. Should the slaughter end very soon, he would suffer an apoplectic stroke.

Now Joan knows what Bob and his pals are fighting for.

Joan always used to look up to Bob as the guiding star of her life, and she was still a good girl when she started working for Bob, whom she hadn't seen for over two years. Her boss had an understanding heart and was always very kind to her, so kind indeed, that he often invited her up to his place. He had always wanted to show her his "etchings". Besides, Sam wasn't stingy and each time Joan came to see him, he gave her the nicest presents. Now, all women like beautiful and expensive things. But Sam wasn't the man you could play for a sucker. He wanted something, wanted it very definitely.....

Poor little Joan! She is still thinking of Bob, yet she is almost hoping that he'll never return.

Poor little Joan! She is still thinking of Bob.......

German propaganda leaflet dropped by Bed-check Charlie

German propaganda leaflet dropped by Bed-check Charlie

On the third day the order came to break camp.

"We're gonna sleep in Leghorn tonight!" Sergeant O'Connor announced. "Get your asses in gear. The trucks will be here in an hour." "Big John" O'Connor had replaced First Sergeant Higdon who had opted to become a platoon leader in one of our rifle companies. Apparently, some men had a need for more action.

From a distance, I could hear the unmistakable rumble of heavy vehicles. Not only did an endless column of trucks appear but also a large number of our Sherman tanks, some already carrying troops on top of their metal shells.

"Get aboard anything that moves," Sergeant O'Connor yelled, as we scrambled out of formation. I picked a Sherman tank, after making sure my section of men were settled in either a nearby truck or on our tank.

We had become an integral part of Task Force Williamson, named after our division's brigadier general. Apparently units of the whole 5th Army, the 34th Division, the 442nd Regiment of Japanese-Americans, the 752nd and 804th Tank Destroyer Battalions, and others all had been doing their part in making headway to Leghorn while we were relaxing in reserve during the last couple of days. Now we'd join them in a major flanking maneuver to the west while part of the 34th Division fought and diverted the attention of the remaining German forces at the southern end of the city.

General Mark Clark, commander of the 5th Army, stepped out of his jeep in front of the tank I had hitched a ride on. I watched as he shouted a few words to Colonel Woods who had also jumped out of his jeep but didn't slow his pace as the two talked and walked together in quick time. I learned later that he had given our battalion commander instructions to occupy and hold the seaport for at least twenty-four hours after it was taken. The general gave our column and the colonel a snappy, respectful salute as he drove away.

Without firing a shot, my tank and my battalion entered beleaguered Leghorn just as it was turning dark, passing through groups of excited, cheering Italians who had come out to greet us when they saw the white stars on our vehicles.

"Grazie! Grazie, Americani!" they shouted ecstatically, tossing flowers and offering us bottles of wine they had somehow managed to conceal from the despised Tedeschi. These spontaneous outbursts of joy and relief occurred often throughout the war; but, we never tired of these exuberant greetings.

Much of the town seemed to be in a shambles, and the docks had been scuttled by the Germans. But where was the enemy?

The premature elation quieted suddenly when a Volkswagen carrying a German officer and driver who obviously had been away on reconnaissance attempted to return to what used to be their headquarters in the city up until a few hours ago. In the gathering darkness, they were within a hundred yards of our column before they could distinguish our insignia. The recognition was simultaneous. As the surprised German driver tried to turn his vehicle around, our men opened fire. This plus the menacing guns on our tank turrets, which had begun to swing in their direction, convinced them that their best bet was to get the hell out of there on foot. A single round from the Sherman's 75mm gun made a blazing wreck out of the Volkswagen. Machine-gun fire cut down the driver before he had gotten far, but the officer made it to the doorway of the closest building and got safely inside before a second round from the tank brought the stone doorway crashing down around him.

Deadly snipers and small pockets of resistance remained scattered throughout the town as, one by one, they either retreated or had to be destroyed. I got off a few shots, making use of my rifle for the first time when my squad became pinned down by sporadic rifle fire from an apartment house at the end of a dead-end street. With the element of surprise taken away from him, the stealthy jerry moved on to locate somewhere else, and the shooting stopped. Now that I had finally used my rifle, I'd have to ream out the barrel and lube it tomorrow, if I made it through the night.

Only my regiment remained the night in Leghorn to handle stragglers and the occasional scrimmages that occurred. Other regiments had moved out with orders to take advantage of the enemy's retreat and go the final ten miles to Pisa and the Arno River as quickly as possible. We would join them in the chase the next day.

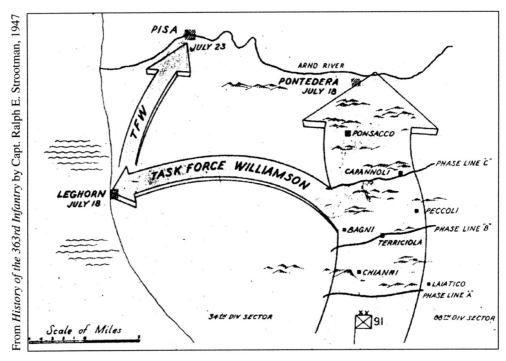

From History of the 363rd Infantry *by Capt. Ralph E. Strootman, 1947*

The 91st Division's push north to the Arno, July–August 1944

Those last few miles of Marina di Pisa lived up to its early promise to be the most treacherous kind of combat zone, an unprotected open field cob-webbed with a maze of marshy, lowland canals and heavily strewn with anti-personnel mines. In almost hand-to-hand combat, our bedraggled rifle companies finally managed to break through to the river valley marshland and low-lying hills just south of the Arno River. By now we were used to the idea that the enemy was desperately determined to give up ground only if they were forced to. For days they fought us furiously, viciously, yard by yard, inch by inch. Kesselring's catchword for this bloody, life-or-death marathon had to be *delay*.

Delay the Allies at all costs! With precision and by-the-book rearguard action, he made our men pay dearly.

Suffering extremely heavy casualties to our young officers and enlisted men, our dog-tired regiment licked its wounds and attempted to regroup. Enlisted men had to rapidly become second lieutenants in the field, replacing the courageous killed or wounded officers we had lost to these surprisingly obstinate defenders and their deadly weapons.

The Wehrmacht's automatic machine pistol, the frightful Schmeisser, a one-man armory of death and annihilation, had badly lacerated anyone who attempted to cross those narrow canals. As it barked its blood-curdling brraap, its rapid-fire staccato bursts, I couldn't help but be ridiculously reminded how it sounded like the quickly ripping canvas of my beach chair back home. Brraap! Someone had named it the burp gun, and it stuck.

The Schmeisser, along with the ubiquitous Shu mines, buried anti-personnel charges about the size of a Cracker Jack box that always tore off a foot jaggedly at the ankle when detonated, had taken their frightful toll on our men. In spite of this, our troops had to be alert and ready to move on toward the important city of Pisa to catch and destroy the slowly retreating enemy before he had a chance to regroup and solidify his position.

But, the Germans had other plans. When we dared to take advantage of our apparent victory to advance those last lousy two-and-a-half miles along and around the narrow highway leading towards our objective that was teasingly within sight, they immediately blasted us with lethal artillery barrages. What's more, their use of the dreaded 88s had increased noticeably, continuing to pelt us from everywhere at once, it seemed. To proceed pell-mell against this wall of ferocious, demoralizing fire would be folly.

We found ourselves completely frustrated by this enemy's super effort and terribly clever defensive action. Although restricted and temporarily repulsed at times, our advance had never been as totally and completely blocked as it was now. For all intents and purposes, we were thoroughly stalemated, unless we were willing to accept the tremendous amount of casualties required to maintain our momentum. We could only wait for the brass to make the decision.

"Dig in!" The order came from up and down the line. We could only wait while headquarters groped with the frustrating problem of the alternatives facing us.

Our S-2 and G-2 intelligence units surveyed the surrounding countryside looking for an observation post the enemy could use to direct these withering fusillades. They ruled out all such spots in this level countryside except one.

Directly ahead, less than a mile and a half from where my men and I waited for orders in the partial protection of an olive grove, the awesomely tilted

Leaning Tower of Pisa protruded weirdly above the tree line. Through the mist of the Arno River, it seemed to hang suspended on the horizon like a surrealistic Dali painting. Our men had dubbed it the tiltin' Hilton.

Since that first sighting, I have learned that the tower is 185 feet high, leans to the east sixteen feet from center, and has eight arcaded stories. Started in the twelfth century and completed in the latter half of the fourteenth century, it had taken several generations of builders a span of some two hundred years to inadvertently make it one of the seven wonders of the world.

It must have been about 10:00 P.M. that night when I heard someone shout, "Sergeant Weckstein, the colonel wants to see you."

I double-timed it from my slit trench to the battalion command post about sixty yards away. "Sir?" I saluted, waiting for his attention.

"Sergeant, the general wants you to take a radio man and leave at the crack of dawn tomorrow. Get yourself as close as you can to that tower. Stay within the cover of the olive groves, but for God's sake, be careful. Try to watch out for mines."

"We think the Germans are using it for an observation post," he continued. "Too damn many casualties. You might have to level it." He paused.

"We've got our cannon company, a couple of batteries of 105s and 155s already zeroed in for maximum effect, and even a destroyer offshore ready to help with their big, six-inch guns, if you need it." His repeated use of the pronoun *you* gave me a hint at what would come next. He continued in his usual, understated tone of voice. "If you see anything that looks at all suspicious, don't wait. Call down fire."

"Yes, sir!" I saluted again and left, agog at the task that was handed me.

This could be an historic, red-letter day. I found myself scared but in stage center, a vainglorious kid already applauding myself as the possible star of this drama yet to be enacted. There wasn't a single doubt in my audacious, twenty-three-year-old mind that I really was about to do the deed, to direct sallies of doomsday fusillades against one of the world's most famous monuments.

It was easy enough for me to find the company's radio technician, Tech Sergeant Charles King of Canton, Ohio, a quiet, guitar-playing, dependable sort of guy. I repeated the colonel's orders, which he accepted without much sign of excitement. I, on the other hand, still quivered with the thought of the task ahead.

Dawn came very soon. I don't think either of us slept much. The sun had barely lightened the sky, and it was already uncomfortably hot and muggy without a breeze to stir the grayish green olive leaves in the perimeter of our bivouac area. Sergeant King and I ate a K-ration fruit bar and drank strong, black coffee. We smudged our faces with mud and readied ourselves for the important task as Sergeant Brown and a very drowsy J.P. wished us luck.

We each took a deep breath and moved out stealthily, vigilantly, feeling a great deal of trepidation about hidden minefields that might be anywhere in our path. We knew no Allied soldier had been there before us.

Through the early-morning haze, I could just make out the ghostly silhouette of our lop-sided target as it appeared to dodge between the trees. We'd have to get closer, a lot closer. Our bodies bent low to the ground, we crouched and stumbled slowly along the perilous way towards our objective for what seemed like an eternity. King had begun to sweat conspicuously. He had that clumsy radio to lug around, and I felt sorry for him.

An hour later, when I thought the timing and distance should be about right to take a first serious look, we settled in behind the trunk of a fallen oak tree on the edge of a grove from where we'd attempt to conceal our activity. I rested for a minute or two and wiped the sweat off my steamed-up eyeglasses. Then I adjusted the telescope's lens to accommodate the distance, about three quarters of a mile, and set it to balance in the crook of a tree branch. Sergeant King had removed the bulky radio from his back and was busily fine tuning it. As quietly as possible, he called the command post for a good read. This had to be done quickly; we knew that the wily enemy had an excellent way of triangulating on our position from our radio signals.

This finished, I pressed my stomach onto the sun-parched dirt. Saturated with perspiration and itching almost unbearably in my sweaty, flea-infested clothes, I carefully focused first on the highest point, the broad circular campanile of the tower. I could easily make out the shadowy silhouette of the old bells, quiet now, but nothing moved. I took my time training the scope ever so slowly up, down, and across each elaborately ornamented balustrade, attempting to discern anything that might be hidden within those black recesses and arches.

For a moment, I indulged my senses. Somewhat hypnotized by the awe-inspiring tower and its artistic mastery, I tacitly noticed the elegance and grace it was really meant to convey. Momentarily, I dismissed the cunning enemy who most probably had been using it to wreak havoc on our troops, yet I knew that, if even a mouse dared scamper within my sight, my brief musing would cease immediately. Like a bat out of hell, I'd have been fast enough on the draw to send the deadly message to fire. The words, "This is Able George One. Fire!" would have been enough.

The morning sun grew hotter by the minute as my mind leaped back into reality. I looked again, this time with no need for further aesthetic gratification. I indulged myself in hoping against hope for even the slightest sign of a possible target. Then, to my utter amazement and chagrin, the marble tower suddenly turned into a vibrating mass of white, quivering gelatin, undulating crazily in a rapidly pulsating kind of dance.

I hadn't counted on such intense heat waves. No one had. This unexpected stumbling block completely thwarted my ability to focus. It was as if I were attempting to look through a bowl full of wiggling Jello.

I ached with a desire to grab it, to take a firm hold with my bare hands and steady the convulsive thing. If only I could be allowed even the slightest suspicion, the slightest reason, to give the order to fire. Finish the damn job!

In retrospect, I can easily recall that the animal within me would have been glad to send the tower to kingdom come in spite of its frustrating shimmy. Militarily well-trained by now, the impatient savage in me thought of the casualties resulting from its probable use as an observation post and yearned to blow it to smithereens, but as yet I had seen nothing move. Not a damn thing moved, not even a single pigeon. A whole division of the Wehrmacht could be hiding within those wobbly cavities, for all I knew, without any possibility of being spotted. I waited and watched, hoping for the sight of just one shiny uniform button or any skulking shadow to make its presence known.

Should I fire anyway?

Since I was a kid of fourteen, I had often played a mind game, a kind of mental solitaire, in which I reinvented myself as devil's advocate and put myself in the other guy's shoes whenever I found myself in some difficult situation. Simply wanting to date or merely speak to a girl had always been one of the more difficult windmills I had to conquer. In this game, I would conjure up the unconscious ego force of one of my more brazen cronies and ask myself, how would he act and what would he say? This temporarily mollified whatever prurient fantasies I entertained, solving the problem for that moment at least. Whether I chose to act upon these imaginings was unimportant. It was just something I did in a pinch to gain perspective.

Eventually, I got pretty good at this game and found it very useful in honing my perceptiveness in a multitude of ways. Absurdly, this became one of those times.

It took only seconds to reinvent myself as a six-foot, blue-eyed, blond twenty-three-year-old, a typical, goose-stepping, Aryan storm trooper who used the name Kurt Reinhardt. His family home was near the German city of Hamburg, a pretty, two-story cottage with geraniums draping from almost every window sill.

Thinking as Kurt, I didn't particularly want to leave this lush setting along the Elbe, especially since I loved to fish from the little wooden dock behind the house and where I often roamed hand-in-hand with my lovely Hilda along its marshy shoreline. It was there I first made passionate love to her under the sheltering shadows of the weeping willows. I'd miss her most of all.

76

But the siren call of my fatherland could not be ignored, so I joined my eager-spirited compatriots to rid the world of its despised Jews, Gypsies, and Russian Reds and to reestablish ourselves once more as a truly superior race worthy of ruling the world, as it was meant to be. Didn't our fuhrer firmly assure us that any sacrifices we made would be worth the glorious end of our holy quest?

So, now is my chance to show those gullible Americans what we're made of. Just let them try to get past our 88s, our artillery, our Schmeissers! As I sit eight feet back, deep within the shadows of the tower's sixth level, they'll never see me cautiously rotate my binoculars in a 180-degree arc. We'll keep knocking the fools off like clay pigeons in a shooting gallery, and soft-headed idiots that they are, they won't dare fire back at this holy shrine.

So thought the imaginary Kurt Reinhardt while I angrily struggled to adjust my own uncooperative sights, all the while playing the puppeteer with this imagined enemy. That bastard Kurt was probably correct in every respect except one. Shrine or not, I had my orders. And orders or not, I'd gladly flatten him along with that grotesque tower if the damned sun would only give me half a chance to see him move.

Thinking about that fictitious enemy as a real personification of evil only tended to frustrate me more, making my collar steam hotly as I grew more anxious than ever to rid the world of him and everything he stood for.

It was an agonizing dilemma. I could either act out the drama, take my chances, and blast away at the tower right now without real confirmation or simply blend in with nature until the air cooled off much later in the day.

Stop wiggling! Hold still for a few friggin' seconds, damn it!

The hell with orders, I thought. I'll just go ahead and fire.

But it was the enemy who had the advantage of the blazing sun that morning. Then it happened. That real-life dilemma was abruptly taken out of my hands by Kurt, of all people, or some other sly enemy spotter, whoever and wherever he was.

The sky directly above us suddenly exploded with ear-splitting bursts of black smoke. Sergeant King and I became the very unwilling recipients of a hail of horrendous shrapnel that began to rain down all around us. With no overhead protection from the log we had used for cover, we could only retreat as fast as possible and dodge the hot, metal sleet that followed us.

It seemed that the tables had been turned as my two-man mini-patrol came under the withering airborne attack, very possibly directed from their observation post within one of those hidden niches in the bell tower, as I had imagined it would be.

As we moved swiftly and dodged through the trees, King radioed back that our position had become untenable. Amidst the cackling sound of static, we received a most disconcerting but welcome reply from Sergeant Brown back at the command post.

"Get your asses out of there! The friggin' generals have decided to spare the tower anyhow. Come on back."

"Roger, out." King wasted no time with small talk. Out was what we wanted and out we got, as fast as possible, zig-zagging back through the olive groves while the devastating black bursts followed too closely. They missed their two human targets, however, and we made it back safely.

I've often had reason to look back at that extraordinary, historic incident, wondering if it hadn't been some cosmic, ethereal force that had stayed my hand and saved that fabulous tower from destruction. To this day I can't help feeling that, had it been any other observer out there instead of me, the results could have been entirely different — catastrophic!

That brief moment that I had thought was wasted in sensitive contemplation of the tower's elegance while everything else around us seemed to be steeped in utter chaos might very well have been the finger of God restraining me, harnessing for one portentous moment the remorseless brute that lurks in all of us.

Now, fifty-five short years later, I can honestly say that I've often relived that day in my mind, rationalizing what might have been. An Italy without Pisa's magnificent, listing tower would have been a tragedy of timeless proportions, too awful to contemplate at this point in time. I know full well that my actions that day could have been the highest form of sacrilege.

Yet, if I could have been sufficiently sure that destroying the tower would have saved the life of even one of my comrades, I'd have done it in a flash. I will never know for certain if I had waited too long or, for that matter, if the enemy had even used the tower. Solving that mystery is still up for grabs.

To hell with you, Kurt Reinhardt! My turn will come later.

Chapter 10

Toward the Gothic Line

The last few miles to Pisa and the Arno River had to be anything but an easy run. They were strongly defended and protected by elite SS Wehrmacht along the obstructive terrain on both sides of the river bank, and the Allied forces had to throw everything they had against Hitler's headstrong army in order to gain control of the river valley beyond. In the long run, it was simpler to try outflanking maneuvers and send constant, jabbing patrols rather than chance costly, head-on attacks in order to gain our objective.

Personally, I never got to see the inner city of Pisa, until some forty-four years later, because we opted to avoid the direct frontal approach, but the historic city was soon destined to fall into Allied hands.

After more than a week of this constant night-and-day struggle, fighting to the death for every foot of those few bloody miles to the Arno, our division, alongside the 1st Armored Division and the British 8th, finally disgorged the enemy from the southernmost bank of the river. Still, we sorely needed to get to the other side, the wide open valley side.

Although the enemy had managed to evacuate most of their artillery across the river during their retreat, we were happy to see a hodgepodge of destroyed Panzer tanks, some still afire, and military vehicles of all kinds that had been left abandoned. They had either been in a terrible rush to get to the other side of the river or their fuel supplies weren't getting through. At this point it seemed to me that their ability to continue to defend against our advance had taken a direct hit and life should be easier for us from now on.

I was wrong.

Taking potshots at us the entire time, our slowly retreating antagonists would stop to lick their wounds but never once gave up their determination to sting and harass us. Their night patrols, as well as our own, busily probed each other for weak points, with the short-lived fire fights usually ending in a spectacular show of blinding flares and tracer bullets.

The bullet-ridden, bloated bodies of what once were men floated slowly and tragically down river. Mortar barrages and devastating machine-gun fire followed closely behind each other's hostile scouting parties, creating more havoc for those who still remained upright, those amazing infantry patrols who dared steal across the narrow Arno River on a nightly basis.

By mid-August our engineers had completed a detailed analysis of the Arno and it's marshy banks. During that time, over a thousand green replacement troops had to be brought in and indoctrinated as quickly as possible while we remained stuck on the wrong side of the river.

The division had little choice at that point but to hang fire and wait until a few days later when our night patrols finally reported unusually minimal action north of the Arno. We crossed to find that the Germans had, at last, acknowledged their losses and retreated to the mountains in the north, their next main defense line.

Our big push to those towering, pine-covered mountains and the dreaded, formidable Gothic Line we had heard so much about would come too soon. We knew there would be a great many more casualties when we assaulted those menacing Apennines looming ominously in the hazy distance, less than fifty miles off across the broad, pleasant looking Florentine valley.

That was August 15, 1944. While we waited and prepared to push on, the 91st Infantry Division celebrated the second anniversary of its reactivation, having also served in the First World War. No formal ceremonies could be held, but Commanding General Livesay expressed the pride and satisfaction he felt for his troops in a terse bulletin sent to each company.

> Our Division is now of age. It has met the enemy under the most trying
> circumstances of terrain and has driven him back with heavy casualties.
> I feel certain that the German high command has this Division registered
> as one of the Allies' first-line fighting divisions. The campaign to the
> Arno, the taking of Leghorn, and the investment of Pisa leave no doubt

in my mind but that I have the honor to command an organization of top-class fighting men.

Major General William G. Livesay

Once we reached the beautifully lush foothills of Tuscany alongside the north side of the winding Arno River, I was delighted to see and meet men from every part of the world who, like us, were involved in this chase to rescue human dignity and freedom. Soldiers from the Polish Brigade, the British 8th Indian Division, the Scots Guards, the wild and wooly 2nd New Zealand Division, a tough and stoic British 4th Division, a Palestinian Jewish brigade, and others poured down out of the hills into the vacated Arno Valley. All joined up on the edge of the fertile Etruscan valley ready to fight side by side against our despised common enemy.

Besides sharing vital intelligence information, we were occasionally lucky enough to share booze and bull sessions with the men of this universal alliance and did so whenever and wherever the opportunity arose.

I can truthfully report that I have never observed any group of humankind indulge themselves in and handle the hard stuff, anything alcoholic, as easily and shamelessly as those Kiwis, the fighting men of New Zealand. During the blistering heat of the summer, they informally donned shorts and khaki-colored undershirts as uniforms, displaying to advantage their enviable almond-tinted bodies. Coarse, bold, and gregarious, they were always a delight to socialize with. We'd curiously try to savvy their quaint, difficult English dialect.

Those macho Kiwis offered an unusually strong sense of protective security if one had the good fortune to find himself fighting on the flank of their brigade. On the other hand, we also appreciated the British brigades and Scots Guards who also did a masterfully straightforward job but with considerably more reserve and unbelievable stoicism. One example I can recall of their coolness under fire occurred a few months later in the frosty climate of Mt. Freddi in the high Apennines.

"They've been blasting away at us pretty heavily," I said to the veteran Scots Guards captain who had chosen to visit my observation post for "a bit of a look-see" after a particularly vigorous German artillery barrage had lasted longer than usual. I asked him why he thought the German artillery had been more active that day.

With classic British aplomb and understatement he looked me square in the eye and, with the slightest hint of a smile, said, "Just a wee bit of retaliation, don't ya know, sergeant."

Somehow I couldn't help but have mixed feelings, feeling somewhat more relaxed yet a little put down after his flippantly humorous answer.

With a view to the forthcoming lethal struggle we were to face once we powered our way through those precipitous mountains, the 5th Army generals decided to move our 91st Division to a special training area, to be temporarily replaced on the front lines by the 85th Division.

All regiments gathered near San Gimignano to learn more river-crossing techniques as well as how to fight in the frigid climate of the mountains before us. Our training included special emphasis on destroying pillboxes and hidden emplacements because it was commonly known that the enemy had plenty of time to strategically place and heavily fortify its notorious Gothic Line.

Putting us through our paces was hardly restful, but at least we were temporarily out of sight of the enemy and safe from the everyday terror we had so recently known and could never become used to.

Sleep, a most precious commodity, was a priority whenever and wherever we could get it. Good, hot food was next, followed by cleansing our grimy bodies in portable field showers. As humble as these activities were, to me they seemed more heavenly than a vacation in Waikiki. The nearest thing we had had to a bath since the battle for Pisa more than a week before was known as a whore's bath. We'd fill our metal helmets with water then splash our genitals and anything else we could reach by hand.

The pleasant country villagers seemed extremely happy to have us in their neighborhood and made us feel most welcome to visit them in their simple, stucco-faced homes. J.P. and I took full advantage of every opportunity to mingle, find a family or two who were particularly congenial, enjoy their company, and bring them foodstuffs that we'd finagle from the company kitchen.

"Grazie, Americani! Grazie," was their ever-constant greeting after the less-than-friendly, sullen Germans had been driven from their town. Those thankful, demonstrative words followed us wherever we went and made us feel like marvelously heroic saviors.

"Buon giorno, signora," we said, as J.P. and I greeted a kerchief-headed old woman sweeping her doorway, hoping we could bring a smile and a reply to our clumsy attempt at Italian.

"Buon giorno!" she said and smiled at us broadly. The poor woman displayed an absence of most of her front teeth but seemed genuinely grateful at our attempt to converse in her language.

"Giuseppe!" she called out to her husband as she stopped sweeping, "Americani soldatesca sono qui," announcing our presence to the stooped, elderly farmer who was hoeing the soil nearby. He straightened his back as best he could, and when he got closer, we could see his outstretched hand, the nervous smile.

"Hallo!" he said, to our surprise, in English. "My name is Giuseppe Manzetti." In an engaging attempt to speak our language, he continued. "Escusa my Engalish, per piacere. Once I liva in America for two years."

"Great!" we responded, almost in unison. As our faces lit up, he seemed to grow more confident. He invited us in and grew quite talkative, telling us how he had once emigrated to live with a relative in New York. It seemed that fifty-five years before, when he was a mere lad of twenty-four, he had become dismayed by the hustle and bustle of New York and, just as soon as he could, returned to the tranquility of bella Italia.

"I don't blame you. You have to be very brave or very crazy to live in New York City," I responded. I spent nine of my early years there after three years in an orphanage in Pleasantville, upstate.

J.P. and I were full of curiosity, so who better to respond to our many questions than this venerable, quasi-bilingual paesano? We relaxed into his simple, rush-seated wooden chairs and settled around a spacious stone fireplace in which was suspended a steaming black pot of hand-wrought iron that appeared to be at least as old as its owners. This had to be their only cooking area, and the old woman stirred the glowing ashes often with strong, wrinkled hands. The aroma from the pot grew stronger during the next half hour, tempting me to politely ask what she was cooking.

"Salsa di pomodoro, tomato sauce," Giuseppe responded. "You lika to eat, how you call it, lunch with us?"

Would we ever! J.P.'s chowhound appetite was renowned in our company's mess tent, and I could see him grin and lick his lips in anticipation. The change from Spam or mutton would definitely be a blessing. Since these most agreeable people seemed to be thoroughly enjoying our company as well as we theirs, I nodded happily and responded with appropriate fervor, "Si, si! Mille grazie!"

Exuberant J.P. had already learned better than I the colorfully descriptive Italian words for thanks that meant we'd truly be thrilled to death. He stated them then with a dramatic bow and a flourish, something in which I could hear the beautifully musical-sounding words *piacere* (pee-a-cherry) and *felicita* (feh-lee-chee-tah).

At that point, I thought that Mama — we had learned to call all women over fifty Mama as, almost without exception, they seemed to relish that salutation — would have offered us a bacchanalian feast if it were in her power to do so. Instead, she beamed with obvious pleasure and busily laid out assorted chipped ceramic plates on their warped, rickety, old oak table, saying something under her breath to Giuseppe about vino, whereupon his deep-set black eyes shone several shades brighter.

Excusing himself, he left and returned a few minutes later with two unmarked, straw-covered bottles from which he wiped away the soil they had probably been buried under. One was obviously the color of Cabernet, the other the color of water. Then he brought out three shot glasses along with mix-and-match tumblers.

Mama busily set about putting a second and larger pot of water onto a hook overhanging the red-hot coals while Giuseppe slowly, carefully uncorked the bottle of clear-colored liquid, first smelling then gingerly pouring the pristine liquid into the little shot glasses.

"Primo la grappa! Salut!" he said simply. "Very strong!"

Neither of us had ever tasted grappa, this fiery liquid which was reputedly nicknamed white lightening by those of our drinking buddies who had found the courage to try it. The old man watched with delight as J.P. and I sipped and reacted to our first tiny draught and its searing, electrical effect on the palette.

This was no ordinary liquor! We quickly discovered that its graphic sobriquet of white lightning was most apt. Humorously, I waved my hand in front of my gaping mouth as if to cool the effect of this liquor that was probably nearly 200 proof alcohol. After its first impact wore off, we simultaneously exclaimed, "Wow!"

Mama, looking up from stirring the richly aromatic sauce and watching us, almost fell on the floor laughing. It was probably the best laugh she had had in years.

J.P. and I toyed lovingly with what remained in our glasses, very slowly draining the last fraction of an ounce of that powerful secret weapon and soon began to feel some of its potent effect. We were offered refills, and J.P. accepted a bit more, which may or may not have proved that the Irish can always outdrink a Jew. Personally, I have no doubt that it's true.

The old man asked if we'd like to look around his tiny farm. As we followed him, he sadly pointed out where he had kept his pigs, chickens, two cows, and a mule. All had been confiscated by the German soldiers. Nothing much was left now except a small patch of vegetables, his acre and a half of grape vines, and some kind of freshly sprouting grain. During these terribly hard times they had to make do and live on anything that could be scratched from the crusty soil.

Returning to the house twenty minutes later, Papa, as we now called him, announced "Mangia!" and we eagerly followed him to the rough, wooden table.

Giuseppe uncorked and poured the darker bottle of homemade wine while he began to tell us with exaggerated hand motions and blanched, old lips how he had had to hide everything of value, including his wine, because the German soldiers would help themselves to anything. His eyes plainly expressed that what had bothered him most was the loss of his livestock, taken away almost two weeks before by the retreating troops. Those he couldn't hide.

Again we heard the phrase that we would hear repeated throughout the countryside as we pursued our enemy. "Tedeschi tutta porta via." I've often wondered if we Americans would have behaved as rapaciously if I had been doing the retreating. Very likely. But no matter who the plunderers were, it was these hapless, cordial Italians who were left high and dry.

Some might rightfully say that the Italian people weren't totally without blame, having permitted Il Duce and his Fascist army to join and enthusiastically become part of Hitler's Nazi hordes. Only when they realized too late how the ravages of war would affect their own personal lives did they take a second look and recant.

It's a well-known fact that these romantically sensitive Italians haven't produced the world's best soldiers and statesmen in this century nor ever since the height of the glory days of Rome, but this comparatively small, boot-shaped country does happen to possess the world's most amiable people. And to this day, it remains my deep-felt belief that they have to be this planet's most charming and ingratiating human beings.

"Do you have any children?" J.P. asked Papa.

An unexpected silence fell over the room. His broad smile disappeared.

"Si. We had two sons. Roberto was-a killed in Africa. Penso," he said, hesitating for a moment as his voice caught, "we hope-a and pray to Santa Maria every day that the other one may be a prisoner. He disappear. Not come home. The lasta time we hear from him was from Sicilia. We no hear from him since."

Because we had always found everyone so warm, so unusually cooperative, J.P. and I had almost forgotten that Italy had once fought against us and changed sides during the Sicilian campaign just a few months before our division arrived on the scene. His son, "the other one," could easily have been our enemy.

"Here's to the end of all wars!" I toasted, taking my first sip of wine. That was answered by a chorus of "Cin cin!" (pronounced chin-chin) meaning "Cheers!"

"Finire il guerra!" Giuseppe responded, too loudly in his attempt to conceal watery eyes, as we lifted our glasses again. His gentle smile was beginning to return as it would be bad manners to make his guests feel anything but joy in sharing his hospitality.

"Buon appetito!" Mama announced as she brought to the table a steaming bowl of tagliatelle con suco pomodoro. Our eyes feasted before our mouths did at the wonderful sight. Papa served his two American visitors first while Mama looked on with pride at her culinary achievement, apologizing for the lack of cheese and cursing the Tedeschi for it.

Long after we had had our fill, we complimented her as generously as it was possible to do in our limited Italian. J.P. rubbed his stomach in mock glee.

Only then did Papa admit to us that obtaining the flour for the pasta was nearly impossible, bragging that he had managed to obtain it from the black market. When J.P. reached into his pocket to attempt to remunerate him, the old man firmly held up his hand and said, "Por favore, no money, please. Itsa make us happy you enjoy."

Without saying a word, J.P. and I cast surreptitious glances at each other, both knowing what we'd bring them the next day, if we were still around.

We said arrivederci about four o'clock that afternoon, promising to return soon. J.P. managed to eat his regular ration of camp chow at six, but I was still nursing the beautiful pasta taste in my mouth and passed. I gave my mess kit full of whatever it was to two of the most astonished, raggedy-ann kids you ever saw who were standing at the end of the ubiquitous garbage line. Contentedly, I nibbled at the canned peaches that happened to be dessert and hoped that those barefoot ragamuffins enjoyed my discarded dinner as much as I had enjoyed Mama's delicious pasta.

Later that night we visited Sergeant Havlichek in the mess tent and with his permission traded most all of my next week's beer ration for gifts for the Manzettis, a ten-pound sack of flour, a wheel of cheese, and a large tin of pre-sliced bacon. I knew they would be thrilled. I also knew I could depend on J.P. to share his ration of beer with me.

That pleasant time with the Manzettis was just the first of our many visits to a surprising number of Italian casas where we were always welcomed with open arms. All were delightfully unforgettable. From then on, J.P. and I would manage to wheedle our way into their households, making it our business to increase our knowledge of the people and their language and enjoying La Famiglia, any family, or whatever was left of it.

Even in the height of battle when I'd requisition a house for use as an observation post or when we based our command post in what was left of some dwelling, the family would be sure to get out of our way and silently remain somewhere in the background. I would try as best I could to offer a smile and talk them out of their fear.

—◦—◦—

Soon, the sudden activity of command post personnel signalled it was time to prepare for the next attack. Sergeant Brown met me as I walked towards the big tent and said, "We'd better get our asses in gear, Weckstein. This looks like the big one."

"Get the maps ready, Sergeant," Colonel Woods ordered, looking more serious than I had ever recalled seeing him.

We were about to break camp and join up with the 5th Army in a back-breaking, all-out assault against the infamous Gothic Line. The thought of those menacing German defenses as well as the many terse warning bulletins from division headquarters were disconcerting, and it didn't take a fortune teller to know that we were in for the roughest battle of the entire Italian campaign.

The pernicious enemy had time to prepare extremely well in order to make our lives a living hell in this mountainous Apennine area, paradoxically just north of the gentle Renaissance city of Florence. They had made full use of Italian slave labor, working these people around the clock to construct concrete pillboxes that were practically invisible, camouflaged fortresses that had roofs covered with three feet of logs and dirt. There could be no room for flanking attacks in the nearly vertical inclines of these mountains; we'd have to hit them straight on.

A few runs by our heavy bombers attempted to soften their resistance, but unfortunately, their well-dug-in positions remained in excellent operational condition. I distinctly recall two or three bombs accidentally dropped much too near our own jumping-off point, some fifty yards behind, where I waited as the noisy procession of B-17s passed overhead. Apparently, someone had pushed that hair-trigger button three or four seconds too soon. Luckily, there were no casualties this time.

Geographically, we had broken the Germans' hold on all the territory between the cultural center of Florence and the mountains. Just a few miles to the north was this dividing line, the snow-capped, rugged mountain range too simply called the Apennines. Its hoary, east-west ridge of icy waterfalls and almost impenetrable gullies had created many streams that flowed through the granite mountain faces, forming some of Italy's largest rivers, including the Arno we had already won and the Po we had yet to conquer.

Why had a vengeful, unforgiving God gone out of his way to erect this mountain chain of three-thousand-foot-high peaks for our enemy's benefit? No way were they less sinful or more deserving than we. It had to be a defender's dream and our nightmare.

This was the site of the Gothic Line. Only a single, twisting, two-lane road was to be our main supply route until Bologna would fall, eight unbelievably long murderous months later.

From Florence to Bologna, the Gothic Line

Chapter 11

The Gates of Hell

If I hadn't already entertained the notion that war was God's ugliest invention, the events I will begin to describe in this chapter concerning the horrendous Gothic Line proved it beyond a doubt. Beyond the names of the many towns, hills, and rivers we fought through, beyond the titles and numbers of the various stouthearted Allied divisions, regiments, and brigades from every part of the world that participated in this huge effort are the personal dramas that are certainly more meaningful, and I report these life-and-death events as I saw them, through my eyes.

Each and every one of the crucial mountain-pass positions we had to face along that highway to Bologna had become a major German stronghold, a granite bulwark I had chosen to name the Gates of Hell. These dauntingly impregnable emplacements had anti-tank ditches ten feet wide and six feet deep, which were doubly protected by anti-tank guns and machine guns prepared for murderous crossfire. Ahead of this were the strategically placed minefields and barbed wire entanglements, Satan's first line of psychological defense.

As if that weren't enough, those reinforced bunkers and concrete pillbox fortifications contained weapons defending every conceivable avenue of approach against armor as well as infantry. What's more, they had cleverly scooped away entire reverse slopes of hills to conceal their larger howitzers, mortars, rolling 88s, and tanks. Huge, multi-tinted fishnets were stretched and ribboned tentlike over those excavations in a hit-and-miss pattern to duplicate the texture and form of the surrounding rugged terrain.

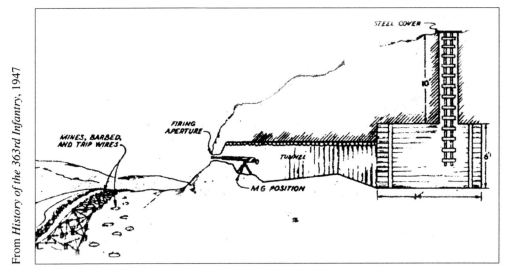

From *History of the 363rd Infantry*, 1947

A typical German dugout in the Gothic Line

The Germans were still in the process of constructing and improving these massive, by-the-book defenses with slave labor when our regiment launched its initial assault against Il Giogo Pass. It was from there that we would attempt to seize strategic Monticelli, the Gothic Line's first and foremost lofty ridge.

On the day before our initial attack, wave after wave of our flying fortresses did a run over the area to soften it up for our infantry. We optimistically assumed our battalion would rapidly succeed after that. The plan was for the 85th and 88th Divisions to quickly pursue the disarrayed enemy through our lines and chase them in the direction of Bologna fifty miles to the north.

Watching the dense smoke and hearing the thunderclaps of a thousand bombs exploding high along the top of the ridge, I felt more elated than I had a right to be. No army could possibly bear up to that kind of punishment without breaking, or so I thought. But, that's not the way it turned out. Like Cassino, it was no walk in the park as we would soon discover. The actual experience was more like a macabre march in a cemetery The bombs our planes had dropped seemed to have little effect. As usual, ground soldiers were obviously needed to finish the job.

Merely attempting to take the low ground of harmless looking chianti vineyards in order to get to the base of bald Monticelli proved to be unbelievably costly because our platoons of infantry were totally exposed to German observers holding that massive hunk of high ground. The Jerries had a field day picking and choosing their targets. They butchered our advancing squads like sitting ducks. No orders had come down to retreat or disperse or take evasive maneuvers. It was all happening too fast.

Soul-piercing cries of "Medic! Medic!" came from up and down the line as it quickly became apparent that the highly touted air strike we had so thrillingly watched hadn't hampered the enemy's capability in the least. Like ants in a hail storm, aid men and stretcher bearers raced in all directions carrying away the screaming wounded, dying, and dead.

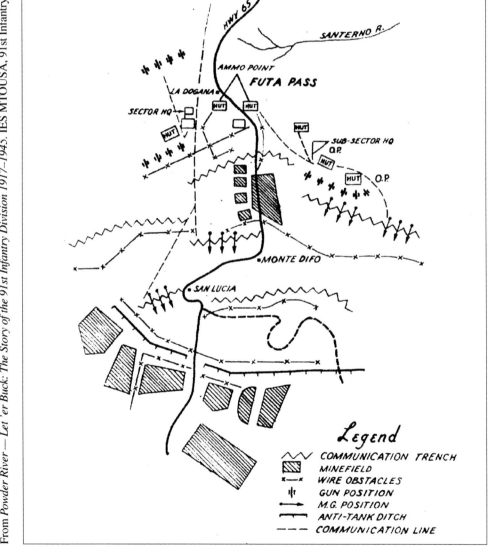

From Powder River — Let 'er Buck: The Story of the 91st Infantry Division 1917–1945. IES MTOUSA, 91st Infantry

Futa Pass, German defense positions

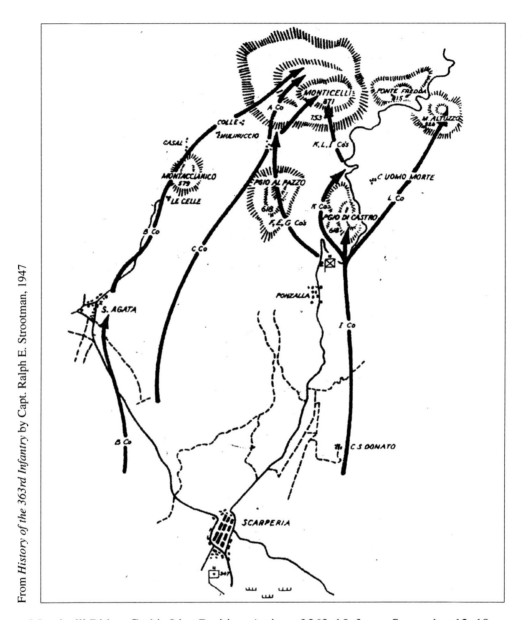

From *History of the 363rd Infantry* by Capt. Ralph E. Strootman, 1947

Monticelli Ridge, Gothic Line Position. Action of 363rd Infantry September 12–18, 1944, supported by 347th Field Artillery Battalion

Those unsung heroes of every battle, the aid men, as well as men con-scripted from other non-medical infantry support platoons to assist in evacuating the wounded, assuredly deserve much more acclaim for their bravery than they've been given.

As further testimony to their courage, here is a passage from the *History of the 363rd Infantry* pertaining to that very day.

The author on leave in Italy

The second chow line, after our soldiers were fed

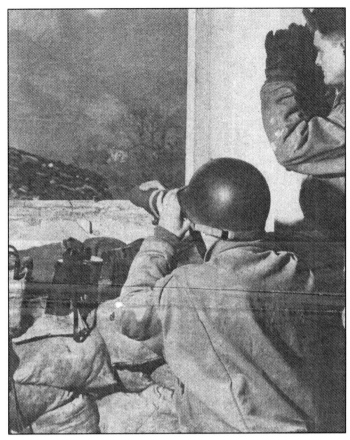

Working with a heavy mortar platoon at an OP

The first day of combat

Dead Germans in front of a Gothic Line dugout

Getting howitzers to the front

Mud everywhere

White phosphorous shelling

The author and
J. P. Dunnagen

Company G near Pianoro

Rounding up prisoners in the Po Valley

The author being awarded the Legion of Merit

It was getting dark as the leading 3rd Platoon, commanded by Lieutenant Robert C. Hatcher, reached the first break in the brush-lined path; here the platoon found what had been a bridge across a ravine. It was now just a pile of rubble lying in the bottom of the ravine. Lieutenant Hatcher led his platoon across safely with the exception of a Medical Corps man who was at the rear of the group and stepped on a Schu mine. The platoon and the rest of the company halted on the southern side of the ravine and hit the dirt upon hearing the explosion as the now alerted Germans opened fire from their defensive positions strung around Monticelli.

Under machine-gun fire another aid man from the 2nd Platoon ran to rescue his wounded comrade and stepped on a mine himself. Two other 2nd Platoon men went to evacuate the aid men and stepped on mines. There were now four men in the minefield. Staff Sergeant Ernest L. Johnson, Private First Class Boyd Rittenberry, and Corporal Willard R. LaMarche from the 2nd, 1st, and Weapons Platoons respectfully volunteered to go into the minefield and rescued two of the men. Joined by Private First Class Michael O'Neill, they returned to evacuate the other two when both Rittenberry and LaMarche stepped on mines. They brought LaMarche out, but permission was refused for them to go back after the others. Instead, the Ammunition and Pioneer Platoon (A and P) was called forward and brought mine detectors to clear a path through which evacuation could be made without further casualties. Helping to clear and mark the minefield, Sergeant Wilbert I. Merx of the A and P Platoon also stepped on a mine and was blown into the ravine.[1]

I had known LaMarche personally, a strapping hale and hearty athletic type who, like thousands of other brave heroes, would now be forced to live the life of an amputee, if he lived at all.

I had seen death and carnage before but never so close, so brutal. It brought on the dry heaves. But under the circumstances I wouldn't let on, couldn't cry, and did my best to conceal the pity and nausea I felt.

Suddenly, our heavy artillery came to life. Our devastating 155mms offered vengeful retaliation as the big shells shrieked noisily overhead. I could even feel their concussion from where I stood as the ground three or four hundred yards away was pulverized into the air. But, it was impossible to breach and enter deeply enough within the heavily fortified enemy bunkers to have an effect. Try as we might, we couldn't stop them, and our casualty list continued to grow

---

1. Strootman, Captain Ralph E., comp., *History of the 363rd Infantry.* Washington Infantry Journal Press, Washington, D.C., 1947. pp. 70–71.

out of all proportion long after the unforgettable cordite smell of smoke from the shelling had cleared the valley.

We had come too far. Retreat was impossible. Our 1st Battalion rifle companies A, B, and C had been ordered to gain a foothold at the top of the strategic mountain at any cost, because this was the first in the long chain of enemy strongholds obstructing our way. Now the 362nd and all battalions of the 363rd Infantry Regiment were involved. The 361st that had already done its share of fighting earlier was being held in reserve.

Two hours passed. The ragged remnants of our battalion's gallant men who had been lucky enough to have dodged the incessant deadly mortar and artillery barrages had made it to a narrow, three-and-a-half-foot-wide embankment about three-quarters of the way up the mountain. Stopped there by barbed wire and machine-gun fire from the concealed bunkers, they could only stay out of the line of fire and wait for further orders.

The better part of a day passed in this stalemate before Colonel Woods had us set up a combined battalion command post and observation post on a narrow, rocky hilltop that overlooked the entire combat zone. Only the small valley separated us from the action.

Then all hell broke loose! Artillery and mortar shells of every size and description began to rain down on our side of the mountain, into the valley, and onto my most essential observation position atop the tiny hill. We were hit with air bursts as well as conventional ground fire, making it a terrifying experience to leave the safety of a protective boulder even to urinate.

This deadly metallic deluge continued sporadically for three days and nights. Any attempt by our companies to probe or advance beyond their present positions just fifty to sixty yards beneath the enemy-occupied rocky crest was met with a hail of devastating machine-gun fire, hand grenades, and well-directed mortar bursts.

My telescope gave me an unobstructed view of the entire bloody battleground from my partially exposed position. It was impossible for us to dig into the steep rocky hillside, so the five of us who comprised this command post's field team had to make use of the largest boulders we could find for protection. Pounded intermittently by their artillery every ten to twenty minutes as we were, I had to quickly locate a large boulder that was concave enough near the bottom for me to scurry lizardlike under it to find a few more inches of protection. Of course, if a shell happened to hit the ground at just a certain angle to where I lay hiding, I would've been a goner.

Fortunately for me, most of the projectiles aimed at our command post either crashed noisily onto the top of our protective boulders or exploded on the far

94

slope of the hill. However, those few ill-fated soldiers of Companies A, B, C, and D who had spread out in an irregular, broken line within my view weren't so lucky.

Because our men were already so close to the enemy troops near the crest, mortars naturally became their weapon of choice rather than the heavier, less accurate cannons that were likely to unintentionally hit their own positions. This well-schooled enemy had become expert in the use of their amazingly accurate mortars. If you listened carefully during the rare quiet intervals, you could hear the metallic klink of the shell as it left the stubby little two-foot barrel. What you couldn't hear at all was the sound of the high-flying projectile itself until a split second before it burst, strewing white-hot shrapnel and untold destruction within a radius of thirty-five feet.

Reprinted by permission of Bill Mauldin and the Watkins/Loomis Agency

"K Comp'ny artillery commander speakin'."

What was left of our decimated companies after the gory first few minutes had begun to dig in to the parched crusty soil of the hillside as best and as fast as they could. I watched, horrified. I had never seen men, our men, being killed and wounded in such vast numbers. Some were frantically digging slit trenches; others tried for the greater safety of the deeper foxhole, especially where they could use excavations left by some previous artillery shell explosion. The mortar shells continued to fall, picking off a man here, two or three there.

Most of the dead and wounded had to be left until the enemy stopped to cool off their mortar barrels. Then medics and litter bearers would rush in to remove them, more often than not in bloody body bags, and take them to the ambulances waiting down below. Although there may have been infractions of the Geneva Convention or whatever rules applied to the battlefield. I can truthfully say, I never witnessed any breach of protocol when either side signaled a need to collect casualties or call a truce. That savagery seemed reserved for Hollywood.

Half an hour later, when the mountainside had finally been cleared of broken, blood-soaked bodies, the enemy mortar barrage pecked away again. Splat! Splat, splat! Harass, maim, kill! A kind of pagan death dance.

I cannot describe how absolutely heart rending it was to watch the gruesome sight of body parts and pieces of American uniforms and helmets floating grotesquely back to earth after the smoke of a telling shell burst had drifted away. I was thankful that from that distance I wasn't able to hear their screams or recognize their agonized faces, faces I knew.

I felt I had to do something, anything, to stop the slaughter.

I couldn't make use of our heavy artillery to get at the crest of Monticelli for fear of hitting our own men scattered zig-zag along the line, so I called on our Company D mortars.

"Dog One, this is Abel George Two. Do you read me?"

"For chrissake, Abel George Two, we've been waiting for your friggin' call. Where the hell have you been?" Unbeknownst to me, they had been expectantly waiting for direction, restrained by their obstructed hillside angle and difficult terrain from being able to make out the targets that were more obvious from my vantage point across the valley.

"Hang tight, Dog One. I'm lining up a target."

Finally! It was my turn! I was frustrated and mad as hell. Until now, I'd been busily dodging shells and reporting what little enemy movement I could see. Mainly, I kept the command post filled in with the locations of our own over-extended squads as they attempted to make headway up the mountain, positioning themselves as best they could for counterattacks. Now that we were badly stalemated and taking one hell of a beating, I would find better use of my time to do what I had learned to do best, direct fire.

Carefully, very deliberately, I trained the scope along the scrubby crest where I knew the enemy had concealed dugouts and foxholes. I caught a subtle movement of a branch and called Company D again. My heart was beating noisily as I spoke into the mouthpiece of the little field radio.

"Dog One, give me a smoke round as close as you can to the top of the hill at coordinate thirty-five. I've got a target."

"Roger."

The smoke given off by the exploding shell a minute later permitted me to see exactly where it landed so that I could better direct the following rounds.

"Beautiful, Dog One. You're forty yards to the right and fifteen over. Try again. This time, no smoke." My directions would have him creep closer to the target gradually while being extra careful not to undershoot the ridge top. Less than a minute later, the next shell exploded about fifteen yards to the left and ten yards beyond my prospective target. If the Kraut had his head up, there was an outside chance that shrapnel might have gotten him.

"You're fifteen left and ten over. Let's do it again."

"Roger."

With the next round I could have kissed that guy on the other end of the radio as I saw a heinie helmet spiral up crazily from where the shell had landed, exactly at the spot I wanted. I thought, Cheez, those things are amazingly accurate! I'll have to call on them more often.

"Great, Dog One!" I yelled into the radio. "That was perfect! I'm planning to keep you guys busy, so keep the line open."

I had tasted blood. From that compelling moment on and during the next few days, I managed to elude Jerries' barrages and focus on selecting my targets. I went mostly on suspicion of what appeared to be artificial landscaping as well as the probability factor. Rarely knowing for sure what degree of success my potshots would have, I fired away almost constantly, like a kid wildly pulling the trigger at moving ducks in a carnival's shooting gallery. I kept those mortar barrels feverishly hot every waking daylight hour, hoping for a bullseye.

Our taxpayers at home will just have to find a way to handle the cost of those shells. I don't give a damn how, I thought, with fierce determination.

Dog Company's supply detail stayed busy during those three nights attempting to carry ammunition noiselessly up the difficult trail to our mortars while dodging German harassing fire that came without warning.

Unfortunately, my personal blitzkrieg wasn't one-sided. Enemy counterattacks came almost as regular as clockwork from dawn of the second day. Even though our men had found some degree of protection in fox holes, the Germans continued to clobber them. Until we could take the crest of Monticelli, the slaughter would continue indefinitely.

From my loge position at the observation post, I watched in amazement as one of our men on the exposed flank of Company B rose from his foxhole and began firing wildly. I saw him wince when hit by small-arms fire, but he cradled his light machine gun in his arms and charged, firing as he went. Then hit again by a grenade fragment, he staggered but miraculously kept on firing. Once more he attempted to charge the hill by himself, only to be cut almost in half by a hail of Schmeisser bullets from a bunker at the crest.

Observing this incredible scene from a distance, I couldn't help wondering who it was and why he carried out that suicidal charge. Someone later told me that the man was Sergeant Higdon, my very first top sergeant. I suspected I understood what had possessed him to take on the German army by himself. A brash, chip-on-the-shoulder, regular Army man, he just had had more than enough of the killing, and the frustration of being pinned down like that had sent him over the edge. First Sergeant Higdon was awarded the Silver Star posthumously for bravery in action.

Day two was quieter. The sound of rifle fire became more sporadic. But when we attempted to send out feeler patrols, the enemy would pick them off and further devastate our dwindling companies with retaliatory counterattacks, occasional machine-gun fire, and mortar bursts. Eventually, they discovered that they could practically roll their hand grenades down the hill at our positions like bowling balls in an alley.

During those terrible days of that living hell on Monticelli, I had somehow learned by osmosis to be a little braver, inspired by the sight of Colonel Woods and his stolid refusal to duck for incoming barrages. As long as I live, I will never fathom his mysterious inner strength and luck as he ignored those porters of death the way he did.

I continued to direct our mortars and cannons all day, watching as best I could for targets of opportunity. Our battalion remained pinned down.

On day three, between enemy barrages and my calling fire, I observed one of our men on the extreme left flank do extremely gutsy, astonishing things. Dumbfounded, I could hardly believe my bloodshot eyes as I watched his amazing actions. These feats are best described in the words of the Army's general orders for his well deserved award of the Congressional Medal of Honor.

> Sergeant Oscar G. Johnson (then private first class), practically single-handedly protected the left flank of his company's position near Scarperia, Italy, in the offensive to break the Germans' Gothic Line. Company B was the extreme left assault unit of the corps. The advance was stopped by heavy fire from Monticelli Ridge, and the company took cover behind an embankment. Private Johnson, a mortar gunner, having

expended his ammunition, assumed the duties of a rifleman. As leader of a squad of seven men, he was ordered to establish a combat post fifty yards to the left of the company to cover its exposed flank. Repeated enemy counterattacks, supported by artillery, mortar, and machine-gun fire from the high ground to his front, had by the afternoon of 16 September killed or wounded all of his men. Collecting weapons and ammunition from his fallen comrades, in the face of hostile fire, he held his exposed position and inflicted heavy casualties upon the enemy, who several times came close enough to throw hand grenades. On the night of 16–17 September, the enemy launched its heaviest attack on Company B, putting greatest pressure against the lone defender on the left flank. Despite mortar fire which crashed about him and machine-gun bullets which whipped the crest of his shallow trench, Private Johnson stood erect and repulsed the attack with grenades and small-arms fire. He remained awake and on the alert throughout the night, frustrating all attempts at infiltration. On 17 September, twenty-five German soldiers surrendered to him. Two men, sent to reinforce him that afternoon, were caught in a devastating mortar barrage. With no thought for his own safety, Private Johnson rushed to the shell hole where they lay half buried and seriously wounded, covered their position by his fire, and assisted a Medical Corpsman in rendering aid. That night he secured their removal to the rear and remained on watch until his company was relieved. Five companies of a German paratroop regiment had been repeatedly committed to the attack on Company B without success. Twenty dead Germans were found in front of his position.

By his heroic stand and utter disregard for personal safety, Private Johnson was in large measure responsible for defeating the enemy's attempts to turn the exposed flank.

As his prime witness, I agreed wholeheartedly with that account. As for the enemy counterattacks noted, I had urgently radioed his company commander to report when and from where those enemy forays were coming, even as I attempted to distract those raiders with mortar fire. This action was partially responsible for the Legion of Merit award I was to receive later.

In one of the attacks, I watched as about a dozen enemy infiltrators slipped slowly over the crest of the hill above Johnson's exposed left flank by ones and twos, appearing ghostly in their earth-colored paratrooper uniforms. From my position a few hundreds yards away, I could see that each of them carried some kind of automatic weapon and were headed around him in a classic flanking maneuver. With Private Johnson out of the way, they could move along the side of the hill, knock off our men one at a time as they waited unsuspectingly in their outposts, and ultimately surround our shrinking forces from behind.

My first thought was to immediately notify the officer in charge of his company.

"Baker One! Baker One! Do you read me?"

"Yeah! What's up?" came the fatigued reply.

"A dozen Krauts are sneaking in at about the eleven o'clock position off your left flank."

No answer was necessary. He had been warned and would probably yell over to his men on the left to get ready. At this point they were strung out in a crooked line about seven to ten yards from each other.

I then made a quick call to Dog One at the heavy mortar platoon and began to work the shell bursts in from Johnson's far left. Within a minute, I had closed in on my target and was pelting the attackers, getting as close as I dared to Johnson's foxhole. With the burst of my first locating mortar shell, Johnson became alerted, looked to his left, and spotted the attack. The rest is literally in the account of his award.

A year later, after the defeat of Hitler's army in Italy, I was selected to help detail the extent of Sergeant Johnson's heroic actions. Having personally observed most of this brave man's unusual exploits, I could assist in documenting exactly how he came to earn the coveted Congressional Medal of Honor.

By now, I had begun to make good use of our heavy artillery fire, directing it miles beyond the top of Monticelli using our 105mm and Long Tom 155mm howitzers. Targeting supply trucks and all suspicious movements I could discern at those great distances, I'd harass and torment their rear echelon. I was always hopeful, and occasionally lucky enough, to score a direct hit. With the invaluable aid of my special telescope, I kept the barrels of our big guns hot. Ever watchful for counterattacks, I'd switch back and forth between observing and the immediate task of clearing the crest of the mountain. But no mortar shell could penetrate those heavily buttressed dugouts except at their rear-facing entrances that I could not see. I prayed for hits and blindly fired away.

The retaliation never stopped. This was one clever enemy and throughout the grueling third day they had already inflicted such terrible casualties on our men that I wondered how we could continue what seemed to be a hopeless impasse.

Those of our men who remained and were not too badly wounded must have been worn to a frazzle, hungry as hell, and, most likely, had to relieve themselves in the hole they remained in to avoid getting killed. I had no possible way of knowing that the situation on Monticelli was rapidly building to a climax. Only later did I find out that enemy information gathered from prisoners and intercepted radio messages indicated Jerry's losses were heavier than we imagined and they were forced to bring in reinforcements from the north. Word came that, while facing our 363rd Infantry Regiment, the platoons of the 4th German Paratroop Division had taken a terrible beating and their numbers were now reduced to a desperate minimum.

Had our own mortar fire and artillery been more successful than I thought? Bless our infantrymen. But, they hadn't been given the opportunity to do much beyond protecting their own besieged positions from the sporadic raids of this gravely crippled foe. The 3rd Battalion under Lt. Colonel Long's driving guidance had been only somewhat successful in gaining a foothold in their sector to our right, but even then, die-hard elements of the Wehrmacht still retained their original positions on the crest.

Obviously frustrated, Commanding General Livesay visited the 3rd Battalion command post and issued this order to the weary colonel. "The 3rd Battalion will follow a rolling barrage up Monticelli at 1400, which will be furnished by Division Artillery Corps. They will be requested to thicken the barrage by firing on targets in the rear areas, but you have to take the ridge at all costs. Go up, and don't stop until you get to the crest."

"I'll get them up there, General," Colonel Long replied, "but I don't expect to have many men left."

Following the General's instructions, the battalion's lead companies were still a few hundred yards from the crest when the draw, up which Company K was attacking, forked in two directions. They started up the east branch and were immediately hit by a well prepared mortar concentration. Suddenly finding his diminished squad of ten men, so exposed on the bare stretch of ground leading directly to the top, Captain William B. Fulton realized he had two choices. Retreat or rush it. His men dropped to the ground each time a close one whined in, and magically all eleven made it and threw themselves into the emplacements the Germans had recently abandoned.

Captain Fulton raised the battalion command post on the radio and announced, "I'm on top of Monticelli. I've got ten men with me. We're played out and I'll be goddamned if I know what to do next!" It was then twelve minutes to three, September 17, the beginning of the end for Hitler's paratroopers on the mountain.

The Germans and what was left of their green reinforcements began a vengeful counterattack — a do or die effort. Lt. Colonel Long took advantage of this opening to send sorties of additional platoons to assist in capturing as much as possible of the ridge. The toll to both sides was staggering as the vicious enemy continued to fight on. But once having a foothold on the crest, there was no turning back for our troops. In danger of being outflanked by a determined force, Jerry's extended outposts on our immediate front could no longer continue to be held without fear of capture or annihilation. During that same day, other regiments of the 91st were attacking in force all up and down the line, diverting what was left of the already over-diluted strength of the battle-weary Germans away from the main pressure point of Monticelli. The stress had become too much.

On the third night and fourth morning, Monticelli became unusually silent. There were no mortar bursts, no bone-chilling machine-gun fire. A blue jay even rasped noisily at me as I trained my eyepiece toward the northwest end of the mountain. The hush was eerie.

The dawn had barely broken through the darkness when Company A radioed our command post requesting permission to test the silence and send a squad up the hill. Scanning the blood-soaked mountain before me, I watched with a mixture of fear and hope as ten men from Company A rose slowly from their protective positions and guardedly made their way to the crest. What guts that must have taken.

Watching suspiciously for any possibility of counterattack, I trained my scope to the far distance and saw the tail end of a truck convoy. It seemed that sometime during the night the enemy had chosen to leave Monticelli. With a sigh of immense satisfaction, I quietly observed their trucks trailing off in the distance as they rapidly retreated to some other line of fortification in the north. Apparently, they had taken more punishment than I had suspected.

I reported what I was seeing to Colonel Woods who was busily phoning regimental headquarters with the news as I gave it to him.

When I accompanied the command post party to the crest an hour or so later, I was amazed at the strewn array of remaining enemy bodies, some already bloated and stinking with the kind of bacteria and maggots that would ultimately win all wars. It was apparent that they didn't allow for time to remove their dead.

How many of these torn up corpses I was personally responsible for I'll never know. I sat down near one of those rear entrances I hadn't been able to observe from my vantage point beyond the crest and without remorse kicked the offensively smelly corpse down the hill so that I could unwrap and eat my fruit bar without distraction before moving on.

Although no tally was taken, I calculated that we had lost at least six men to every one of theirs. It was probably our battalion's most costly single battle of the war in Italy. Too many people I knew and respected had lost their lives or had been severely wounded on the southwestern slope of Monticelli Ridge, and this had been only the beginning of that Gothic Armageddon.

The terrible cost of lives resulting from that savagely fought standoff remains vividly and powerfully etched in my mind to this day, more than any battle that had come before or would come later in that war. I shudder even now as I recall it.

Chapter 12

The Apennines

W e couldn't know it at the time, of course, but there were eight long, terror-filled months to go, a lifetime for too many thousands of brave young men, men who would never again return home.

I was about half right in my estimate of our regiment's casualties over those last, tortuous fifty or so miles. They were staggering. When there finally was time to tally the 5th Army's losses after the war was over, they found that of the 3,000 men originally in my regiment, 1,564 men had been wounded and 535 killed in action. Of my own small section of men — the ten I started out with — most of them were lost.

Like many others, I had survived this first life-or-death encounter, and if I just happened to be one of the few lucky ones who would manage to get out of this war in one piece, I'd consider it a rebirth. Now, fifty-five years after the fact, I do feel as though I've lived two lives.

Getting back to that first life, however, we had yet to fight our way to the crucially important Po Valley once the key city of Bologna fell. Then once and for all we could finally break the enemy's stubborn stranglehold on Italy, hopefully before they reached the formidable and impassible Alps.

Those next few grueling miles of the Apennine mountain range could make all the difference in the war. They knew it, and we knew it.

Now that our regiment had driven the Germans off Monticelli and out of the dreaded Futa Pass, we attempted to take full advantage of the retreating enemy's disorganization but found that the higher we went, the more the cold, fog, wind, and rain became the enemy's allies.

Winter was rapidly approaching, and those seemingly inaccessible pre-alpine peaks offered very little in the way of refuge from the weather. The sudden onset of seasonal rains exacerbated the misery of trying to pursue our antagonist through unbelievable quagmires of muddied side roads and passes. We'd have to chase the Jerries around or up and over the sheer escarpments of those craggy, saw-toothed summits. Meanwhile, they of course tried their best to kill us.

These harsh descriptions of what one thinks of as sunny Italy are not exaggerations as anyone unfortunate enough to have spent that winter with us in the Apennines would surely know. Our feet and faces were the first to suffer the icy temperature. I wore three pair of GI socks plus burlap sacks over my boots against the cold, but even these couldn't keep out the wetness from the rain and melting snow that always found a way to seep in.

Many trees, weakened by the wet ground and the almost constant shelling, had blown over, blocking the muddy highway. There wasn't a dry soldier in the lot; every man, in spite of raincoat, helmet, and combat boots, was drenched to the bone.

As we moved through frigid sleet that alternated with driving rain, the enemy subjected us to continuous artillery barrages. The Germans, long before we got there, had zeroed in along crucial points in the road to demoralize us with this metal storm whenever they felt they were being chased too closely.

I can vouch for the fact that their ploy worked because it tended to affect our morale even more than it injured personnel. Again and again, our disheveled column had to hit the ground along the road's rain-filled ditches, totally immersed in the oozy residue of mother nature's excrement, until each barrage was over. Cursing mad, we rose, cold, muddy, wet, and thoroughly miserable, wishing we were back in the hot, dry Algerian desert.

We had become a sorry looking lot. Several of my men did look like the devil and understandably asked permission to go on sick call and report to the doctors in a medical detachment somewhere to our rear. I could never be quite sure if their ailments were real or imagined, but they invariably did return a day or so later.

Murderous encounters and fire fights continued unabated for the next few weeks. We continued to push our desperate attack and were met in kind by incredibly obstinate die-hard defenders. They must have been as wet and miserable as we were, yet they seemed prepared to meet our assault in every village and farmhouse, through streams that were raging torrents, and on every inch of rocky, high ground.

Our successes, fleeting as they were, could only be measured in yards as our platoons struggled valiantly night and day to dislodge this solidly entrenched foe. Each advance cost dearly. Every once-charming little hamlet tucked away among the pretty valleys or perched ridiculously atop peaks, each and every one of them as well as each deserted farmhouse took its toll in both American and German lives. Every single one of them had at least one Kurt Reinhardt doing his duty for God and country and had to be desperately fought for, sometimes for days at a time.

I discovered that an Italian town usually consists of about a dozen ancient two-story buildings hand-built of stone and stucco and joined in a row along a narrow street. In the center of that line would be the ubiquitous small church and graveyard.

Individual farmhouses were located well away from the town center, often in groups of two so that in normal times the old folks could sleep in separate buildings but close enough to the family so that Nonna, the grandma, could cook and care for the bambinos.

Sometimes I came across the remains of farm animals, mostly horses and sheep that had become innocent victims of the war. Their torn bodies had been reduced to a mound of distorted fur lying silhouetted sadly against the frozen turf of their snow-covered barnyards.

Whenever our snow-suited infantry squads came upon one of these peaceful looking dwellings, the typical procedure was always to advance cautiously and get as close as possible to find out if anyone was inside. It wasn't practical to look for human footprints in the snow because the weather changed so quickly that tracks could be covered in no time by a fresh snowfall or sleet storm. Even if the building appeared empty, it might be booby-trapped, but in these mountains, more often than not Kurt was quietly waiting inside, watching to see how many men we had and which ones were the officers.

One or two of our gallant scouts would generally take the lead at a distance of about fifty feet ahead of the others, crouch low, and slowly make their way toward the objective. When the enemy inside thought the moment was right, two of them would quickly raise their machine gun to a window, or as often happened, one man with his deadly automatic burp gun would attempt to pick off either the closest victims or the suspected officer in charge. At that point, our men would run for the nearest shelter or hit the ground, which was often peppered with murderous Shu mines or Bouncing Bettys.

It wasn't practical for our men to use anything heavier than rifles, automatic weapons, bazookas, or hand grenades. After all, we couldn't arbitrarily destroy every suspect house in Italy with artillery. As a result, our casualties from these skirmishes were heavy.

Whenever I could, I stayed in communication with the companies and would observe a house from my observation post for at least fifteen or twenty minutes before our attack to try to spot any enemy activity or snow tracks. If I saw anything suspicious, I'd either direct artillery fire on that building or warn the squad leader by radio. Alas! Too often the house was around the bend, over the next hill, beyond my line of sight.

Many times I had the feeling that this enemy took great pleasure in playing tit for tat, training their sights on my observation post, especially after I lobbed a few rounds too close to their positions. One instance stands out in my mind more than others.

The colonel had directed a few of our battalion command personnel to follow him to a high point in the vicinity of Mt. Freddi, near Traversa. Our command personnel usually included a radio technician and the intelligence, reconnaissance, and operations team along with a limited number of their assisting personnel on the staff. When we had climbed to the spot he had selected on the map, a lone farmhouse situated about seventy-five yards ahead of our company, the colonel studied the potential base first hand. He wanted to use it as a forward command post for the next attack.

"That looks like a good location to set up your observation post, sergeant," he said to me, pointing to a raised, comparatively barren area about seventy-five yards ahead of the house along a dirt trail.

Without trees or boulders for protection, the position looked to me obviously precarious. Yet from that great height overlooking the entire valley before us, it would give me a truly unlimited view of all the action, theirs and ours. First, I'd have to dig a hole deep enough into that hard claylike soil to give me some protection from their artillery. I'd use my little GI shovel to dig myself in along the existing shallow roadside ditch.

For an hour, everything seemed quiet, but the silence turned ominous. All at once, the enemy let loose every one of the howitzers in their arsenal. Our party had been discovered and singled out as a target. The entire command group, including my usually unflappable colonel, swiftly retreated to safety. But, following orders, I had already positioned myself at the forward designated post, so there I was, out there alone and too far from the command group to ask questions. I had received no instruction to abandon my position, and I assumed they wouldn't go very far anyway. I began digging like crazy, figuring I'd join them later after dark, as was often my practice.

I wasn't aware of it at the time — and it may sound incredible — but at that moment I happened to be the lead man of the entire 5th Army! Not one American or Allied soldier was closer to the enemy positions than I was at that moment, and the German gunners wasted no time in letting me know they knew it. I became the sole target of Lord knows how many artillery pieces. Like a mole, I dug like crazy, trying to make a dent in the hard ground big enough to hide my body. Sweating profusely now, I had to watch helplessly as the shovel slipped, out of my fear-dampened hand, down the side of the steep cliff. I felt sure this was the end for me.

Wham! Wham! Splat! ZZZZZZ! I heard the whir of hot shrapnel hiss past my ear. If concussion didn't get me, the shrapnel or a direct hit certainly would. My only chance, besides getting up and running the hell out of there, which I had never opted to do before and, in any case, had received no orders to do, was to make use of the hard edge of my steel helmet and both hands to dig deeper. It worked, even better than that forever lost pint-sized shovel. I managed to dig a slit trench just big enough to squeeze myself into. I pulled in my arms and stomach and acted out the role of a scared snail for the next two hours.

Scrunched as tightly as I could to the bottom of my slit trench, I quickly calculated that the use of my helmet had increased my odds of staying alive by at least twenty-five percent. Now there was much less chance of flying shrapnel hitting me, unless they decided to use overhead fragmentation bursts.

Had they used white phosphorous shells, as they often did, I'd have been a goner, caught by the rain of white-hot particles that, having once entered the skin, didn't stop burning for many minutes as they smoldered and singed their way deep into the flesh.

I had lost one of my men a month before to this devilish weapon. During that particular shelling, I realized that one of the bursts had hit too close to his slit trench, and hearing his screams, I ran to him, calling for a medic. To my surprise, it was J.P. and another man who arrived on the run. They had been temporarily assigned as stretcher bearers when our regimental casualties mounted to fearful proportions.

As horribly painful as it was to him, that man was lucky because he survived. A few feet away, in another trench, another one of my men lay dead of a concussion from an almost direct hit. Kurt had been up to his old tricks again, and I swore I'd get even.

As I lay there in my trench on Mt. Freddi remembering that previous incident, I noticed that the shelling had tapered off to only an occasional volley. I figured that the enemy's ammunition had begun to run low, and like us, they had to conserve. It was then that I heard one of my men, Private Harry Crooker, hollering at me from the direction the others had taken.

"Sergeant, the colonel wants you to get back to the command post." His voice was like manna from heaven. I had had quite enough of being the bulls-eye for Kurt's artillery practice, and I certainly had had enough of the lone-wolf scene. I ran, following him back to headquarters, minus a shovel and probably a few pounds lighter than when I had arisen that morning.

Once I had returned to comparative safety, it occurred to me that almost every fourth or fifth round that the Germans had pelted me with were duds. They never exploded! After the war, I learned that the slave labor forced to assemble those shells were responsible for a great deal of sabotage. If they're still alive, I'd like them to know how grateful I am and that it would be my greatest pleasure to thank each and every one of them personally.

Our casualties continued to mount heavily, exacerbated mainly by a further drop in the temperature until one day in late September, in a blinding snowstorm, a blessed stop to the fighting was called. There would be no major forward movement of any of the elements of the 5th Army, at least not until our spring offensive almost six months away. We would continue only to parry with patrols and harassing artillery fire.

Of course, they didn't tell us everything. Unbeknownst to us, we had been relegated to remain mired down where we were in the Apennines, winter weather and all, for another half year. At the time, however, it seemed to me like a last minute reprieve from the electric chair.

We kept ourselves occupied during those long wintry months by watching and waiting, firing cannons at the enemy, and sending probing patrols at night to check suspect outpost positions and to keep them from laying mines. Occasionally, from my outpost at night I could see glowing tracer bullets and flares and hear the terrifying sound of automatic weapons during some savage night patrol firefights. I prayed silently for our men, hoping that they'd get back unharmed. Of course, that would not always be the case.

My job during this unexpected intermission was primarily to observe and report and to direct artillery and mortar fire at suspected supply trails across the stream and mine-filled valley from my observation post. However, almost nothing moved during the day nor on especially bright moonlit nights. My O.P. was a freezing cave, much like a camouflaged igloo. This was to remain my temporary home in that snow-covered, north-facing cliffside, the wrong side, for almost six months.

There was a partially demolished estate cottage about seventy yards behind the cave's rear exit, and I made as much use of it, and its outhouse, as I could, especially between six and ten o'clock at night when mutual observation was limited. I would sneak back and forth to my cave, being extra careful on moonlit nights because on a number of occasions I was the target of their mortars when they happened to spot me or my tracks in the snow.

Mortarmen in the Idice River Valley region of the Apennines

Apparently, Kurt was at it again. I could imagine him behind one of those craggy points watching for me to slip out the back entrance of my cave to answer nature's call. I could almost hear him say, "Shoot at the same coordinates I gave you at 6:30 last night. No smoke. You should be zeroed in already, yah? Fire!"

Kurt would then listen for the pop of his mortars as they left the barrel and hear them whistle as they soared over his head towards his assigned target. Knowing those were German sounds, not incoming, he relaxed and let his binoculars discern whatever they could in the semidarkness of early night. If he managed to hit something, it would be impossible to know, except for the signs of blood, if they hadn't been covered over with snow by the following morning.

Wow! That was too friggin' close. Screw you, Kurt! I'll keep dodging your lousy mortars and give you a dose of your own medicine, so watch your ass, Buster. My guys will be more than happy to go night fishing just as soon as I get my ass back to my O.P. I don't think Hilda would like it very much if she has to make love to a hero in a wheelchair, and I'm just the guy who can put you there, Herr Schmuck, so don't hassle me anymore tonight.

Kurt quieted down after a five-minute barrage and wondered how this would all play out. The close calls he had experienced during the last few weeks had unnerved him a little, and he was beginning to nurse strong doubts about ever seeing home again. He hadn't heard from his parents or Hilda in weeks, and rumors were circulating in his regiment about the awesome Allied aerial bombings in his homeland. How could this have happened? Goring swore that this could never take place since the Luftwaffe was the strongest airforce in the world.

This business of having to retreat higher into the boot of Italy was most troubling to Kurt as he was intelligent enough to realize that no war had been won by constant delaying actions and falling back. Counterattacks had been limited to squads and now, with the bad weather, were almost halted.

You never know. These Americans could be foolhardy cowboys and attack at any time, even though the intelligence reports said they wouldn't until the weather changed.

God, how he missed the warmth of his cozy fireplace and the erotic sensual aroma that emanated from Hilda's smooth white skin just before they made love.

Kurt Reinhardt, my imaginary anti-hero, was sadly in need of a morale builder, but I was determined that none would be forthcoming.

I, on the other hand, was fortunate enough to have a number of three-day furloughs during the winter hiatus, and needless to say, those comparatively peaceful days could never be long enough.

Drawing by Radulovich, from *History of the 363rd Infantry*, 1947

Artillery positions above Loiano in the Apennines

During the first week of the stalemate, J.P. and I decided to accompany Alberto, the partisani who had attached himself to our outfit, to visit Alberto's home in Florence. Alberto hadn't seen his family in almost a year, even though they were only about thirty-five miles away.

Having showered and shivered in cleverly portable field equipment, we were issued fresh uniforms, and finally, passes in hand and feeling exuberantly ready for anything, we boarded a GI chain-wheeled, half-ton semi headed for Florence. That unforgettable jaunt into what was to become one of my most favorite cities in the world was the cupid's arrow of my overwhelming love affair with wonderful Italy.

After driving only a few miles down the winding mountain road, we noticed the weather improved rapidly as we neared Scarperia, the beginning of the rolling hills north of Tuscany that led south to the alluring city of Florence.

"Had we only gone this far?" I wondered in amazement. "Had we prevailed over only these few tortuous miles of territory during that six-week-long nightmare?" Unbelievable! But when we recognized the terrain from previous battles in our agonizingly long march past the Gothic Line and up into the Apennines, it finally sunk in. War was certainly hell!

Suddenly, we were in the placid, sun-baked Arno Valley. The warming rays of the sun and the abrupt, drastic change in scenery were like an epiphany. There really was a saner world out there, and we were not about to miss a single second of what it had to offer.

From the moment we left the mountains, I felt excited and astonished at my first good view of Florence in the distance. A large city without skyscrapers, it had all the appearances of a sprawling, five-mile-wide village. A single, huge, eye-catching, red-domed cathedral in its center seemed to take precedence over all the surrounding smaller, less ornate, stone-colored buildings.

I was extremely anxious to explore its streets and alleys. Instead, we made a beeline for Alberto's residence first, bypassing our intended sleeping quarters, the American rest depot in the city's defunct railroad station. J.P. and I followed Alberto through the ground-floor door of the two-story apartment house that bore Alberto's family name, Sechi, on the arched glass window above it.

"Berto!" his mother and younger sister shouted, almost in unison, as they saw him.

Alberto didn't, couldn't, speak. The brave, tongue-tied partisani had a lump in his throat that we had to respectfully acknowledge as we waited for him to regain his voice. We stood there as they hugged, wiped tear-filled eyes, and then began to jabber profusely in the middle of the entrance hall. Finally, when he was again able to speak, he introduced us as his American comrades, and

Mama immediately took us by the hand into her warm, friendly parlor. Having deftly removed the cork from a wine bottle she had hastily procured from somewhere in the next room, she poured the wine into five crystal goblets.

No mention was made of Alberto's father, so we didn't ask. But the pride and the love that they felt for Alberto was obvious in every glance, in every word they spoke.

Mama and Alberto's sister, Maria, spoke together rapidly under their breath. We could make out only a few words, something about wanting to celebrate but having little to share because the war had been a terrible hardship on them without an income. J.P. thought faster than I did at that moment and had a brilliant idea, realizing that with money you can buy most anything. I've always suspected that he was part Scotch, and this bit of pragmatism tended to prove it. We each chipped in about fifteen American dollars that, in those days, must have seemed like a veritable fortune to these impoverished people.

He addressed himself to Alberto as he laid the money on the small mahogany coffee table. "Tell your mother we'd like to share the pleasure of celebrating with you. Do you think she can find the ingredients to make us a pasta fagiole?" In the past, back on the line, we had talked with Alberto often about sharing the delights of this dish. He had raved about it so much that we were dying to sample it.

A few more words passed between them too quickly for us to understand, but we learned J.P. was right; you could probably buy anything if you had the money.

Mama agreed, saying "Si," as her sweet, middle-aged face lit up. She'd try to round up something.

"Vieni. You come," sister Maria said as she escorted us to a comfortable-looking upstairs bedroom and indicated it was ours to share as long as we were in the city.

We stowed our things, apologetically leaving the three of them happily chatting and reminiscing while J.P. and I left the house to go exploring.

I cannot believe there is anyplace in this world that is more exciting for walking and sightseeing than the city of Florence. Because it had been declared an open city after our planes had bombed out most of their bridges, we were able to stroll aimlessly — which I recommend highly as the best way to sightsee in Florence — through a maize of novel streets, busy piazzas, and surprising alleyways. We stopped for a while at the world's most charming bridge and market place, the Ponte Vecchio, which would become a must for just about every one of my future travels to Europe.

Priceless marble and stone statues greeted our view wherever we turned our heads, and I vowed to learn more about their historical backgrounds if I should live to have that opportunity.

Wherever we roamed, we could sense the implied appreciation of our American uniforms and what our insignia represented to the people of Italy. Their genuine smiles and more-than-friendly attitude increased our desire to explore every little nook and cranny and to learn as much as possible from them and about them, and I know we had one hell of a good time trying.

After a few hours of insatiable sightseeing, we recrossed the quaint little bridge over the khaki-colored Arno River. This time we stopped half way, and without saying a word to each other, without knowing each other's thoughts, we reflected for a few minutes on the murderous battles that had taken place down-river near Pisa and thought of our friends whom we had lost just a few miles from where we stood.

Armed with four bottles of wine, we rang Alberto's bell. Maria opened the door. A heady aroma immediately assailed my nose and every impatient pore in my upper and lower palette. Mama's pasta fagiole was almost ready. She had bought a rabbit, various herbs, cranberry beans, and macaroni made from chestnut flour. Regular flour was not available because the Tedeschi had cleaned out the city's supply that was usually shipped in from the Po Valley. She removed one of the half-gallon jars of homemade sauce from the top shelf in her closet to use for the dinner.

The exquisite flavor of the pasta fagiole lived up to its glorious advance notice. Simply put, it was fabulous! Out of this world! I know it couldn't have been the heady wine that had helped create that kind of magnificent, lifetime impression.

That heavenly dish has forever intoxicated my senses since that moment. Even to this day, that thyme- and sage-filled aroma and taste defy imitation. My wife is a very good cook, and desperately trying to please me, she has valiantly attempted to duplicate its magical taste on numerous occasions, purloining recipes out of every Italian cookbook from San Francisco to Italy but, alas, with minimal success. As I have unfortunately lost track of my friend Alberto and his family, we'll just have to keep on trying recipes. Perhaps, if he reads this, he'll show up again, but I'd like him to know that, above all, it's him I miss, possibly even more than the heavenly pasta.

When we retired to our upstairs bedroom long after what had to be the world's greatest dinner, we found that our bed was being warmed by red-hot bricks wrapped in towels and strategically placed under a fluffed-up, goose-down comforter. God forbid we should sleep in a cold bed. What hospitality! J.P. and I were treated like kings the entire time we were there.

On the afternoon of the third day, we reported to the railroad station, found transportation back to our regiment, and dejectedly left the congeniality of

Alberto's family and Florence, only to be greeted by a howling blizzard an hour later as our truck climbed higher into the Apennines.

Reporting in, I donned my triple pair of stockings, burlap sacks, and parka jacket, slogged through the foot and a half of snow, and relieved two of my men, Thomas J. Miller and Charles Lott, at the bitterly cold observation post. Lucky guys. It would be their turn now to go to Florence.

Nothing unusual was happening on the line. By early December, it was quiet enough for me to be relieved once more. This time the rest area would be Montecatini, the world-famous European spa noted for its hot springs.

For the next few days, I was inadvertently billeted in a small luxury apartment with two of my old friends, band members from Division Special Services. It was hard to believe that they actually resided there during these winter months while the rest of us dogfaces were struggling with distress and death in the Apennines. I wondered, had I made a mistake by not attaching myself to Special Service when I had the chance?

A couple of years older and considerably more sophisticated than I was, these lucky guys didn't seem to give a hoot what they did as long as they could keep themselves stoned and balled most of the time, anywhere behind the lines. The two of them, with their live-in hooker Angelina, allowed me a glimpse of the sybaritic side of life that I had never witnessed, preparing me for the ways of the world in which I had not yet indulged.

Cute and sassy Angelina was being kept very inexpensively by these piano- and clarinet-playing sergeants. All she required was her three meals a day, a few pairs of nylon hose, and an ongoing supply of cigarettes and chocolate bars. For these simple things in life, she and her other fellow "puttanas," as I discovered later, would be willing to give their all and then some.

Although occasionally coyly invited by her, I could not quite see myself participating in the menage-a-trois games they often played. My marriage of two years could have certainly played a part in restraining my libido, yet I couldn't help being tempted and curious. Although I had found myself incredibly aroused at times, especially as I watched the obviously exaggerated sway of the hips and shapely backside of Angelina, I suppose it was my Hebraic guilt that kept me from taking a chance and actually doing the deed.

Naïve as I was at that time, now that I had come face-to-face with the human condition outside of my own tight little world, I couldn't deny the fact that these friends of mine were having the time of their life. I knew my body was ready and my senses were becoming more salaciously provoked every day, but I was just not quite ready for it yet. So that's the way my cookie crumbled in the sensual city of Montecatini. My education, however, was to continue.

I attempted to enjoy the town, nosing around the once-fabulous hotels, spas, and boarded-up boutiques that had been all the rage of kings and queens, a place for the wealthy and for lovers' trysts before the war. But it wasn't Florence. Something was missing.

When I returned again to the front lines and my cliff-side igloo, as I stared abstractly at the snow-covered, sheer escarpment in front of me that was enemy-held Montepiano, I found my mind often wandered, and I would hope for a miracle to end the war.

I had bought a new pipe and tobacco in Montecatini. The taste and warmth of its glow felt wonderful in the frosty wind of December. Even so, I would have to be careful of its flickering brightness against the dark, moonless background or it could reveal my position, giving Jerry something to shoot at.

Christmas and Chanukah came and went, unnoticed by me. Then it was New Year's Eve. Not knowing what to expect from the enemy, I remained especially vigilant at my observation post, puffing away at the briar but cuffing it with my palm, alert for any unexpected intrusion. You can't imagine my astonishment when, just before midnight, I heard a rather raucous recording of "Auld Lang Syne" being broadcast from speakers somewhere high up across the valley of this snowy-white no-man's-land. It was followed by two more melodious but unrecognizable holiday chorales sung in German. At twelve midnight, they fired a magnitude of tracer bullets and flares simultaneously into the air, creating a spectacular, noisy fireworks show that lit up the sky on that black night.

Most likely, it was designed to be a show of strength to demoralize us. To some degree their ploy worked. It seemed to me an obvious show of brawn and tenacity, as if to notify us in advance of what we would ultimately confront when our next attack order came. Yet, somehow, their remarkable and unexpected use of music signaled to me the surprising fact that, even in the thick of this terrible war, there still lurked a slight spark of humanity, even in the ostensibly heartless soul of the Nazi soldier.

Despite my philosophic reverie, I would have gladly snuffed out the owner of that absurd spark had I been capable of doing so at that moment. I fully understood that killing was an uncivilized act, but my hatred ran deep. *They,* the despicable Nazi's, had started it, had begun this grim war against much of the unprepared, trusting world — against my people in particular — igniting the fires of hate-ridden dementia that so ardently burned within me now. There remained no doubt in my mind that I would gladly fight them to the death, theirs or mine, then or even now.

Over the next few months, our stockpiles of ammunition and fuel pipelines grew steadily. It was obvious that they were being set in place as close to the front as practical in preparation for the next big push to the north.

During that long winter lull in combat, we had to carefully conserve our mortar and cannon ammunition for the coming major assault that would lead us out of these mountains and into the Po Valley. The Ardennes Offensive, occurring on another front many miles away in Belgium, caused our supplies to be curtailed even further. There could be little doubt that those GIs to the north needed them more than we did at this time, and I was given a daily quota of how many shells I could use.

Conversely, Hitler's troops in northern Europe would most likely take priority for their supplies that might otherwise be earmarked for Italy.

Fortunately for us, with excellent planning, enough of our implements of war remained available for the eventual breakthrough we'd need to crack whatever defenses the enemy had had time to build up during that long winter stalemate. So it seemed that in this Allied and Axis struggle, our forces had a much better supply line than the German forces. Their supplies had to come to them over the difficult Alpine highway while our routes were much more diverse.

We knew by the gradually improving weather and the increasing stacks of gasoline cans along the road that our offensive was due to begin soon, but oddly, our high command chose this time to train my division further. Apparently they decided that, before our push through the flat Po Valley, we would need to learn better field communications with our armored tank support.

Throughout each of these training sessions that usually lasted about a week, our outfit moved far enough behind the lines to alleviate the stress of battle. First we'd shower, change clothes, and rest for a day before starting to work out the glitches inherent in passing split-second information back and forth to our Sherman tanks.

It was during this break that I became aware of some strange goings-on in our rest camp. I noticed field ambulances from our medical detachment and camouflaged tanks from the 1st Armored were parked just outside of our bivouac area. It turned out that one of the ambulance drivers had latched on to a prostitute in the nearby town. Together they had come up with a shrewd financial arrangement. He would drive into town, sneak her into his ambulance, return to camp, and then wait until about ten o'clock at night, at which time they would open for business. He'd stand by at the vehicle's doorway, collect the money in advance, and control the line-up, being sure to avoid any lights as well as having too many customers at one time crowding the vehicle. The line moved quickly.

One night, a boisterously loud tech sergeant who had had too much to drink raised a ruckus because the weary pro had become vexed as she waited too long for him to climax. Annoyed, she pushed him off. And, angry as hell, he complained loudly. An officer nearby overheard the din and went to investigate.

The drunk-as-a-skunk tech sergeant managed to run like a bat out of hell during the confusion after the officer appeared and was never caught. I didn't find out what happened to that non-com businessman, but I'm sure he was immediately reduced in rank to buck private. It was the end of their experiment in free enterprise, at least for the duration.

During those training times, I'd push my advantage with First Sergeant O'Connor to finagle a two-day pass out of him. I figured, what the hell, Florence was just around the corner, and who knew if or when I'd ever see it again.

Often I'd be able to arrange it so that Jess and I could go together; at other times, I'd go alone. J.P. knew by now that I'd spend at least one day going to whatever opera or concert was available. Sometimes I'd attend both in one day as there was always something musical happening in Florence. The Italians and I seemed to share a love for Puccini. They always had his operas showing at one or the other of their many little theaters. I could never get enough of *Tosca*, *Madame Butterfly*, or *La Boheme*.

All good things must end, however. While I didn't realize it at the time, that was my last trip to that Renaissance city until I could afford to return again in another life, almost thirty years later. Of all the extraordinary events that occurred and the prominent places I visited during those turbulent war years as well as the five decades that followed, my strongest and most poignant memories will always be of my brief time spent in the remarkable city of Florence.

Even looking over a map of Italy stirs the memory with the familiar names of each of the many, tiny Apennine towns situated between Futa Pass and Bologna. Livergnano, Querceto, Loiano, and many more are each capable of evoking vivid stories, leaving indelible imprints of heartache and adventure.

Unfortunately, the public never encountered those romantic-sounding names in the overpowering media spotlight. But as a seasoned veteran, I firmly believe that Monticelli and those few winding miles of mountain passes and tiny villages in the Apennines happened to be where the battle for southern Europe was decisively won, bought and paid for by thousands of brave young men who will rest forever in a Tuscany gravesite.

Chapter 13

The Push to the Po

Early April in most of Italy would not garner any special attention because its wonderfully moderate Mediterranean climate remains about the same all year round. In the glacial, wintry height of the Apennines, however, April meant the sight and sound of a noisy blue jay, the early touches of new green here and there other than the ubiquitous pine and juniper trees, and the first flowers. Among the remaining few patches of crystallized snow sparsely scattered on the rocky hillsides, crimson poppies and wild mustard flowers sprouted suddenly along the gullies and clearings. It was a welcome relief from the white of winter and seemed almost cause for a springtime celebration among the men of my battalion.

We were immensely grateful for the change but at the same time more than a bit fearful of what we knew still lay ahead. All military leaves had been cancelled, so we waited apprehensively to hear those sobering words. They came soon enough, accompanied by the same old sickening feeling in our gut.

"OK, men, check your equipment. We're moving out in two hours."

That gave me just enough time to check for rust in the bore of my carbine and resettle the extra underwear, tarp, and blanket in my knapsack that I would need during the last few frigid months.

I had just returned from Florence where I attended the largest Passover service ever held in Italy and maybe in the world. Several thousand GIs of my faith, all from the Allied forces, had congregated at the unusable train station downtown to participate in a massive Seder and delicious repast of typical holiday fare. Apparently, back home our rabbis had managed to persuade the producers of matzos and kosher wines to subsidize the auspicious festival.

I remember praying silently and passionately at the conclusion, after "Rock of Ages" was chanted in unison, knowing very well that this could be my last Passover. Someone had once said, "There are no atheists in foxholes." I could swear to that.

I returned to base knowing that the busy rail junction of Bologna, about twenty-five miles to the north, would be our next goal. Aerial photos had shown the destruction of the depots and the bang-up job our Air Force had done of mangling the maze of train tracks that led to the center of the city. Its only importance to our division now was to make limited use of it as a geographical jumping-off point once we reached its outskirts.

Now that the crucial hour was almost here, every unit of our division would join up with every conceivable Allied fighting force in Italy from wherever they happened to be to move forward together across the broad no-man's-land. Hopefully, we could now deliver the long-awaited knock-out blow and push through to the fertile wheat and rice fields of Italy's bread-basket, the Po Valley. Everyone was ready to go and itching to get the damned war over with.

It would have been wonderful if it were that simple. But ever watchful for the very first sign of our expected all-out attack, our antagonists threw everything they had at us as we attempted to descend the Apennine highlands before the valley. While never underestimating the lethal strength of these headstrong Germans nor the fact that they had had plenty of time to erect well-defended fortifications and camouflaged artillery positions during the last six months, we were nevertheless surprised by their tenacity, their potential to detain us at all costs.

We had hoped that the enemy would be demoralized by their heavy losses in other parts of Europe as well as at the Russian front, but that was wishful thinking. Instead, those defenders of the black swastika acted more like a rattlesnake that refuses to die after decapitation.

It would take three more grueling weeks of fierce, bloody combat to get them to release their death grip and remove their vicious fangs from each peak, valley, gully, village, and farmhouse to the south of Bologna. All the while, with the aid of my trusty telescope and my back-up of mortars and artillery, we continued to pound the living daylights out of their remaining well-entrenched defenses. But they chose to make each town a stronghold, leaving us little choice except to indiscriminately raze almost every peaceful village and farmhouse along our route as we blasted away at them in our mad push to the Po.

Many of those former townspeople had moved to nearby caves, carrying their valuables with them to avoid the ravages of both armies, while others had simply departed to wait it out with their kinfolk in the more placid north. Escaping south through the front lines would have been impossible for them, at least until after we arrived on the scene.

The remains of Livergnano

Our battalion and company command posts made use of those pulverized little villages as our headquarters for a day or two before moving on. It was interesting to note that, after the first day that we occupied each horribly shell-torn building, a few of the heartier villagers would reappear to try again to set up housekeeping as best they could. Little by little, those desperate people would begin to rebuild their crumbled walls and ceilings with any handy refuse. They were amazingly stoic and forbearing in their brave effort to return to their former way of life.

I couldn't help but admire them and attempt to help those long-suffering individuals. After all, it might have been my fire direction the day before that had ravaged their homes.

Although beleaguered by both sides, the Italians somehow always appeared to feel very much more comfortable with Americans than they did with the despised Tedeschi. I've often asked myself why. Aside from their rescue from an uncertain fate at the hands of the Germans, my guess was that they enjoyed both our Hollywood image as the bold and audacious Yankee and our laid-back, earthy good humor.

I found that most Italians really had a secret love affair with Hollywood and assumed that all, except for small minority of the so-called ugly Americans they might have come across, were reasonable facsimiles of that delusive image. Perhaps because of their uncomplicated lifestyle and the innate romance in their souls, continental Italians have always loved our cinematic reputation for being footloose and fancy free. They also took notice of our great need to please. Thus we supplied all the fairy tales lacking in their own often unpretentious lives and fulfilled their desire for fantasy. Whether they were city folk or country folk, it didn't seem to make much difference.

In contrast, what could the straitlaced, constrained German offer? As much as he'd occasionally try to be good-natured, and as pleasant as his smile was, this wasn't Kurt Reinhardt's style and never could be. Inherently, the German disposition, even if doing his utmost to be congenial, usually came off as being too uptight to the Italians.

⊶ ⊷

In mid-April, I was busily engaged in my usual fire direction from our command post near the devastated hilltop city of Pianoro when one of my wisdom teeth began to act up. The colonel arranged for a jeep to chauffeur me to the MASH unit, about five miles behind the lines. I felt like a goldbrick and guilty as hell for taking the time off. This was the first out of 550 days on the line that I had to leave for illness or any reason. Why I felt so remorseful is still a question I ask myself.

I can't remember the name of that marvelous field dentist, but within one hour he had sat me down in his operating tent, shot my gum full of novocaine, and hammered away at the remains of the impacted tooth. He cleared the cavity, asked if I wanted to stay for another day, then surprised at my response, he sent me on my way, back to Pianoro.

One would think that I'd have been more than happy to get time away from the front, but strangely, that was not the case. For whatever intangible reasons I have yet to fathom, I truly missed the company of my men and the dangerous arena of our busy command post.

I returned to our battalion command post to find that we were ready to move out again to face the Nazis' last line of defenses and artillery that continued to blast away at us and block those last few miles to the Po Valley. But then, in the midst of managing to dodge their harassing 105s that threatened us each uncertain moment, we were suddenly given another reprieve.

Sergeant Brown answered the crank-up field phone and handed it over to Colonel Woods, who paced nearby. In his quietly official way, the colonel responded only with a minute or so of "Uh-huhs," then finally ended with a firm "Wilco, out." He sighed profoundly before relating his news to us in the command group.

"That was the general. Another regiment will be relieving us and going through our forward positions in about two hours. We're supposed to sit tight and hold this location until they tell us what sector they want us to cover."

The enormous consequences of this unexpected news didn't hit me immediately. It hadn't quite sunk in to my fatigued brain that my fighting days were almost at an end. Then it finally dawned on me that I'd probably live at least another day and maybe a lot longer, if their artillery didn't get me and if I didn't do something stupid like getting blown up by a booby trap or stepping on a land mine. I exhaled noisily and promised myself I'd get drunk that night if I could find someone who had a bottle.

While fresher units fought the fierce three-day battle to push the enemy off the rugged hills just south of Bologna, those of us who had been relieved — and relieved in more ways than one — remained in a state of numbness. Our heads hadn't yet caught up with the last-minute change, and we dangled in a state of limbo.

It felt as though the weight of the world had been removed from our shoulders. By that time we knew we were winning and were anxious to get the misery of the battlefield over with.

It was a wonderfully indescribable feeling to think that we could now try to relax there at our decaying Pianoro headquarters. In that seemingly irretrievable ruin of someone's former residence, there was absolutely nothing left. There were no comfy chairs, no mattresses; all the good stuff had disappeared. For the moment, at least, we could take whore's baths, doze between nuisance barrages that kept pecking away, write letters, and wait for orders to join the fray once more.

On the second afternoon of this reprieve, we were astonished to see a bedraggled, middle-aged man and his pretty, raven-haired daughter of about eighteen come through the framework of our austere billet, what was left of his doorway. They had apparently been living in a cave nearby, and now that the noise of the war had sufficiently receded to a moderate rumble, they felt safe enough to venture back to the house to see what remained. The stairway to the nearly roofless bedrooms upstairs had been blown away, but with the aid of a rickety ladder, the man managed to climb up to the shattered second story, leaving his daughter downstairs. We could hear the father scrounging around through the debris out of our view.

Corporal R____, who had been gaping at the girl, as we all were doing, suddenly jumped up from where he had been squatting and rapaciously seized her. In the few seconds before I had an opportunity to separate him from her, he had begun to tremble uncontrollably and ejaculated prematurely without benefit of unzipping. Wide-eyed, the poor frightened girl never uttered a word but spat at him as she left the structure in a huff.

After a few minutes, her father, unaware of what had occurred, paused as he came down the ladder to look around momentarily at the ruins before he left. He silently dabbed at his eyes with his fingers before he, too, vanished into the countryside.

"Fresh, spirited American troops, flushed with victory, are bringing in thousands of hungry, ragged, battle-weary prisoners . . ."

I was disgusted. Did nice, clean-cut, all-American young men do this kind of thing? My growing education in the strange, dark ways of humankind had taken on new meaning. After that odious episode, I found myself avoiding the abhorrent company of Corporal R_____. I fervently hoped that, after the war, the stupid bastard would clearly remember the soggy feeling of her spit and see a good therapist. Obviously, war brought out the best and the worst of human nature.

It had started to rain again. Later that afternoon, I watched as the muddied, serpentine road in front of our command post became unusually active with trucks, tanks, and tank destroyers. A battalion of foot soldiers straggled past, already dolefully exhausted, their anguished eyes staring at nothing in particular as they shuffled sluggishly towards the front.

The distinct rumbling of artillery bursts somewhere off in the near distance reverberated almost continuously, letting me know that my counterparts in other observation posts had to be extremely busy and miserably wet. I walked back into the C.P. and stood close to the slowly burning ashes in the fireplace, shivering at the thought of the fierce battle that was raging all around us, which would hopefully put an end to the bloody fighting. I sat listening to the distant detonations, passively waiting, feeling a lifetime away from the action.

The letdown finally hit. I was so tired of the war that I could have cried. Few civilians can even begin to imagine the gut-wrenching fear, the sounds of death, the pain and butchery suffered on a daily basis by the dog-face infantryman. But there was also a second kind of mental torture, the conditions he had to live with constantly, freezing or frying through all kinds of relentless weather, jumping up from his soggy slit trench to find a place to answer nature's call at all hours of the day or night no matter what, trying to open a can of cold beans with fingers too frozen to maintain a grip on the GI can opener when he became desperate enough to eat anything. There are too many examples to list here and too much of it for young men to keep on taking without cracking. I had come close to that point on a number of occasions but would never let on. Everyone else around me was probably in the same boat.

Our three-day hiatus in Pianoro finally ended with the fantastic news that we had badly beaten the enemy who was finally falling back. We were to join up quickly with all the other units of the Allied forces in Italy to help sweep the broad Po Valley clean of the retreating, hopefully disorganized enemy.

Intelligence had logically assumed that the Wehrmacht would most assuredly make good use of all natural geographic barriers between Bologna and the Alps, especially the Po, Adige, and Brento Rivers. We could be sure that Field Marshal Kesselring had planned thoroughly to slow us down by planting mines on roads and bridges and placing small defensive squads and 88s at almost every hedgerow or river bank. On the other hand, our own generals had tasted victory and were relentless to cut them off before they could retrench.

As my regiment rejoined the battle, we rapidly bypassed Bologna a mile to the east of the main highway and took part in the grim chase on foot, they as the fox, we the hounds. Coming down out of the high ground, I passed what used to be a railroad yard and couldn't help but mentally compare it to a king-sized erector set that had been twisted in all directions by a very angry child. It was immediately apparent that our fly-boys had accomplished their mission and done their job well.

Although the landscape to our immediate front was as flat as Kansas, some fifty or so miles ahead I could clearly discern the startlingly high peaks of the snow-capped Dolomite Range. Displaying razor sharp pinnacles that pierced the sky as far north as the eye could see, these were only the beginning of the formidable Alps. They spread their frightening bulk across the entire top of Italy very much like a wide cuff on a boot.

The threat conveyed by that disturbing sight sent shivers down my spine as did the thought that we might have to follow the retreating Jerries through the icy Brenner Pass high up into those cloud-capped ridges.

Quite suddenly, the sky began to roar with the thundering forays of American prop-driven P-51 Mustang fighter planes as they made devastating runs across the wide, pastoral valley. Now that the enemy had been forced out of the shelter of the Apennines, they were easy prey for our Air Force pilots who had been called upon to execute the first strike, to destroy the enemy's ability to retaliate, and especially to target all armored vehicles and heavy weapons, anything that moved not having a white star painted on it.

The damage these fighters were inflicting was too distant for us to observe, yet I could tell by the crunching explosions followed immediately by dense columns of oily, black smoke that our airmen were devastatingly right on target. The echoing staccato of their rat-a-tat strafing signaled the fact that we were witnessing the end of the enemy's resistance as there seemed to be no opposition, no anti-aircraft guns to slow them down.

Somehow I found it important that I conjure up Kurt Reinhardt as he viewed the few bedraggled men that still remained in his depleted section. He too felt as painfully tired and frustrated as the others.

"Gott in himmel!" he uttered aloud as the American plane began its run again, relentlessly peppering the trenches he and his men were occupying on the far bank of the river. "Where the hell is our Luftwaffe?"

Kurt realized full well that their planes might have been needed more urgently elsewhere, on one of the other besieged fronts perhaps. But how could Goring leave his fighting men, his courageous Italian Wehrmacht, so totally high and dry, such easy targets for these verdammte Americans pilots? Frustrated, Kurt radioed his command post.

"Was gibt? We need some anti-aircraft guns up here!" he yelled. "I can't hold this position long without counterfire!"

There was only static on the other end of his line for an answer as another American fighter plane made its slashing run along the river. This time the plane's gunner hit two of his remaining seven-man squad, part of the automatic weapon crew he had been ordered to command to hold off the enemy.

What enemy? Since he had left Bologna with orders to create a 200-yard defense line along the 400-mile Po, the only enemy he had seen were these bastard American mosquitos that, bite by bite, had been nibbling away from the air at his comrades. His original twenty-eight-man platoon had been reduced now to only five.

Between the horrible screams of his wounded men and the frightening bark of the incessant strafing up and down the line, Kurt could only curse and wonder at the inextricable hell he found himself in. He reread the inscription on the belt buckle of the nearest wounded infantryman as he tried to calm the man and stop him from screaming. "Gott mit uns" was the terse phrase inscribed on every Nazi soldier's buckle. He took special note of its message again, wondering why God ignored his prayer and didn't appear to be on the Third Reich's side during these last few schrecklich hours.

As for me, I joyfully watched those planes kick up the dirt all along the tree-lined river. Maybe now I'd get Herr Leutnant Reinhardt off my back once and for all. Everyone knew that the war was almost over, so why didn't that tight-assed heinie give up and cash in his chips while he still had a few left?

He was at the end of his rope. Rat-a-tat, rat-a-tat. God, how he hated them. "You'll have to kill me before I give up!" he screamed idiotically at the top of his voice, waving his fist after another quick pass of the fighter plane.

Hearing him, the four frightened men in his machine-gun crew who were still in one piece whispered stealthily among themselves, "Herr Leutnant must be going out of his mind." They assumed that, since he was one of those crazy zealots, he was mad enough to expect them to go down with him. Nuts to that! They had had enough of this endless slaughter, but how could they simply throw down their arms and surrender? If they didn't drown in the river trying to evade the American plane's spattering bullets, Herr Leutnant would probably shoot them himself. Nothing was worth this, not the fatherland, not the fuhrer, and especially not this crazy SS officer! Only one choice remained.

Kurt watched in a helpless stupor as his men fled, scrambling up from that accursed river bank along a line of beech trees leading to the north, away from both the verdammte Americans and from their verruckt Leutnant Reinhardt.

By the time Kurt regained his composure, he found himself alone with the two torn-up bodies that once were his gunners. Seething and almost hysterically distraught, he thought about his own probable fate. Not sure where to direct his anger, he grasped the back end of the unmanned machine gun and turned it skyward, waiting feverishly for the next speeding aircraft to pass over him.

He had some fifteen minutes to ponder his untenable dilemma before the next strafing run. Kurt could almost understand the desertion of his low-brow crew, but he, as an officer and loyal member of the party, would never cut and run, even if it meant the end of him. It seemed to him that a hero's death was to be his most probable way out of this hopeless predicament, and if that's the way his life was going to end, so be it. Heil Hitler!

His feelings of futility and blind anger waned with each passing minute, and intermittently he began to fantasize, indulging in occasional dreamlike images of home, of his parents, and of Hilda.

He heard the frightening, unmistakable rumble of several approaching prop-driven executioners who were bent on interrupting his illusions. He jerked the trigger. The pilot of the second plane had a better angle and put two bullets low into Kurt's left shoulder that tore off the surrounding flesh and bone as they exited still blazing hot through his clavicle, just a few inches from his heart.

Bleeding profusely, he laid there disoriented and in excruciating pain until a German ambulance finally found him and took him along with seven other wounded men to an overcrowded field hospital near Verona. He wasn't conscious enough to be aware that they gave him plasma, hurriedly dressed his shoulder, and sent him off to a more permanent hospital near Bolzano, on the mountainous Austrian border, for further medical treatment.

For weeks he'd remain in a mental fog, mostly induced by pain medication, never having had a chance to realize how lucky he was, compared to hundreds of his comrades-in-arms whose broken, torn-up bodies lined the muddy shores of the Po River. If he hadn't lost too much blood and infection didn't get him, Kurt might just make it home.

Inasmuch as this enemy soldier was only a representation, purely a figment of my imagination, I would decide how to deal with his fate later, after the war had ended.

In the meantime, because there was no longer any high ground nor any tall buildings to serve for my observation post, the Colonel had relegated me to motorized reconnaissance patrolling.

I sprawled out on the hard back seat of a jeep, clasping my carbine, while Lieutenant Fabian Allen, our new platoon leader, sat watchfully alongside the driver, windshield down and ready to man the mounted machine gun. He had joined us recently to replace the overly fearful lieutenant we had lost during our first introduction to battle over a year and a half ago.

Lieutenant Allen had been a line officer who led an infantry platoon up until this time and who had proven himself in battle, having been awarded the Bronze Star twice. One could feel confident with a leader like that, and I was pleased that someone of his stature had at long last taken full command of my section. I felt relief rather than envy, glad to give up most of my responsibilities at this stage of the game. Too many second lieutenants had lost a leg leading their platoon across minefields, and I seriously shunned the possibility of a field promotion at this point in time.

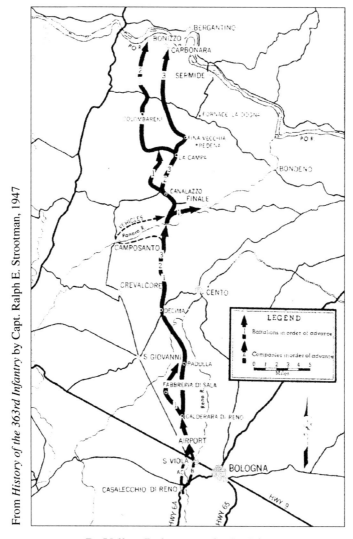

From *History of the 363rd Infantry* by Capt. Ralph E. Strootman, 1947

Po Valley, Bologna to the Po River

In our jeep, we carefully checked out much of the Po Valley south of the river, and within a few days, the lieutenant and I found ourselves on the road with radio instructions to head for a bridge that headquarters thought might have remained standing and may not have been mined. To us, that *may* and *might* were two extremely important words.

Our orders were to attempt to make contact with the retreating forces. That meant we'd probably have to first locate that bridge, check it out and be among the first of our advancing troops to cross the river, and then, as ridiculous as it seems now, we'd actually try to draw enemy fire to locate their positions. This was just like our training days in Oregon, except that we trained as a whole platoon then, not just with the single jeep we had now.

As we approached the river near the little town of Carbonara, the lieutenant's fist closed more tightly on the trigger handle of our loaded machine gun while I held my carbine at the ready. I borrowed the lieutenant's field glasses and scanned the town on the other side. It appeared to be empty of residents and deathly quiet, almost always a suspicious sign.

Fortunately for us, the antiquated, 300-foot wooden bridge hadn't been booby-trapped. This retreating enemy had apparently been disorganized and in too much of a hurry to take the time to wire it. Of course, if they were still in the vicinity and wanted to, a single shot from an 88mm could blow all three of us to kingdom come. We held our breath. In an eerie kind of silence, we slowly made our way across the narrow span to Bergantino, the pretty little village on the north side of the river.

Going about five miles an hour, we passed to the far side and into the outskirts of the village. Suddenly, we were swamped by at least a hundred villagers who had remained hidden until then. Seeing the white identifying star on our vehicle, they emerged clamorously with joyful shouts of "Viva Americani! Grazie, Americani!" They crowded our jeep, palmed kisses in our direction with both hands, and would have crowned us kings, it seemed, if we had willed it.

We thoroughly enjoyed the greeting until Lieutenant Allen asked the man who appeared to be the leader of this welcoming committee the all-important question. "How long ago did the Tedeschi leave?"

"Maybe twenty, thirty minutes," the man answered innocently, grinning inanely.

Holy mackerel! They were most likely watching us from the hedgerow, waiting to ambush us, for all we knew.

Our driver eased through the elated crowd and maneuvered our jeep northward to make contact, as our orders had stated. We drove at a slow, steady pace for another 150 yards up the tree-lined road when we heard the unmistakable crackle, the nightmarish burping sound of Schmeisser bullets. They snapped the air around us, fortunately missing us from a nearly impossible shooting range of about 300 yards. The unexpected little skirmish scared the daylights out of us as well as the crowd, scattering them back into their houses and cellars like scared rabbits.

Needless to say, we too got the hell out of there and back across the river as fast as our jeep driver could turn the thing around. Unable to fight any kind of shooting war by ourselves and having accomplished our mission to locate the enemy, we reported back to the command post rather than be foolhardy. It seemed our foe was almost in full retreat and appeared to have no heavy weapons because if he had, he could easily have disposed of us. Rather than engage us, it was obvious that he had merely wanted only to hold us at bay while escaping to the next defensive position.

Breathing easier on the way back to our command post, we watched with a great deal of pleasure as a group of our fighter planes made still another strafing and bombing run farther up river, feeling timorously secure in the fact that our guys should easily be able to see that dingy white star painted on the hood of our jeep.

We could hear the rumble of tanks and the sound of machine guns and sporadic rifle fire on our left flank as we headed south, signifying that more Germans had been caught attempting to cross the river. The reverberating sound of the mop-up continued throughout the noisy night, but on the morning of the next day, an uncanny hush hung in the air. The silence was proof that what little that was left of the enemy had escaped to their next line of defense along the Adige River, approximately twelve miles north of the Po.

Meanwhile, all along the line, thousands of Germans had surrendered or been taken prisoner, only to became a disconcerting problem for our busy troops as to how to dispose of them. I clearly recall passing a column of several hundred unarmed enemy soldiers, hands behind their heads as they gloomily shuffled southward, with only two American foot soldiers carrying tommy guns to guard them. No doubt these former goose-stepping warriors were thrilled to walk anywhere at a normal pace, forever disqualified from the pointless fighting. They would most likely have kept on marching even without the two escorting sentries.

This exhilarating sight was now being repeated all through the Po Valley, with the exception of a few stubborn pockets of SS, the elite guard, and the sparse remains of their mobile artillery that were intent on fighting on. These unforgiving Kurt Reinhardts created road blocks using their worrisome 88s in a vain attempt to slow us down.

I questioned a German corporal who seemed to be leading a squad of straggling prisoners along the side of the road in hopes of gaining some information about the location of the main body of his troops and armor. He shrugged his shoulders and answered that there was no main body anymore, just a few SS officers following orders to harass us to give their army time to regroup and work its way up into the Alps. Had they succeeded, they could have held us at bay indefinitely in that impossible mountainous terrain.

His story sounded credible, and as they seemed harmless without their weapons, I radioed my squad to watch for them and show them the way to regimental headquarters. Then I watched the backs of those eight defeated men as they dejectedly plodded down the road.

To keep the German army from reaching the Alps, our bombers had already begun daily runs in the vicinity of the Brenner Pass, the Alpine doorway to Austria and Germany. Once again, we didn't get to see the telling results of their destruction from our obscured position.

Everyone sensed that the war was over, except those few bands of Nazis with die-hard officers like Kurt Reinhardt that we came across occasionally. Frustrated by their refusal to surrender, our combined air and ground forces doubled the pressure, hammering away at them the next day with everything in our arsenal. Unfortunately, we couldn't help but suffer a few of our own casualties from mines and small skirmishes along the way, but compared to theirs, our losses were relatively miniscule.

As our battalion moved out to regroup in the vicinity of Treviso, a few miles directly north of Venice, I again joined Lieutenant Allen in what was to be the next-to-last day of combat, reconnoitering for stragglers and die-hard enemy pockets of militia along the Po River roadsides and trails. We came upon a grotesque scene so unbelievable that to me it resembled some huge, Hollywood-like movie set. We were tongue-tied, shaken by the sight of hundreds of mauled bodies, Tiger and Panzer tanks smoking or aflame, and vehicles and equipment of every type smashed and scattered haphazardly as far as the eye could see along the once-scenic valley's fields and river ditches. It appeared to us like a ghostly graveyard of immolation solemnly dedicated to Hitler's madness, the last dark act of a modern-day tragedy.

Contrasting greatly with that strange, macabre scene was its backdrop of flourishing green fields, poplar-lined cart trails, meadows of waving wheat and rice, and clumps of wild, red poppies as far as the eye could see. Ambulances, theirs and ours, searched for survivors in the midst of this massive destruction. There weren't many. The rest, the mass of mangled corpses, had to be disposed of and so were taken away in canvas body-bags by trucks and ambulances.

We stopped for a moment to stretch, to smoke, and to take in this spectacle that was like a sight out of the Dark Ages.

I heard a whimper coming from one of the German bodies nearby. Hardly breathing, he had been left for dead. I kneeled beside him, this hapless former enemy in his early forties as he barely emitted another groan. His wound was not obvious to me; possibly a concussion had gotten him. I waved down one of the passing ambulances, which had by now thoroughly earned the reputation of being called meat wagons, that rushed him away. I often wondered if he survived.

Later that day, we returned to our base near Treviso only to find that we would be moving out again in the morning to mop up a few fanatical zealots who had been causing trouble near the Adige River.

There was a persistent rumor among the men that the Germans had finally tossed in the towel. Nothing official was announced until our battalion had settled for the night in a large compound that appeared to have once been a stable and agricultural warehouse. The rumor turned to prayer-answering reality when each company in the battalion was notified at last by field phones and special messengers sent around with the historic bulletin: the war was over!

One would have thought it would be cause for fire works and great celebration, but we had waited and prayed for it for so long that the remarkable news was accepted calmly and passively, with only a strange numbing relief as the prime emotion.

The combination of our massive air power, unyielding armor, and persevering infantry had put an end to the war in Italy with the official surrender of a badly beaten German army on May 2, 1945. During the preceding two years, we had irreparably destroyed at least twenty-five of their supposedly invincible divisions, close to half a million men, one heck of a lot of manpower.

The remarkable effort of the individuals in our medical detachments, engineers, artillery, and every service company who went through much of the same hell on many occasions as our infantry did should not be underestimated. Each and every one of them had contributed greatly and, in many cases, most valiantly to bring the war with Germany to its conclusion. I salute them all.

Every man who fought in that war would no doubt acknowledge the amazing feats of unsung heroism that were enacted over and over again on a daily basis, always above the call of duty, by those incredibly courageous infantryman. Although I too wore the blue rifle infantry badge, in no way could I compare myself to those gutsy guys down on the firing line.

Although I felt quite proud of my part in the war, I was especially in awe of our 1st Battalion dogfaces, the incredible warriors of Companies Able, Baker, Charlie, and Dog, who had survived and who now were ready to fight the Japanese somewhere down the road.

Chapter 14

Alberto Remembers Rome

A few guys sat on the hard ground playing poker while others slept in the shade or quietly daydreamed of home, but my merrier drinking buddies had already been basking in a kind of double afterglow following the day's exhilarating news. I never knew where these characters managed to find the hooch, but I didn't care as long as they shared it. Rather than pass the afternoon alone, I decided to join in the light-hearted banter with this happier, livelier, and somewhat inebriated group.

Then I noticed Alberto sitting fifty feet away, his forehead pressed heavily on his arms, fingers locked and tightly clasped around his bent knees as he stared sullenly, wet-eyed, at the dry turf beneath him.

"What's up, amico?" I asked discreetly as I walked over and joined him, sipping a mix of black coffee and cognac from my clumsy, weather-beaten canteen cup. He should have been dancing with joy at the demise of this hated German enemy and for the chance to make a new life as something other than the adventurous partisan soldier he had volunteered to be so many months ago back in 1943. "Why so sad?"

He lifted his head slowly, and with a tormented look I had never seen him wear before, he gazed at me.

"Sergente, I have never talked about Edda, my sweetheart," he began, choking up again as he mentioned her name. I waited.

"What happened in Roma when the Tedeschi came into the city I had hoped to forget, but ...." He shrugged, waved his arms in frustration, and abruptly stopped talking to avoid breaking up again.

I figured that if he could get past the critical emotional point, I might get to hear the rest. Whatever it was, I felt he needed to get it out in the open and so remained quietly by his side until he would be ready to talk again.

"You came into the war a few months later and never knew what kind of hell the Germans made out of that beautiful city. *Our* soldiers didn't want to fight the Americans! As soon as we could, our commanders signed an armistice to get the Tedeschi off of our backs, and we became your ally. September of 1943, I think? I was twenty years old when I joined my friends in the partisani movement."

Alberto had partially regained his composure, and as he spoke, his deeply felt words seemed to release more of the pent-up ghosts that were haunting him. He continued, more openly now that he had my ear. For a fleeting moment I could almost see traces of his old self as he tried to smile.

"I met Edda in school during my first year. We were both studying to be teachers when the craziness started. I was staying in the house of my cousin, Lorenzo, near the river. It wasn't too far from the school. When I met her, I couldn't help myself. I fell in love with her right away, and we would have been married ...." His voice caught again, and he paused self-consciously before going on.

"Those bastard Nazis took over the whole city. I mean, they took over everything! They stole anything they could lay their hands on, and their officers were the worst. For almost a year they did everything they could to make us hate them more. They were angry because our leaders capitulated and joined the Allies, and for the nine terrible months that the Tedeschi occupied Roma, they took any damn thing they wanted. After a while hardly anything was left for the people. With no rice or pasta, not even flour to make it with, we were forced to deal with black marketers if we wanted to eat. Can you imagine an Italian living without pasta? Che fa male, it hurt terribly to see eggs sold for a dollar each and rice for $175 a sack. And meat — forget it. We were allowed only three and one-half ounces a month for each person. If we could find it.

"Every few days their soldiers would raid a section of the city, take people right out of their bedrooms or off the streets, and send them to labor camps like slaves!" Here he had to pause again before going on.

"Edda's father was killed fighting for Mussolini in the African war. Her mother was Jewish and worried terribly about what would happen to her and her daughter when the Gestapo found out. How could the bastards not find out, especially if you lived in the Jewish section of the city. That's where they had to go to live after her father died.

"It was almost impossible to spend evenings with Edda because the Germans made a curfew, sometimes nine o'clock, sometimes five, if they wanted to punish us for something the underground had done the day before.

"Because I wasn't Jewish, her mother made me feel like an outsider, a gentile, but we really loved each other very much, and I know we could have found a way to get married anyway, after the Germans left."

I wanted in the worst way to ask what happened. I knew he wasn't married. Probably sooner or later he'd tell me. I waited, but he changed the subject.

"My cousin was afraid to ask me to join his group of anti-fascist partisanis because he thought I might be too young and my mother would never forgive him if anything happened to me. But when winter came and we watched our people suffer and freeze because all the coal was taken to hotels where only the Germans were staying, it helped make my decision. Young or not, I was already anxious to join. I could hardly wait!" He paused again.

"Coffee?" I asked, offering Alberto my canteen cup.

"I have some grappa in my bag," he said as he reached in and brought out a small bottle of the white lightening, took a swig, then poured some into my half-empty cup.

"Many anti-Fascist political refugees were able to hide out in cellars," Alberto continued, "even in the basements of some Catholic schools. But then the Gestapo placed guards on the streets, especially around the neighborhood where my Edda lived. It was almost impossible for me to come and go without attracting attention."

Sergeant Brown and the other merry jokers who were squatting a few feet away began to laugh raucously at someone's off-colored joke, momentarily interrupting Alberto's narration. When the noise subsided he continued.

"I became very worried because Edda was losing a lot of weight. Everybody was, but she had already lost about twenty pounds. Edda weighed only about ninety-five pounds when I met her so was pretty skinny to start with. I tried to steal for her and her mother whatever scraps I could. Watching her lovely body waste away like that, I couldn't just do nothing! I begged my cousin to get me into the local partisani so I could at least do something. He understood and sympathized with me.

"The next day he took me to become one of his compadres. 'Be very careful!' my cousin said. 'Try to look innocent, like we are just out for a walk. Those bastards have spies everywhere.'

"He took me to an apartment house near Porto Portesi, about a mile from his place. We had to walk. The Tedeschi had already taken all the bicycles and automobiles. Also, someone had killed a guard near the Colosseum the night before, and as a punishment, they ordered that no busses or street cars were allowed to go out all day. German sentries were all over the place, but they couldn't stop and ask everybody in the city where they were going, only the ones who looked suspicious or wore the black clothes of a devout Jew. If they didn't like the way you looked or you answered them in a strange way, they'd send you to a work camp or, worse, to a camp in Germany. No one ever came back from Germany.

"Even the elevator wasn't working that day, so we walked up to the fifth floor and Lorenzo rang the bell, two short and one long ring, I remember. The person inside was expecting us, and I figured that Lorenzo had gotten word to him somehow, although he would never have used the telephone. We could hear the radio inside. It was loud, playing a symphony of some kind. Wagner, I think. Lorenzo told me later that the loud music I heard, usually music written by German composers, was purposely meant to drown out our voices in case the Gestapo was listening.

"We couldn't see the person who looked out at us through the tiny eyehole of the door, but it opened quickly and closed fast behind us. A short, middle-aged man was looking me over like I was a piece of meat while Lorenzo whispered something to him. I was scared, but I thought about Edda. I wasn't going to leave. She, and Italy too, needed me very badly. I would do what I had to do, join the war against il sporco Nazis and the Fascisti pigs!"

Alberto's voice rose when he stated those last words, and the twisted scowl on his face almost frightened me. I could plainly see the venomous hatred he had for our enemy. I doubted that he and the other partisans could ever forget, as I wouldn't. Quivering with repressed emotion and the continuous flow of the potent grappa, he refilled my cup as he went on, more anxious now to vent his vehemence about his traumatic time in Rome.

"After that, my cousin and the little man quietly told me all the rules for fighting our underground war, what I should and shouldn't do, and especially to forget to remember the first names of anybody I would work with. Last names were never to be mentioned, even between us. And how we were able to sneak out at night without the German guard seeing us is a secret I'm not allowed to tell even to you, amico.

"Nine other partisanis were there when I made my first raid three nights later, on the edge of the city near Via Ostiense. We had to loosen a track to wreck any train that happened to come through. The only Italians who were traveling on trains then were the Fascisti pigs anyway, and it was just as well that they got it along with the Tedeschi. Late that night I watched from behind a house. Two German guards lit their cigarettes, smoked, and talked to each other most of the time, not taking their duty too seriously. Whenever they walked further away from where we were hiding, we would, how do you say, open the tracks more, little by little, trying not to make noises they could hear. It took us more than an hour to finish. Four of our men were ready with knives and guns with silencers in case the guards discovered us.

"We knew the whole city would suffer terrible punishment after we finished each raid, but we had no choice. We had to do what we could to fight back. We couldn't just stay home and do nothing. Dio, we were fighting a war!" He sighed deeply then, to my surprise, cried out most painfully.

"What I didn't count on was that the bastards would raid the poor, working-man's part of the city after we had burned one of their supply trucks. They rounded up a thousand people, mostly Jews, to work and die in German concentration camps. My beautiful Edda and her mother were taken away, and I know what the chances are of ever seeing her again. No one comes back, not from that hell!"

Alberto stopped talking after sobbing out those last portentous words. I wanted to cry with him, but after the many horrors I had already witnessed during the last year and a half, no tears would come. Choked up and speechless, I sat there, glassy eyed, silent, my trembling fingers ridiculously patting the back of his hand as I took another big swig of the potent grappa. The burning hot liquid oozed down my gullet, only slightly relieving the pain I felt for him in my heart at that moment. I knew there was no way I could lift him out of his acute depression, and I was too liquored up to try. Soon the strong drink dulled but didn't completely eliminate our mutual gloom.

J.P. came by and joined us, unaware of our hopelessly morose, inebriated state. His timing couldn't have been better as it precluded any further dispiriting talk of Alberto's Rome.

I didn't realize it then, but that would be the very last time I would see my unusual friend Alberto. He wasn't around the next day or any day after that. I could only guess that, while the rest of our regiment remained another four months in Italy, he had gone home to begin a new life.

I could only assume why it was that he didn't say good-bye before he left. The poor guy had already lost his sweetheart under very traumatic circumstances, and now that the war had ended, we'd all be leaving him for our homes in America. Even as courageous and stouthearted as we knew he undoubtedly was, his having to face the inevitable loss of his newest Army buddies, his best friends, could have been too much for him to bear.

I, for one, understood, but I missed him terribly.

Chapter 15

Tito and Trieste

The big war had been won, but the battle for Italy, at least a healthy
chunk of it, wasn't over yet.

After sharing the anguish of Alberto's Roman tragedy, I sat dumbly on the
floor, mentally and physically exhausted, in a pathetic state of intoxication. Just
minutes before involving myself in my comrade's alarming state of mind, I had
been called to a special meeting at the command post and given the unsettling
news that we had to face a new enemy, Marshal Tito's Yugoslavian Army. I'm
sure I must have shuddered in anticipation of what would come next, but in any
case it certainly sounded better than a quick trip to the Pacific.

The new instructions from Colonel Woods sounded serious. As he stood
facing me, he said, "Sergeant, Marshal Tito intends to grab the whole peninsula
that the city of Trieste is situated on. Some of his troops have already taken up
positions there. Others will be infiltrating soon, and the chiefs of staff are
depending on us to stop them."

He paused a few seconds, looking me squarely in the eye as if the whole
damn thing were my fault, then continued.

"I'm assigning you a jeep and driver, and I need you to locate every one of
Tito's armed outposts in the city. Where he has a squad or company of troops,
our plan is to match him with a company of our own, positioned right across the
street. We have to pinpoint these Yugoslavian partisans and find out exactly

where they are, what weapons they have, and how many men there are. The 2nd New Zealand Division has had an earlier start and is already busy at it, so keep an eye out for them.

"The whole battalion is leaving for Trieste first thing in the morning," he added.

I wasn't sure whether to laugh or cry. In any event, it was going to delay my plans for a two-week furlough in Los Angeles to see my wife again before heading out to the Japanese theater of operations. On the other hand, summer was almost upon us, and the weather had turned pleasantly warm. It was wonderful for enjoying the mild, northeastern corner of Italy and the sunny Adriatic Sea that I had often heard about. As there was no choice in the matter anyway, I decided to be pragmatic and make the best of it.

I had wondered why all the men in our 1st Battalion, about two thousand of us, were issued new uniforms and weapons, just one day after the Italian war ended when they had not been issued to any other outfit in the entire American 5th Army. Now I knew the reason. Obviously, the State Department wanted us to make one hell of an impression on the Communists when we arrived in Trieste. We would quickly let them know that our will would be a hell of a lot stronger than theirs if push came to shove.

I was well aware that Tito's informal army of resolute partisans had done a lot more than their fair share of fighting off the German invaders. Somehow I felt close to each and every one of them who might have aided our cause, whether Socialist Red, Pink, or whatever. To have thought of them in any other way than comrades in arms at that time would have been inconceivable, and I had hoped that they would have felt the same way toward us. I had been given a job to do and, of course, I would do it but with unfeigned respect for this politically near-sighted new rival.

The next day, trucks took our battalion to our billet, the castle of San Giusto overlooking Trieste from its commanding height on a bluff above the city. The other two battalions of our regiment moved farther inland to the vicinity of Gorizia, an agrarian region about forty miles to the northeast.

This imposing, seventeenth-century castle loomed majestically near the top of the gradually inclining palisades. The castle, a throwback to the feudal era when every city required protection from foreign invaders, had been constructed with everything a castle should have, with the exception of a moat. All of us enlisted men sacked out in sleeping bags on the dirt floor along murky, unlit hallways deep within the confines of the castle. As I left this antiquated fortress each morning to check over the city, the quixotic boy-child in me felt as if I were a knight-errant and the jeep my prancing white steed as I valiantly went forth to slay a dragon or two and most likely rescue several damsels in distress along the way.

Trieste, an important seaport northeast of Venice, straddles a gradually sloping headland off the comparatively calm waters of the Adriatic. Parts of the city are perched precariously on steeply rising cliffs while, oddly, other parts farther inland are as flat as a table. Where the hillside slopes more gently, there are tall, multistoried tenements and busy shopping centers like those in any large, cosmopolitan city. The city appeared to me very much like a small version of Milan.

I knew that Trieste was a city of about a half-million residents and gloriously situated on the sea. Apparently Tito was no one's fool. If he could somehow manage to occupy and retain this fantastic area for his country, it would be akin to Canada taking over the city of San Francisco in our country. After all, didn't Stalin grab everything he could lay his hands on? So why shouldn't Tito grab Trieste for Yugoslavia?

My driver and I toured the city as we had been ordered to do, checking against the coordinates on my map to become better oriented to this new gameboard and precisely noting and reporting by radio what I could see of Tito's little bands of militia. Wearing mostly civilian clothes, they would have been much more difficult to spot except for their captured German rifles and Russian-made carbines slung over their shoulders. They made hardly any attempt to conceal their activities, and so it was easy for me to see them sitting in open windows or sunbathing bare chested on open-worked balconies of apartment houses, always with their weapons. Generally, a squad of about fifteen or twenty men would move in and commandeer a first- or second-story apartment located at strategically busy corners. There was nothing clandestine. Like us, they apparently had instructions to make sure they would be seen and to appear contentious.

My job was a snap because it didn't appear likely that anyone was ready to take pot-shots at me, which was a pleasure after those devastating 88s and 105s.

After my report was turned in, I would get a kick out of noticing that a group of our men moved expeditiously into a building across the street or in that same general vicinity a day or so later. I never asked how they, or we for that matter, managed to confiscate those residential locations without displacing civilians who lived or worked there.

This kind of checkmate combat was becoming fun, and I couldn't help but enjoy the hunt and think hey, Navy, look! No carrots, same glasses, but they want me to use my eyes again!

During this daily reconnoitering, I saw what appeared to be an opera house in the heart of the city. It occurred to me that opera houses always had a maestro, a musical director. As my vocal lessons and coaching had abruptly stopped when I was drafted, this might be a great opportunity to get some practice and pick up where I had left off.

A delightfully dour janitor with a Jerry Colonna mustache was lazily polishing the brass appurtenances at the elegant marble entrance. In Italian I asked about the maestro's schedule and when I could see him.

"Our opera company is doing *Tosca* in Venice. He'll be back next week," the old man responded, with some fearful hesitation, no doubt wondering to himself why an American soldier wanted to see his esteemed professore.

When I returned about six days later, I found the maestro working upstairs in his private studio. He was considerably older than I had imagined he'd be. With an oversized ascot bow tie and a full mane of bushy, gray hair and dressed in a shabby tweed suit, he was the perfect portrait of the stooped musical conductor, the lionized genius I assumed he had once been before the war raised havoc with the arts. He looked up from the opera score he was perusing at his beat-up, old spinet, wiped a black handkerchief across his eyes, and studied me with genuine astonishment.

"I would like to study and review solfège with you while I am staying in the city," I said, after introducing myself. "How much would it cost me for that and one hour of voice lessons?"

The shocked expression changed to one of relief. His cordial smile and response was slow, deliberate, unforgettable, and typically Italian.

"Yes, I can work with you," he said. Smiling broadly now and displaying teeth stained by years of smoking, he squinted his old eyes in amusement. "But no money, please. Just bring bread, coffee, cigarettes, or anything you can. Food is more valuable than the lira."

Our battalion had to move out of the city before I could take advantage of his gracious offer, and I'll always regret having procrastinated and not grabbing this opportunity earlier. Even one lesson would have been a marvelously memorable experience.

On our fifth day in Trieste, a well-dressed, well-educated, attractive young woman brazenly approached the entrance to our command post in the castle. It was early, and she found me getting ready to drive off for my daily exploration.

"Will you help me, please?" she said in English, her voice and her eyes begging for attention. As I have never been known to ignore the plea of any pretty young petitioner, I stopped to listen.

Her problem, she whined sweetly, was that the Yugoslavian intruders had confiscated her family's apartment by getting the keys from the building's janitor. "They came yesterday and took away the keys. I protested, but they called me names and warned me not to go near it until they were finished with it."

Her story intrigued me. What gave these Socialist partisanis the idea that they had a right to commandeer the property of Italian civilians? This was my first real confrontation with totalitarianism, and I didn't like it. Something about this situation reminded me of the unscrupulous Nazis. It reeked of oppression, of iron rule.

"My mother and father are terribly frightened. We would report this to our mayor, but our government is so busy with so many urgent problems that it could take much too long a time."

It was impossible for me to know why the Reds had singled out that particular apartment of all the apartments available to them in Trieste. There must have been other factors that I wasn't aware of. Maybe they wanted it for another one of their outposts. I was feeling indestructible and acutely omnipotent at the time, having played my significant role in defeating the all-powerful Wehrmacht. Interested and ready to help, I know no other reason why I offered to try to get her apartment back.

The local Yugoslavian Army headquarters was a few miles northwest of the city, and I headed for it on the following morning, after receiving the colonel's permission, as the trip and the mission seemed to fall loosely within the scope of reconnaissance. With the inflated image I had of myself, I felt ready for anything, and thirty minutes later, having received the location and information I'd need from the distraught young woman, I found their command post. Three uniformed guards stared at me with curiosity before I attempted to pass under the ominous hammer-and-sickle banner into a simple, two-story, stucco house.

They saw little reason to be unduly suspicious of me because I carried no weapon. At that point in time I saw no need to carry my carbine. Yet I did at all times wear my unmistakable blue-metallic insignia with its embossed rifle denoting that I was an infantryman. Not surprisingly, that and my cocky attitude seemed to command a lot of respect, even from these zealous partisanis who led me to a menially appointed office in the rear of the building.

With fist closed and elbow bent, my right arm extended high over my shoulder in the comradely, Socialistic salute, I greeted the officer who appeared to be in charge of operations.

He smiled at my gesture pleasantly enough, and rising from his desk, the tall captain offered me the same salute in return. As he did so, I noticed a change in the expression around his eyes, as if to say, "What are you trying to pull? Why are you making like a Communist?" I had figured that it couldn't hurt to appear brotherly and minimize his suspicion of me as being a right-wing anti-Socialist.

I couldn't speak to him in his Slavic tongue, so I asked in Italian which language he preferred I use.

"Deutsch, bitte," he replied, to my surprise. He pointed to the chair near his desk for me to occupy.

Fortunately for me, most Jews who were brought up on the streets of New York in the 1920s and 1930s had to know some Yiddish, a European dialect derived mainly from German. We absorbed it by some kind of osmosis from our grandparents and, in many cases, even our parents. With a modicum of difficulty and unaccustomed hand waving, I explained to him that I was trying to do a good deed for this apparently helpless family in the city and asked if he could please help me and do me the favor of returning the keys in question.

"Ya?" was his response, meaning by his questioning tone that I was to continue and give him more information.

For the next ten minutes, we verbally fenced with each other, sometimes communicating in three languages as I tried to reassure him with my best demeanor and mock complaisant smile that I most certainly had no ill intentions, no hidden agenda, and no disrespect for his position in the matter. I repeated that it was a terrible hardship on those poor people not to have a roof over their heads. He looked at me strangely. At this stage of the game, I had no intention of arguing too loudly about his unruly act of confiscation.

He barked an order to one of the guards, and almost before I realized it, they placed a set of keys in the palm of my hand. At the very least, these people are very well organized, I thought, to be able to get those particular keys so fast. But why?

I thanked him profusely and raised my fist once more to salute him, feeling strangely as if I'd won a bloodless battle. Exhilarated by this success, I left quickly and immediately headed directly for the apartment. My curiosity had suddenly been aroused as I held the enigmatic keys.

The address the young woman had given me took me to the most affluent part of the city, to the twelfth floor of an elegant looking, twelve-story apartment house. Could this be the right place? I was surprised by its resemblance to some of the posh, canopied, high-rise units I remembered that dotted Wilshire Boulevard in west Los Angeles.

Leaving my driver with the vehicle on the broad thoroughfare in front of the high-class tenement, I rode a gilded elevator to apartment number 1004, as she had directed, turned the key in one of the elegantly carved double doors, and entered a veritable Shangri-la.

In my naïve twenty-four years, I had never envisioned the opulence that was spread before me as I slowly walked through the marble and mirrored foyer then into the colorful explosion of an expansive main sitting room. Here the massive, rust-colored, silk-velvet sectional sofa and mahogany grand piano were only the first of several fascinating objects to catch my eye.

Whoever these people were who owned this place were anything but poverty-stricken. I could understand now why the partisans had chosen this particular apartment to borrow. To their way of thinking, it must have seemed the height of decadent capitalism. I'm sure that one of their high-ranking officers, maybe Tito himself, would certainly have known how to make good use of it.

The imp in me saw that this could be a most enjoyable experience, if I wasn't too quick to notify the fearful signorina that I had managed to get the keys. Our battalion would probably be in Trieste for a bit longer, so why not keep the news of the transferred keys under my hat for a little while? I would simply tell the woman that I had been promised the keys soon and then return them to her just before we left the city. That should at least satisfy her to the extent that the apartment was not going to be permanently occupied by the dreaded Yugoslavian partisans, whom these northeastern Italians feared and distrusted almost as much as they did the Germans.

Why shouldn't I use it instead?

I don't recall that I ever saw the woman again. I believe I gave the keys to the building's janitor but only after several exciting adventures took place there.

Chapter 16

Here Today, Dead Tomorrow

Jess Dunnagen and I began regular visits to my Shangri-la apartment almost daily, generally in the oppressive heat of the late afternoon after my troop-movement reports had been turned in. Private First Class Day, my driver, would drop us off, then J.P. and I would open the windows to let the cooling sea air waft through while we lounged around in our lush surroundings, indulging in fresh fruit and whatever brandy or wine we could find in the local stores. Making like million-aires, we listened to music and decided the political future of the world from our comfortable down-filled sofa for an hour or so before return-ing to base.

Almost constantly, we'd tune in to the sound of good, old American pop music emanating paradoxically from the German-made Blaupunkt radio in this luxurious Italian home, except for those private times I felt like tickling the ivories on the magnificent Steinway piano.

Whenever time permitted, we continued to enjoy this luxury, sometimes chatting and flirting with talkative neighbors, having only to report back hours later when we'd telephone the command post to have a driver meet us down-stairs. More often than not, we just walked the pleasant mile and a half back. Life was good!

After having discovered this unusual prize, I stupidly began to invite some of my other friends over, mainly to show off the place. Word got around, and suddenly I found myself with more friends than I had ever had before. My ego trip had begun to backfire. It wasn't long before a couple of officers in our company asked me for a set of duplicate keys. They wanted to use the apartment when I wasn't there and suggested, "Wouldn't it be nice if we could make some kind of congenial arrangement for not getting in each other's way." One doesn't ignore a request from a superior officer for obvious reasons, the main one being that I could possibly lose all of my rights to the flat. Needless to say, the keys were duplicated.

A few days later, I entered the apartment one evening to find two extremely attractive women sitting around and chatting innocently with the lieutenants as they all enjoyed their drinks. One bottle of cognac remained unopened on the coffee table, and the half-empty second bottle was being proffered to me.

"Have one on the house, sergeant," said Lieutenant B_____ as he smiled, offering me a snifter. Then, in a distinctly firm undertone that was accentuated with a very obvious wink, he added, "But please do me a favor. Drink up and get the hell out of here. We really need the place for a while."

I recall at the time hearing music in the background. On the radio, Jimmy Dorsey was sweetly tootling away one of my all-time favorite tunes on his clarinet, a romantic ballad called "It Had to Be You," when the second couple rose and began to dance, hands suggestively caressing each other's bottoms.

Blushing, I took the lieutenant's hint and left the apartment, confiscating the jeep and driver that was waiting for them downstairs. I was sure they wouldn't be needing it for a long, long while or at least for a few hours.

"How about *those* Eyetye hookers!" Private G_____ remarked. The tires protested loudly as he sharply handled the first corner.

"What hookers?" I asked.

"Didn't you get a look at those broads with the lieutenants?"

"Those were hookers?" I asked incredulously.

He laughed at my simpleminded innocence. "Wake up and smell the friggin' roses, sergeant. The town's full of 'em."

I thought back on those two women, gorgeous, exquisitely dressed, and acting well within normal social conventions, until the dancing began. How could I have known their shady profession? I had had little or no exposure to that dark, dissolute side of life, at least not until Private G_____ hit me with it. Then I remembered Montecatini and Angelina, the overworked, under-respected pro, who had neither the classy look nor the manners of the two women I had just come in contact with. The variance was interesting, to say the least, posing questions I vowed to grapple with later.

No, I hadn't just fallen off the turnip truck, but I was comparatively naïve, socially too young for my years. I had, of course, seen many exaggerated caricatures on the silver screen of scantily dressed, overrouged streetwalkers who in no way resembled those sophisticated ladies of the night I had just left at the apartment. Those women upstairs looked downright appetizing.

I had occasion to see these and other officers come to the flat later with different women, each one strikingly more beautiful than the other. Curious, I finally worked up the courage to ask Lieutenant B_____ how it was possible to find so many lovely, high-class prostitutes so quickly and easily in a town like this.

"Sergeant, when your stomach is empty, you'll do damned near anything to fill it!" He responded brusquely, grinning at my naïve question.

I had my answer. It was supply and demand, need and money. Apparently you could buy just about anything and anybody you wanted because there always seemed to be someone willing to sell themselves for the right price. Here was a valuable lesson, I thought, as I recalled those times in Africa and Naples when I had been offered sisters and virgins for practically nothing, for a couple of lousy bucks or a carton of cigarettes.

It soon appeared that it was no longer to be solely my apartment; a month later, half the Allied forces in Trieste seemed to be making good use of it. Here was still another very important lesson. I should have learned to keep my big mouth shut. This was one hell of a way to get a liberal education.

About 9:30 one evening, I arrived to find three New Zealanders using the place. I never found out how they had managed to get in or finagle the keys to the apartment, but one doesn't argue much with these incredibly physical Kiwis who were as drunk as hoot owls, playing the radio too loud and raising an awful racket.

Feeling like an intruder, I introduced myself and offered to leave them and their girl friends alone if they would only keep the noise down. Before I could leave, I was stopped by an imploring glance from one of the three prostitutes. As soon as she had the chance, she whispered something to me in her language, knowing that these men didn't have a good grasp of Italian. It seemed that the man she was with was soused to the gills and was threatening to kill her.

On the better side of caution, I decided that I ought to hang around and wait in the smaller of the three bedrooms out of sight. The last thing I needed here were MPs or the local police.

By 10:30, the other two couples had found their way to bedrooms. The third man, a formidable hulk, the one the woman had earlier signaled to me that she had been prepaid to have sex with, sprawled awkwardly on the overstuffed sofa, on the verge of passing out. I prayed to God he wouldn't vomit. Bleary-eyed, he kept trying to sing the words to "Waltzing Matilda," and with each pause, he bellowed every epithet he had ever learned as he attempted to persuade the frightened women to perform every sex act imaginable or he'd "damned well cut her bloody throat." I seriously doubted that he could have even gotten it up in his condition.

In the meantime, I remained concealed and out of sight, very much like a voyeur watching and listening in dismay to his rambling depravity, anxiously wondering where it all would lead. Off and on he'd fall into a drunken stupor, pass wind and belch, alternately snoring and snorting loudly, then he'd wake himself up between grunts.

When finally he quieted down, I turned the lamps down in the parlor and returned to my comfortable brass bed. In the meantime, the sensuous woman had gingerly slipped away from him and out of his sight had tiptoed barefoot to my bed, frightened out of her wits. He muttered something in his besotted, semi-conscious state about "killing the bitch" and made a clumsy effort to find her in the darkness.

"She's gone," I assured him. It didn't seem to bother him much. He was too far gone to do anything except mutter under his breath and fall back onto the sofa in a drunken stupor.

With hoarse whispers and sign language, I suggested that she get underneath my brass bed, hide from him before she should attempt to leave the apartment, and give him a chance to fall asleep. Almost hysterical with fear, she complied. Five minutes later, I heard his resonant snoring was more rhythmic now and less spasmodic. Hopefully, he would be "out" for the rest of the night.

About twenty minutes later, I felt my own testosterone heat up and almost reach a boiling point with the thought of this very appealing, wholesome, young whore cringing fearfully within a few feet of my growing desire.

"Ssh. Silenzio," I whispered, forefinger to my lips, as I joined her on the throw rug under the wire bedsprings. She didn't protest, and we laid there for a while longer with my arms around her. Although she was fully dressed, I was incapable of resisting her sexy, warm body, and with her implicit compliance and cooperation, we consummated the instinctive act. It was her way of thanking me for rescuing her from the hostile brute.

When I finally felt that it was safe enough, I noiselessly let her out of the apartment a little more than half an hour later. Holding her shoes in her hand, she thanked me again at the door with silent, exaggerated lip movements, sighed heavily, then unexpectedly gave my cheek a sweet, little peck.

I soon fell fast asleep, finally and fully relieved of the persistent libidinous pressure that had been mounting steadily within me for too many months. But I did remain awake just long enough to contemplate the consequence of this, my first real transgression, naturally forgiving myself and regretting the fact that I had never even gotten her name.

The three rugged New Zealanders and their two remaining puttanas awoke early, appearing none the worse for wear. They were certainly a stouthearted bunch. If they suffered any hangovers, it wasn't apparent. They were pleasant enough at eight o'clock in the morning, but I was more than happy to finally see them leave. Georgie, the guy who had been the troublemaker, only casually asked about the woman he had been with. I told him again that she had left after he fell asleep, which seemed to satisfy him.

⊷ ⚌✦⚌ ⊷

May on the Adriatic is as good as it gets. I found time for my men and I to visit the pebbly seashore below the castle, do a little swimming, and sunbathe for a couple of hours in the late afternoon whenever we could.

On my second visit to the beach, there were two frolicking nymphs playfully cavorting in the water. They were laughing and busily splashing away as I waded out to where they were, looking forward to a bit of fun and flirtation. The prettier of the two apparently had a similar notion as she began to splash me in return, teasing me to swim and chase her.

When we tired of that game, she continued to chatter endlessly as we flopped onto my khaki blanket, slightly separated from the others. I couldn't understand more than a third of what she was so gregariously prattling about, but I did manage to learn that her name was Gina and that she often came to this beach to enjoy the sun and water.

I sat up, hands across my knees, and puffed away at my pipe as I contemplated this svelte, suntanned, unusually talkative girl next to me and wondered what she'd look like with her long, dark hair dry and wearing street clothes. Her two-piece bathing suit revealed only that her breasts were a bit smaller than average, but from the hips down, she was firm, shapely, and quite appealing.

Instinctively, my game plan was to learn more about her and, at the same time, learn more of the language, which she was more than willing to teach me. But I'm quite sure that in the more carnal recesses of my sex-starved mind there lurked a certain curiosity to test the limits of this free-spirited young woman.

I asked how often she came to this part of the beach and when she was likely to be here again.

"Tomorrow, if you want. Can you bring American cigarettes? I love Camels," she responded in a lyrical tone that flowed off her tongue so provocatively as to more thoroughly arouse the excited animal in me.

It was time for us to get back to the command post for dinner, but her flashing smile as we said "ciao" alerted me to the possibilities of an unusual adventure. I'd be crazy not to return and bring her at least a pack or two.

The next day she was there, as cute as I remembered. After saying hello, I handed her a pack of Lucky Strikes. Her eyes lit up like Las Vegas at midnight while she hurriedly ripped off the cellophane.

"Grazie, Anello, grazie!" She bent towards me and kissed my cheek. I lit her cigarette and relit the still half-filled bowl of my pipe.

"Why Anello? Perche?" I asked, wondering why she had called me by that name.

She responded that her nickname for me had all the letters of my first name, that it was the Italian word meaning finger ring, and that she liked the way it sounded more than Leon. I couldn't disagree. Gina continued to call me by that musical sounding name until I last saw her a few weeks later.

My courage rose several notches higher, and I told her that tomorrow night I'd like to come get her and take her to see my apartment. "We could dance, if you like. You like good music?"

She nodded her head as she blew a smoke ring. I had never learned to do that.

"The American music on the radio is very good. We'll have a few drinks, and I'll bring candy."

I'm sure I sounded like an awkward adolescent teenager, but I could see her eyes sparkle when I mentioned the word candy. A shortage of sugar and cocoa had left these people famished for anything sweet.

"You like chocolate?" I asked and then thought to myself, how dumb! Who the hell doesn't like chocolate? "I'll bring some Hershey bars."

"OK, Anello mio! You come get me at seven o'clock tomorrow."

She gave me the name of a square and the corner where I was to pick her up. I'd grown very familiar with the city by then as a result of my daily reconnaissance missions, and I took note of the fact that it was only about a half mile from the apartment.

She was there when I drove up. I had seen her only in a bathing suit or beach robe, and seeing her then in two-and-a-half-inch heels and dressed up only added to my infatuation. She was as cute as all get-out in the clingy, knee-length, printed silk skirt she wore. Eyes flashing, Gina had already leaped agilely into the jeep before I could get out to do the gentlemanly thing and assist her in.

Being somewhat of an introvert, I had always derived a great deal of pleasure from the company of more communicative, fun-loving, uninhibited people, and this young woman certainly seemed to fit the bill. I was looking forward to the evening with keen anticipation, knowing that she'd at least keep the night lively.

She gasped noticeably, as I knew she would, as soon as we entered the apartment, oohing and aahing at everything in sight. I laid my week's ration of two chocolate bars and a bottle of local brandy on the coffee table in front of the sofa. The sun had dipped behind the palisade, and its remaining glow cast soft shadows in the darkening living room. I'd refrain from turning on the lamps as long as possible. I turned on the radio. All Europeans seem to love our jazz bands, so I had very little trouble dialing in to the familiar smooth riffs of the Duke's classic, "Sentimental Journey," that flowed like honey through the single speaker.

When I turned back to her, I saw that she had already ravenously finished off the first of the candy bars. A piece of the chocolate had escaped her mouth onto a corner of her lip. I made a move to wipe it away, but she held my extended hand, giggled like a schoolgirl, and said, "Kiss it off, please." I did, slowly. That simple act of touching her velvety skin with my lips had suddenly increased my ardor, spawning what I felt was an obvious carnal bulge that she couldn't possibly miss.

Embarrassed, I moved away to the rhythm of the slow beat, hoping she might not have noticed, and held out my hands for her to join me in the slow fox-trot. She rose to take my hand as I waited, but something had suddenly changed. The once bright and shining, irreverent, daredevil look that I had become used to seeing in her features had taken a 180-degree turn since the Hershey bar and the kiss.

Gina retained the smile, but something about it was immensely different. That new smile and her amber-colored eyes had taken on the look of a wild, carnal grimace. Instead of dancing, she turned and unceremoniously pushed me down onto the sofa, straddled my lap as she faced me, and with her skirt raised, began to gyrate her body in an unmistakably sensual manner. All the while, she contemplated me through half-closed, strangely amused eyes and continued the tantalizing motion for a few more minutes.

For a while, I was awestruck and couldn't believe what was happening but was delighted that it was. I was ready, and she knew it. Pulling me up by my hands, she found the nearest bedroom, and from then on, I just left everything entirely up to her. She seemed to enjoy this wanton release and to take special satisfaction in the fact that she could control me like a robot.

Almost twenty minutes later, no longer the joking, game-playing, talkative young woman I had previously known, she dressed quickly, explaining that she had to leave and that she preferred to walk back alone to where I had picked her up.

"Did I do something? I hope I didn't hurt you." This new serious side of her shook me up. What the hell could I have done?

"You were wonderful, Anello mio. No, it's not you."

When we said good-bye, the hug seemed sincere enough. For a brief moment, she peered into my eyes and kissed my cheek as she had done the day before, then she fled like a modern-day Cinderella.

I wondered why she didn't come to the beach anymore. Not knowing where to find her, I didn't see her again until a few nights before our battalion had to leave the city two weeks later.

"You know a girl named Gina?" one of the officers asked me.

"Yeah! How did you know?"

"She asked about you yesterday and wanted to know how you were."

Taken by surprise, I asked where he saw her.

"She has her office in a bar downtown. For chrissake, sergeant, didn't you know? I had a date last night, and Sophia introduced her to me while we were having drinks."

My mouth must have dropped open, and I looked at him stupidly.

"Don't tell me you didn't know she was a pro!"

I shrugged and walked away. No, lieutenant, I thought to myself, I really didn't know. How could I have known?

The more I thought about our last meeting, it began to make sense. Still, it was hard to believe, and I spent the rest of the day wondering about the enigma of her personality, half schoolgirl, half demimonde. Even knowing the truth about her, I found myself missing that fun-loving part of the vibrant, twenty-one-year old Gina, pro or whatever.

Among other things, curiosity caused me to visit the bar he had mentioned. I held my breath as I saw her toying with a brandy snifter in the company of an elderly, baldish individual who, I assumed, might have been her pimp, her father, or her customer. He was making entries into a notebook, ignoring her.

"Anello!" she said when she saw me. "What are you doing here?"

I could see by her expression that she would rather not have seen me under those circumstances. I was sorry to see that there was no sign of a smile on her face.

"Tonight could be my last night in Trieste, and I had hoped to spend it with you," I replied weakly.

Gina didn't say anything for a minute. The old guy looked me over like I was a piece of questionable merchandise then got up and left the table.

"What would it cost to spend the whole night with you?" I asked, taking her hand.

"Pazzo! You *are* crazy! Why would you want to do that?"

"I don't know, maybe for old time's sake." I couldn't think of anything else to tell her, but I think she understood.

She squeezed my hand tighter as her eyes searched around the bar. "Be here at 9:30, and bring a carton of cigarettes."

If she didn't smoke them herself, she could easily get $20 or more for that carton, which was a lot of lira in those days, unless Baldy took half of it. I didn't really give a damn. I didn't smoke cigarettes anyhow, so I had nothing to lose by giving her my ration.

I told her I'd be there. I walked out of the bar, wondering what had come over me. Just a short time before, I was as unsophisticated as any wide-eyed fourteen-year-old. Now, temporary though it was, I had become involved in an illicit affair with a prostitute, obviously doomed from the start.

I think she had some kind of youthful infatuation with me, too, and realizing that she couldn't legitimately pull it off, had shown every sign of feeling sorry for herself. I wasn't sure whether I should feel guilty or proud.

Home seemed at least a million miles away, and considering the war news, I almost forgave my transgression, convinced that my odds of ever getting back home in one piece were pretty damned grim. The latest scuttlebutt circulating around battalion was ominous; when we left Italy, we were to go directly to Camp Bowie in Brownsville, Texas, to prepare ourselves quickly for the coming invasion of Japan.

Somehow, there was an immature kind of solace in the fact that I wasn't alone. Almost every infantryman I knew, married or not, seemed to have shared the guilt of straying at one time or another, making one almost feel chicken for not participating in this rampant phenomenon. I'm quite sure that this need for carnal monkey business could never be understood by others who were not thoroughly inundated with the idea of being here today, dead tomorrow, especially not by our mates at home.

I did spend that last night with Gina. I felt I was much more the man now than the naïve corporal I thought I remembered from way, way back in 1943, only a few lifetimes ago.

Chapter 17

Borderline Occupation

Marshal Tito was doing everything in his power to imitate Stalin by laying claim to the seaports of Trieste and Fiume, the city of Gorizia, and hundreds of other Italian borderline villages and verdant square miles. He would have loved to grab everything on the map situated to the north and east of Venice. With the imminent defeat of the Germans, he and his National Liberation Army assumed for some ungodly reason that they were entitled to gobble up those fringe territories for Yugoslavia, that is until the Allies swooped into this disputed territory en masse, virtually overwhelming his forces and firmly putting an end to his willful aggression.

Now that we had more or less stabilized the situation in the important port of Trieste, our battalion and its complement of service troops were moved again. We were trucked out of the city to a much more pastoral area noted on the map as the Italian territory of Venezia Giulia, much of it closely abutting the western border of Yugoslavia.

The other battalions of the 363rd Infantry Regiment, about six thousand men, plus numerous brigades of the British 8th Army, had already deployed troops over the entire countryside near the city of Gorizia, mainly to convince any remaining Slav forces that they couldn't simply walk in and take over.

It seemed that our generals didn't give a damn what we did while we were occupying these territories as long as we kept up appearances, looked mean, and acted strong.

Personally, I took the move as an opportunity for R and R, rest and recreation. I wanted to make the most of this occasion to holiday in that peacefully pleasant countryside where the inhabitants were a homogenized group of Italian and Yugoslav individuals. Because all of these people were farmers and common workers, it was understandable that their politics favored the Socialists on their eastern border; something in the promise of redistributed wealth appealed to them.

Our battalion billeted in the small village of Prevacina on May 20, 1945, relieving an attachment of the 2nd New Zealand Division that had preceded us. I now shared the wooden floor of one of seven rooms in a two-story, stucco house with about six other men from my headquarters company.

The nearest adjoining Allied troops were a brigade of turban-wearing Indians who patrolled the river about a mile from us. They pretty much kept to themselves, and we didn't see a need to intrude on them.

The little town of Prevacina had a population of only about 300 citizens, most of whom were females because many of their men hadn't returned from the recent wars and most likely never would. Everyone spoke both Slavik and Italian but made no bones about leaning towards Socialism and Yugoslavia, displaying their bias at every opportunity. At least once a day, groups of five to thirty-five Yugoslavian partisans would brazenly parade up and down the little main street in front of our command post, defiantly chorusing hearty marching songs in wonderfully rich, a cappella harmony.

Music seemed to run in their blood. The field hands, which included almost every person in town, trudged off in small processions almost daily to pick or plant crops of corn or potatoes, singing their workers' chanteys loudly and rhythmically. The sound was a catchy, deep-pitched counterpoint that I'd heard only once before when Russia's world famous Don Cossack Chorus had performed in Los Angeles.

Impoverished as they were and despite their subdued defiance, all of these people seemed complacent in their simple, rural lifestyle but for one singularly interesting exception. Surprisingly, one of the most popular songs in the village was titled, "America, America, America Voglio Andar," emphatically meaning "I want to go to America." It had a very catchy, unforgettable melody that I find easy to recall even today because I enjoyed singing it loudly along with them, meaning it as much or more than they did.

J.P. and I were having a ball, spending every spare minute of our time at the tree-lined brook that flowed nearby. We hadn't been assigned any special tasks, so we would make for its cool, clear, refreshing water or bask on its huge, sun-warmed boulders as often as possible. It was at these occasions that we'd sense the immense pleasure of our recent victory as well as the joy of living. Very often we'd chat with the young people as well as some of the partisan soldiers from the village as they, too, enjoyed getting away from their toils in the sultry, summer heat.

After a week or so of this all-expense-paid, once-in-a-lifetime vacation, headquarters requested me to join a small party of one lieutenant and four men to return to Monticelli in order to document Sergeant Oscar Johnson's extraordinarily valiant actions at the Gothic Line, actions which ultimately won him the rare and coveted Congressional Medal of Honor. Our report was to be used in submitting the recommendation for that award.

The four-day trip would be a big deal in the annals of the military, we were told. Reviewing and detailing the circumstances of Sergeant Johnson's three days of incredible daring against the Germans would forever be a feather in the cap of the 363rd Infantry. I had been a principal witness to his remarkable deeds and was more than proud to be chosen.

When I returned to Prevacina, I quickly rejoined J.P. in pursuing our fascinating hobby of making friends and learning languages. He told me that several of the men in our battalion were putting together a musical variety show, which included a small band and comedy routines. They wanted me to be their vocalist and assistant director.

I figured, why not? With no combat to be fought at the moment, I became an integral part of the show, singing pop ballads and creating corny slapstick skits. Our little troupe's reputation grew to the point where we were being asked to travel to other battalions all over the encamped peninsula, treading the boards so to speak, on fifteen-foot, prefabricated, wooden outdoor stages. What a hell of a way to fight a war.

Headquarters made a point of sending me a memo that the 5th Army was going to hold a talent contest in the city of Milan in ten days and asking me if I would like to compete as a soloist. No prize was mentioned, but as far as I was concerned, just the trip to this glamorous city would be prize enough. To get into the contest I would need an accompanyist. I didn't have to think twice. Sergeant King, who was my radio man during the Pisa incident, had been accompanying me on his guitar in our little musical show, and now that the muscles in my vocal chords were finally stretching back into shape from these recent workouts, I felt I was ready. I figured I'd probably lose though, considering the talent that would be drawn from all those many thousands of men, but win or lose, five days in a Milan hotel was not to be sneezed at by a guy who had become used to thinking that sleeping on the floor could be great if only they'd let you sleep.

I was limited to two songs and felt that my best numbers at the time were Gershwin's great standard, "Embraceable You," and "The Donkey Serenade" for a big ending encore, if one was needed. On the week of the contest, we arrived in Milan, somewhat startled by the immense size of the city, and found our pre-arranged hotel to be about a block away from the theater we were going to appear in. Our room was on the first floor overlooking the hustle and bustle of the busy street.

This had all the earmarks of becoming a fascinating adventure, but not in a million years could we have guessed how much of a diversion this would turn out to be until that very first night. To our astonishment, the local city council had arranged to throw a street party right outside our window.

The new regime of anti-Fascists wanted nothing worse than to have cause to celebrate, so when the news came of Benito Mussolini's hanging a few days before, there couldn't have been a better reason. One hell of a bash was in order.

Many people may at sometime have attended a block party, but unless they've attended one in Italy, they don't know what they're missing. I've never had the good fortune personally to attend a Mardi Gras in New Orleans or Rio, but I'd be willing to bet that the spirited fervor, the no-holds-barred air of festivity during the wild shindig that took place on Via Garibaldi that particular night could rate right up there with them.

Wine and grappa poured freely from huge, wooden kegs set on flatbed trucks colorfully festooned with red, white, and green bunting. These were arranged about a hundred feet apart all along the winding, quarter-of-a-mile-long avenue. Seven or eight combos of roving musicians played and sang lustily as they sauntered up and down the overcrowded, four-block dance floor. Almost without exception, everyone wore colorful costumes and were either drinking and eating crusty little antipasti or singing and dancing to the wild rhythms of the nearest group of musicians.

For Sergeant King and I, with the aid of the bottle of cheap cognac we had bought, the Army quickly became a distant memory, many years and miles away from our first-floor balcony window. All lingering thoughts that bordered on the life-and-death hostilities of only a few weeks ago appeared to be gone from everyone's memory, especially for these hordes of merry Italians who, for the moment at least, no longer feared the brutality of violent conflict. It just wasn't in their nature to be anything but amiable. All they needed was an excuse.

We spotted a pair of adventurous looking lasses dressed in peasant costumes strolling beneath our sill, and they asked if we'd join them. Perhaps it was the other way around; I can't remember.

"Vieni! Avanti!" they shouted above the din. The sight of our American uniforms and my response in a mix of English and Italian seemed to hit the perfect chord with them. We left the apartment, and all four locked arms from that point on, joining in the intoxicating merriment surrounding us, parading boisterously up and down that gayly lantern-lit avenue.

It must have been about two in the morning before we felt it might be time to ask them in. They plaintively rejected our invitation then warmly kissed us good night, showing more than a little regret. Of course, that was in 1945, a romantic, much more innocent time.

I do not know if such street parties still occur in Italy today, but if they do and if I could possibly know the date and place, I'd do all in my power to be there again, this time with my lovely wife to share the experience. And if I could possibly shake J.P. loose from his ubiquitous grandchildren, so much the better.

On the following afternoon, I left Sergeant King, who I knew had no interest in the classics, to head out on my own. I wanted to find out what was happening at the world-famous La Scala opera house. Why I fall into these things, I don't know, but there happened to be a young woman there having some kind of language problem at the ticket window. With my newly bolstered ego, I volunteered to try to assist her.

"I wanted loge tickets for the ballet this coming Friday, and the fool just doesn't understand me," she complained, in a combination of broken English and classic German, waving her arms in frustration.

In my questionable Italian, I explained to the man seated behind the iron-barred window what I thought she needed. He said, "Aah," meaning he finally understood, muttering under his breath something about Tedeschi as he handed me her tickets and asked for six hundred lira.

The young woman seemed more than happy to pay it. She told me then that she was from Basel in Switzerland and that her name was Anna Berman.

"Jewish?" I asked, testing. She flatly said no, but I suspected otherwise for I'd never met a gentile who bore that name. Wherever I had traveled in Europe, no one freely admitted to being Jewish. Understandably, the yoke of persecution wasn't easily disposed of, and yet, sadly, I found the phenomenon still to be almost as true today, more than fifty years later.

The program that afternoon was a symphonic concert. Because the two of us, Anna and I, seemed to be alone at the moment and because I hated attending this type of thing by myself, I asked if she wished to join me. She said she would be happy to.

Unlike the heart-on-their-sleeve, impetuous Italians, she seemed impenetrably reserved but implied that she was grateful for my company. I saw no need to push the relationship. Simply being with someone of the opposite sex seemed gratifying enough as we sat innocently holding hands in the first balcony of La Scala, drinking in the aura of that world-renowned opera house.

I wondered what she might be thinking about this strangely constrained American soldier next to her. We parted after the concert with no fanfare and only veiled questions to myself about my own ambiguity. I had that eerie vacuous feeling as I watched her cross the piazza and disappear. I felt alone again, unadventurous, wanting badly to go home.

The talent contest started at 1:00 P.M. the next day. Just before it was my turn to perform, a choir of about 200 men, Japanese-Americans, more than likely from the 442nd Nisei Regimental Combat Team, sang delightful Hawaiian chants. They were good! They couldn't lose. With that many voices and their harmoniously plaintiff island sound, who could argue with their right to first place?

I did my first number immediately after their applause died down, sounding to myself like Minnie Mouse after the thundering quantity of voices of my previous competitors, but I gave it all I had. I was truly surprised by the applause from the audience and so offered my encore. Allen Jones I wasn't, but the audience seemed to take great pleasure in my rendition of "The Donkey Serenade."

When the judges had made their decision, I was not surprised to learn that the Japanese-American choir had won first place. However, I was amazed to find that I had placed second among all the talent represented in the entire 5th Army. In reality, I had won nothing, but it was certainly an exhilarating experience.

Our Milan excursion at an end, Sergeant King and I returned to Prevacina the next day just in time for our regiment's first sharp encounter with the Yugoslavs.

Someone had spotted a horde of about 2,000 shabbily uniformed soldiers who didn't seem to belong to any Allied outfit in the vicinity. Rifles and automatic weapons carelessly slung over their shoulders, they were marching westward toward Trieste on a main road about 300 yards south of our village. Like a trail of ants, they had probably come from somewhere beyond the Yugoslavian side of the nearby border on the deliberate instructions of Marshal Tito.

To my mind, their purpose seemed simple: to test us and try to infiltrate. With any success, they would attempt to occupy some of the territory that had not been awarded to them in the final Allied armistice agreement, trying to bluff their way through and gain as much ground as they could finagle along the way.

Quickly apprised of this flagrant breach of agreement, Colonel Woods immediately instructed the commander of our Sherman tank attachment to have our three armored vehicles move out into clear view and turn their menacing gun turrets in the direction of the oncoming crowd. Our own battalion of foot soldiers came out to watch, trying to be as obvious as possible in this game of bluff and bluster. The scene was like an event in an ancient Roman arena in which the final outcome was predictable. The odds were definitely not in their favor, but with instructions to probe our will, they insisted on proceeding.

Our tanks rumbled down the country road, their gun turrets and mounted machine guns slowly turning point-blank toward this ragtag partisan army before coming to a dead stop 150 yards from their column. The colonel's orders were to wait and hold our tanks' forward movement where they were but to keep those clamorously noisy motors running for the obvious purpose of bending this foe's morale.

From where I stood, I watched, fascinated, as the partisani commander who led this small army finally held up his left hand, and their advance came to an abrupt halt. Then after a minute or so, two white flags waved at us from the head of their procession, signaling that a conference was in order.

Buckling on his side arm, Colonel Woods and his driver jumped into the nearest jeep and headed straight for the alien group. I stood transfixed as I watched the one-sided negotiations that were taking place. I knew the crisis was finally over fifteen minutes later when the long column did a sloppy about-face and, like a weary, elongated centipede, slowly receded back to wherever it was they had come from.

When he returned to the command post, the Colonel immediately telephoned division G-2 to apprise them of the event. He reported that after they saw the armor and the military force we were prepared to expend, their leader had acted pragmatically, bending to our firm determination. After a short attempt at arguing, with the aid of his interpreter, his final words were clear, realistic: "We have just finished fighting a long war against our common enemy. Let's not begin the process again."

Tito's desperate ruse had failed, and to this time, none of the disputed territory was ever ceded to the Yugoslavian Socialists.

What was amazing to me was how little the American public knew, or understood, or even cared at that time about the degree of embitterment and desperation inherent in this supposedly friendly ally's territorial greed. We did know that these Yugoslavian partisans had earned our great respect for their costly battle against the invading Germans. What these stouthearted partisans had accomplished within the limitation of their small, underground army was truly worthy of our highest praise and regard. But their intense desire for a Socialist world, their blind rush for radical changes, seemed acted out in imitation of what then appeared to be the successes of Stalin. Impatience led to bluff and bad timing. Tito had tried to bite off more than he could chew. I felt sure his people must have become too weary of war and its terrible cost to pick up the proverbial gauntlet we had thrown down that day.

After that aborted attempt, there appeared in our village dozens of strangers who wore the raiment of those same tattered soldiers and who roamed the streets, appearing here and there in small groups. Obviously, they had been instructed to keep an eye on us, swing the homogenized village further over to their side, and watch for an opening.

Unless they caused clear-cut agitation, there was little we could do. As troops of occupation, we could only keep an eagle eye on these pockets of insurgents and try to avoid trouble. To emphasize our presence, we held company and battalion parades regularly, purely as a show of power to let them know we'd take no nonsense from any quarter, just in case they happened to have any more daring ideas.

Despite all this political posturing, it was still easy enough to become friendly with these newcomers as most of them were quite affable and often joined J.P. and I near our favorite spot by the brook. A good number of these potential agitators were young women, hard looking and militant. We'd often attempt to draw them out and exchange ideas with their group while flirting coyly, careful not to get too heatedly involved with them over politics. Initially reserved, they loosened up quickly as all of us sat around casually in our swimsuits.

A mixed group of both sexes listened most intently to J.P. and I spout off about our strangely antagonistic, differing points of view. They seemed to take a great interest in our two-party system of government. Tongue in cheek, J.P. would call Harry Truman and his Democratic congress dupes of the Communists, and I would loudly argue that if Jesus happened to be a Democrat, the Republican right wing would take great pleasure in nailing him to the cross again. Our overly serious audience struggled to understand our strange jargon, our quasi-humorous bantering, but mostly they seemed amazed at how we could appear to really despise each other's political factions and still remain the best of friends. Of course, we tried our best to explain, but I seriously doubted if their peculiar, Slavik single-mindedness would ever permit such absurdity. Time has, unfortunately, proven me right.

During June, our last month of occupation, the brass suggested that we could hold weekly dances at the small meeting hall next door to our command post. Because we already had the makings of a five-piece band, it was a simple matter to announce to the small village that everyone was invited to a dance on the following Thursday at 8:00 P.M.

The turnout was better than expected. I don't think that these gentle, rural folk, who happened to be caught in the tortuous maze of divergent ideologies, had had much pleasure or enjoyment lately, especially in this extroverted way. About sixty female villagers, both mothers and daughters, attended along with a few dozen of the partisani outsiders.

Coincidently, our ration of beer had arrived earlier that day, this time in unmarked wooden kegs rather than in the usual Budweiser aluminum containers. Someone said the delicious brew had been imported from Switzerland, and I could easily believe it. I've never tasted any lager as good.

The heady combination of music and great brew helped make that evening of our first dance unforgettable. The crowning touch came later that evening in the person of Elsa, a surprisingly knowledgeable, English-speaking partisani who had very recently joined our clique at the stream.

166

As Elsa listened to me sing a few ballads with the band, her twenty-four-year-old mind chose to forget our fundamental differences for that moment, or so it seemed. More than once I caught her gazing at me in a way that led me to believe that, if nothing else, it would be fun to dance with and talk to that pleasant looking young woman and overlook her party line. What did I have to lose?

To hell with politics! I left the stage and brazenly walked over to where she was toe-tapping with two of her male comrades and extended my hand as an invitation to dance. Elsa appeared genuinely surprised by my invitation and firmly grasped my extended hand. Before I could take two steps, she had guided me onto the dance floor while I tried to fathom whether she or I would lead.

She was at least as tall as I was. Her leathery skin and shapely, uncommonly muscular body belied the fact that if she shed fifteen pounds of sinew and curled her long, stringy, ash-blonde hair, she would most assuredly have made herself much more attractive to men. Apparently, it was in the nature of these militants not to care very much about outer appearances, and she fit the mold perfectly.

The band was playing their limited version of "Moonlight Serenade," which was about as much as I could handle on the dance floor. Anything faster for me would have been disaster. I had never learned to jitterbug.

After having danced two or three sets with her, there was no doubt in my mind that, more than anything else, the woman's real interest lay in converting me, in reforming me from decadent capitalism to her form of Socialism. I listened politely for a while as she kept insinuating her propaganda. I soon found myself humming along with the band when she'd stop for a breath, not wishing to enter into two-sided polemics that I knew could lead nowhere. Finally, she noticed my apathy, and giving me up for a lost cause, Elsa returned to her comrades but not before she had teasingly rotated her pelvis against mine two or three times to let me know in a most unsubtle and unladylike way that she was prepared to give her all for the cause if only I had been more inclined to share her point of view.

Everything in Prevacina reverted to normal on the day after the dance, but when Elsa happened to pass me on the narrow street the next morning, she emitted a scornful little laugh and remarked in a lecherous half-whisper, "Stupido! You don't know what you missed last night."

Maybe. I smiled weakly and took off in another direction to pick up my mail. What I might have missed didn't seem as important to me then as my letters and packages from home. The mail clerk had two letters from my wife and a package from my aunt Ethel in Florida.

Receiving mail overseas was, without a doubt, everything it was cracked up to be in those old Army posters. I lost no time opening the butcher-paper wrapped box.

J.P.'s insatiable stomach quivered in anticipation as he watched wide eyed. The excelsior fell away exposing a tin of cookies, a small kosher salami, and a can of gefilte fish. The salami was short lived as I shared chunks of it with the guys around me within smelling range.

Later, I opened the can of rare, priceless gefilte fish. Marinated in a heavenly aromatic salt brine, the ground-up patties are usually savored with a touch of a red beet-flavored, sweetened horseradish. Having no horseradish of any color handy, J.P. and I were about to devour it plain when I watched him do the unspeakable and profane. He smeared his soft fish onto a slab of white bread and then proceeded to slowly layer it with a slice of his ham, ridiculously followed by a slice of American cheese. I choked and broke up laughing as my chowhound buddy proceeded to desecrate the age-honored, ethnic delicacy in this manner, but he devoured it that way in spite of my hiccups and protestations. My aunt would have had a fit. Watching him savor the combination, however, I had to admit that he thoroughly enjoyed his wacky club sandwich, ultimately washing it down with Swiss beer.

Dinner time came and went. As far from an area of overt poverty as we seemed to be, I found it inconceivable again that, even this far north, we still had those lines of skinny, barefoot kids waiting at the garbage end of our chow lines. They were happy for any unwanted scraps from our mess kits and for the mess sergeant's remaining soggy coffee grounds. Behind the doors of many of these unpretentious houses, our garbage was often their main course and our coffee grounds reused and savored for their beverage. I can never forget the pathetic look on their grimy little faces as the waifs hungrily stared at us whenever and wherever we ate. I knew that most of those leftovers would be shared with the family, yet interestingly, we never saw anyone over twelve openly solicit for food. Adults refused to humiliate themselves. Hungry as I'm sure they often were, their pride wouldn't permit it.

Thinking of the strange hash they probably concocted out of our leftovers made it easier for me to comprehend why they might look to any political scheme that offered more promise of feeding what was left of their war-diminished families. Hopefully, my kids, the ones I was now seriously planning to have when I got home, would never know this kind of want, this kind of hand-out.

For over three months, our battalion continued to occupy, patrol, and control the Italian-Yugoslavian border territory that summer, each man restless with one vexing question uppermost in his mind and waiting impatiently for the answer. The European war was over, so for God's sake, when the hell would we be going home?

Chapter 18

Home at Last

Apparently, we had made our point. No more incidents occurred, and it seemed as though Marshal Tito had at last understood our message and was finally ready to toe the line. It was time for our battalion to say ciao to Prevacina. Other more permanent soldiers of occupation would take our place and make friends with these most agreeable townspeople as we hoped we had done. In a wishful, selfcentered way, we wondered if they would miss us.

Hallelujah! Our replacements arrived early, and we boarded the same dusty trucks they came in on.

The entire regiment traveled south all day, finally settling into an open bivouac area seventy miles north of Naples. We happily accepted the bone-jarring trip as part of the discomfort necessary to get us closer to those ships in Naples waiting to take us back to the United States. Army engineers had already erected tents for us along a level, grassy plain, and we sensed that this, the Volturno River valley, would most likely be our final staging area this side of the Atlantic before our departure from Italy.

Only another few days or so before shipping out, I thought impatiently. Not much to do until then except to laze around and wait. It was the beginning of August, and there were things yet to happen to me before I boarded the ship for my long awaited trip home.

According to the news reports, American forces were delivering serious blows daily to the Japanese in the Pacific theater of operations, and it didn't look like we'd soon be needing our steel helmets and rifles. These and other items that had once been life-or-death essentials were being packed and crated to be forwarded to a dockside in Naples for shipment back to the United States, probably to be used by us again later in some bloody, hell-bent invasion of a distant Pacific atoll.

On August 3, 1945, after Spam and eggs, I was summoned to regimental headquarters by the regimental commander, Colonel Fulton Magill, who unofficially advised me that I would be receiving the rare and distinctive Legion of Merit medal.

One of the other officers, Major Floyd Pinnick saluted and handed me a copy of the five-page commendation, and as I read it my hands trembled, my eyes dampened. Among other things, it stated "for exceptionally meritorious conduct in the performance of outstanding service."

I hadn't realized that such an extensive history of my actions had even been noted, let alone recorded by a clerk at headquarters. The full official recommendation was outlined and signed by Colonel Woods.

Headquarters 363rd Infantry

United States Army

APO 91

Subject: Recommendation for the Award of LEGION OF MERIT

To: Commanding General, 91st Infantry Division

1. Under the provisions of Army Regulations 600-45, as amended, it is recommended that LEON WECKSTEIN, S/Sgt, 39687321 1st Bn Hq Co, 363rd Inf, be awarded the LEGION OF MERIT for exceptionally meritorious conduct in the performance of outstanding services.

2. From 4 July 1944 until 20 October 1944, he rendered outstanding services as intelligence sergeant of the 1st Bn, 363rd Inf.

3. Since he entered combat on 4 July 1944, S/Sgt Weckstein has rendered continuous and outstanding service as battalion intelligence sergeant 1st Bn, 363rd Inf. During this period he has established himself as an observer of superior ability whose reports and observations are sought after by all intelligence agencies in the regiment. He has proven himself to be unusually rugged physically and mentally by undergoing hardships imposed by extremely difficult terrain, disagreeable weather, and hard fast moving enemy action. On two occasions his courage and physical stamina carried him through three actions that completely depleted his section. On several occasions he

was the only remaining NCO of the forward battalion OP. Exhaustion and battle fatigue have, in more than one instance, depleted the NCO and enlisted man complement of the battalion commander's group. Never, however, has S/Sgt Weckstein absented himself for any reason. He has, at different times, continued to observe when individuals alongside of him had become casualties. His mental and emotional stability have made possible continuous keen and accurate observation of enemy activity. He has assumed the job of sergeant major for the forward CP group, organizing the group for local security, arranging for rations, writing up and transmitting reports, performing the duties of operations sergeant, reconnoitering for new OP locations, sketching key terrain features, and numerous other duties outside of those normally assigned the intelligence sergeant. Always these various jobs have been handled in an excellent manner.

When the battalion is off the line, S/Sgt Weckstein organizes classes for his section. His leadership and teaching ability are much in evidence during the conduction of his classes. Members of his group are far above average in sketching, map reading, range determination, and target designation due to his diligent teaching procedures. Every member of his section is qualified to adjust mortar and artillery fire and frequently do so. His co-workers are apt aerial photo readers, and their work as observers is greatly enhanced by this aptitude.

Recently, S/Sgt Weckstein has assisted in making an apparatus which gives azimuths in mills and degrees to a given point. This instrument has greatly facilitated pinpointing targets, thereby enabling mortar and artillery fire to be brought down more quickly. He has at present one of the most efficient battalion sections in the regiment. This section was developed by him under two different S-2s. He has lost three key men by enemy action and lost two other members to key positions elsewhere. Each time he was the nucleus around which a new and better section was developed.

The high degree of efficiency in the section is due to the interest taken by S/Sgt Weckstein in each individual man. The result of his unceasing effort to develop the section through training of personnel is very evident. The interest and enthusiasm S/Sgt Weckstein attaches to his work has greatly aided the development of confidence in his men, both in themselves and in S/Sgt Weckstein as their leader.

Specific examples of S/Sgt Weckstein's ability to organize and command are set forth in the following:

On 13 July 1944, S/Sgt Weckstein established an OP ahead of rifle protection on hill 577 near Chianni. The battalion had received severe shelling the day before and had engaged in several small arms fire fights, and at that time the unit on our left was meeting considerable resistance. His task in establishing this OP was hazardous and required great courage and a high sense of duty.

On 26 July 1944, the battalion CP was located in a poplar grove south of the Arno River near Pisa. The forward elements along the river were widely dispersed which made possible enemy infiltration between groups into our rear positions. S/Sgt Weckstein elected to work his way forward to a knoll from which he could observe the area in question. His route forward was exposed to observation, and his position was very precarious as several good approaches led into it from suspected enemy held areas. He remained in observation in this position for several hours.

His organizational abilities have been demonstrated on numerous occasions. One outstanding indication was at San Miniato while operating a battalion OP at the hotel. During the period of 10–12 August, he organized a series of company OPs using the battalion OP as the base. Each company had two OPs, and each was given a sector of responsibility to observe. A communication system was set up so as to control all OPs at all times. Working in conjunction with the artillery and 81mm mortars and with his company OP series, it was made possible to locate and destroy two enemy OPs, two machine gun positions, a convoy of six trucks loaded with troops, and two camouflaged SP guns.

On 13 September 1944, from the battalion OP at Cofaggio, near Scarperia, S/Sgt Weckstein located a pillbox in the 362nd Infantry area and adjusted 155 artillery fire on it. He also located two houses north of Mt. Calvi from which machine guns were firing and adjusted artillery fire on them.

On 14 September 1944, the OP was on hill 579 and observing Monticelli ridge. The hill was almost barren and very rocky, offering little concealment or cover. It received intense artillery, mortar, and small arms fire all day. S/Sgt Weckstein was on the scope all day. He located five enemy occupied bunkers on Monticelli ridge. He called for artillery fire that silenced two of them. He located barbed wire entanglements, enemy fields of fire, and communication wire.

On 15 September 1944, S/Sgt Weckstein did outstanding work as an observer during the bitter and bloody fighting on Monticelli ridge. At 1645 he noticed the first counterattack forming and called for artillery and mortar fire on the enemy activity north of the ridge. From this time until dark, he reported many kinds of enemy activity, and his direction of supporting fire caused many casualties. He located and made precision adjustments of artillery and mortar fire on three pillboxes in front of C Company. He was on the scope from sunrise until sunset. His superior officers had so much confidence in his ability to use the twenty-power scope that it was reserved exclusively for him.

On 16 September 1944, S/Sgt Weckstein remained at the scope all day; his observation of enemy activity enabled cannon, mortar, and artillery fire to inflict heavy losses on enemy equipment and personnel on Monticelli ridge. Intercepted messages from the enemy revealed the desperate conditions of the enemy at this time.

On 17 September 1944, before dawn, S/Sgt Weckstein took his twenty-power scope to B Company's position on Monticelli ridge. He selected a position on the left flank. He was under MG and mortar fire from the left front and rear. From his position he could observe the approach routes from the left flank and warned the defenders on this ridge of the German counterattacks.

On 25–26–27 September 1944, S/Sgt Weckstein picked up much enemy activity and aided in precision adjustment supporting fire on enemy positions on Mt. Freddi. The OP was on the hill to the south of Mt. Freddi and received severe concentrations of artillery and mortar fire. At this time his entire section had become casualties, so he operated alone. This was one of the hottest OPs the battalion ever occupied. The weather was extremely disagreeable. In spite of this, S/Sgt Weckstein stayed at his scope and continued his observation.

On 14–17 October, the OP was located in a road cut near Querceto. He observed enemy activity as our troops captured C. Torre and C. Fiume. He located several tanks and much enemy activity near the Belmonte sector. He worked with the artillery officer, aiding in precision adjustments of fire on enemy activity observed.

On 19 October 1944, the battalion OP was located in C. Fiume, southwest of Mt. Belmonte. The location of the battalion on our right had been reported during the night to be on Mt. Belmonte which made necessary a movement of troops up on its west flank to protect it. At first light, S/Sgt Weckstein started a careful observer's study of Mt. Belmonte. In a short while he had definitely located troops belonging to the unit on our right, and the report based on his observations was the first accurate information the unit's battalion headquarters and division headquarters had of their whereabouts. This information radically changed the conception of all headquarters concerned of the situation.

From this same OP, S/Sgt Weckstein located four tanks which were taken under fire by artillery and cannon and several machine gun nests which were fired on by mortars.

During the course of the three days S/Sgt Weckstein occupied this OP, it was repeatedly taken under SP fire, and many direct hits were registered on it. However, S/Sgt Weckstein remained observing practically the entire time during daylight.

S/Sgt Weckstein, intelligence sergeant of the battalion intelligence section, observed through the twenty-power scope from sunrise to sunset on numerous occasions. His six-man section was cut in half by casualties the first month of combat, only two of his original section still being with him. He has spent much time and effort in building up his section of replacements through teaching and example into one of the best in the regiment.

One day through his observation, two enemy OPs, two machine guns, and a convoy of six trucks carrying personnel were knocked out by artillery fire. On another day he picked out and aided in adjusting fire on pillboxes that were holding up the advance of the battalion. He was the first to observe potential enemy counterattacks and directed fire on them. On one day he established his OP with the front line companies to better observe the counterattacks of the enemy. During this four-day battle for a strategic military objective, his entire section were casualties, and he operated alone in one of the hottest OPs that the battalion ever had.

S/Sgt Weckstein has stayed at his scope observing during intense artillery and mortar barrages. He has proven himself to be unusually rugged physically and mentally by undergoing hardships imposed by extremely difficult terrain, disagreeable weather, and hard fast moving enemy action. His skilled observing and reporting are recognized as superior by all the men and officers in the battalion. His unceasing and tireless devotion to duty are an inspiration to the men and officers of the battalion. His sections uphold the finest traditions of the Infantry and the Army of the United States.

4. I have personal knowledge of the facts set forth above.

5. Rank and organization at the time of services performed: S/Sgt, Hq Co 1st Bn 363 Inf.

6. The entire service of S/Sgt Leon Weckstein 396687321 during and subsequent to the time cited above has been honorable. The services rendered by him may be considered as completed in connection with the phase of the Italian campaign, termination 20 October 1944.

7. Previous awards: none.

8. Proposed citation: Leon Weckstein, for exceptionally meritorious conduct in the performance of outstanding services.

Lt. Colonel Ralph N. Woods

My hands shook as I returned their salute. He told me I would be ordered to appear in a special regimental dress parade to receive the medal from our division commander, Major General Livesay. Out of three thousand men in the regiment, twelve others also were singled out to receive the prestigious award, but only three were given to people within my own 1st battalion, one of whom was my revered Lieutenant Colonel Woods.

I don't mind saying that I was one proud soldier. I wasn't sure that my size-fifteen shirt could hold my newly attained self-esteem without popping a few buttons. I was treated now with respectful deference by one and all. I was left pretty much on my own for the next few days until the presentation of awards would become official at the upcoming regimental parade.

During that respite, I had plenty of time to muse on the probable fate of my imaginary personal enemy, Kurt Reinhardt, as he recovered slowly and painfully in a hospital near Munich. His grievous wound would leave him with very limited use of his arm, and I could see that his full recovery, if it happened at all, was going to take many years.

"I believe it would be better for you to recuperate near your home in Hamburg as there's little more we can do for you here," the German military doctor said, with a frown. "Your family can visit you whenever they want until you get out of the hospital."

Kurt agreed. The extreme pain had begun to subside, and he felt it would be more practical to be released from a hospital near his home town, hopefully within a month or so.

The war had ended for him forty days before, and during that time, he had often relived within the dark recesses of his mind the battles he had fought. These gloomy reveries that would come at any hour of the day or night would always end in frustration from unfulfilled promises from headquarters of more heavy artillery and Panzer tanks that never came. He had given up on fresh recruits long ago.

And the verdammte Luftwaffe, he thought. What in the hell happened? Goring's heilige invincible airforce had seemed to be in hiding; they had been nowhere in sight. Herr Hitler, in my opinion you and your lousy blitzkrieg really deserved a worse fate than your easy suicide.

A few railroad tracks had already been repaired as Kurt's almost empty second-class coach traveled slowly toward the hospital near Hamburg, allowing him time to absorb the unbelievable sight of terribly devastated, once charming German cities along his main route. He had no idea that this had been happening. Of course, one couldn't believe the Allied broadcasts, but now it seemed that Goebbels and Field Marshal Kesselring apparently hadn't wanted to apprise their front-line troops of the magnitude of the destruction in their homeland for reasons that were now obvious.

Feeling the sudden stab of pain in his shoulder, he again was only too aware personally of what damage that Jew Roosevelt's air power had done. But this, he thought, looking out the train window, God in heaven, how could it have happened? Where were our anti-aircraft guns?

When Kurt had left for the front only two years ago, the Third Reich had stood proudly, its potent German armies poised in all parts of Europe to deliver the decisive, crushing blows that would permit his country to rise again to its preordained position of leadership of the world. Now, in only such a short time, the country lay in ruins. What went wrong?

The lieutenant's former arrogance, his once youthful idealism, quickly turned to despondent resignation with the sights he saw from the train window. Obviously, Germany had been thoroughly beaten, but could it ever, like the proverbial phoenix, rise again from the ashes? He wondered. From what he was able to see from his dirt-encrusted window, it didn't appear likely that it could ever happen, at least not in his lifetime.

Rumors of the Russian Communists taking over all of Germany had spread through the hospital, and he was truly frightened of that possibility. But what could Germany do now without its leaders, with its army mutilated? What would America and England do? That bastard Stalin was most likely too shrewd for their naïve statesmen and would have an easy time gaining the upper hand.

The train slowed to a stop when it reached Berlin. Kurt looked in amazement at the unbelievable destruction, at the strange soldiers in the station. A combination of flags and uniforms of every kind, American, English, Russian, everything except swastika banners, proved to him that his fatherland could never again be what it once was. The punishment had been too telling.

Two uniformed guards with side arms came aboard the train to check the passengers. One was Russian, the other British. Had these former antagonists already formed some kind of an alliance he didn't know about? There were so many questions, so few answers.

With difficulty, he silently returned his traveling papers to his bag after the guards left. The readjustment was going to be schrecklich and frustrating as hell to do even the slightest chores with one hand. Doctor Mueller had told him frankly that he'd need a lot of therapy and, due to the damaged nerves, not to expect to have even limited use of his arm for at least a year or so, if ever.

An hour later, Kurt gasped as the train entered what was left of his Hamburg, his city. "Gott in himmel!" he managed aloud. Is there anything still standing? Having reached the nadir of his expectations, Kurt broke down and cried as he hadn't done since he had lost his pet schnauzer to a speeding car when he was nine. Most of the passengers bound for Hamburg had already left the train, and as this was the last stop, he stayed behind and took the necessary time to shed bitter, pent-up tears, lamenting the lost way of life that he once knew, knowing it would never be again.

An ambulance was waiting for him and one other patient. Let them handle the amputee first, he thought. That would give him enough time to splash some cold water on his eyes, adjust his cap, and try to look like the proud officer he imagined he once was.

After he had settled into his new hospital surroundings, Hilda and his parents came to visit him. The emotional reactions of Frau Reinhardt and his father were predictable. Concerned for the well-being of their son, they articulated emotional, hateful epithets at their former leaders, all the while bewailing Kurt's bandaged wound. They, more than he, had already been aware of the senseless futility of his former patriotic fervor and did their best to assuage his disappointment in the fuhrer, attempting to convince him that Germany would most likely rise again but without the fanatical madness of such a shameful dictatorship.

His parents left him alone with Hilda, hoping the woman would lift his morale and influence him to accept his lot and be satisfied making a future with her. Seeing and being near her should ease his obvious dejection.

"You don't know how much I've missed you," she said, when they were alone.

"All my thoughts have been with you too, liebchen. I could hardly wait to come home to ... y-you." The painful, chronic torment had returned for a split second, jarring him as it was occasionally prone to do.

Brief as it was, his pained exclamation frightened her. She couldn't help but notice and winced inwardly while saying nothing to him, but something within her pragmatic mind rebelled at that moment. This was a different person from the handsome youth who left her only a couple of years ago. The thought of laying her head against that scarred, misshapen shoulder frightened her, and she did all she could to keep from running out of the hospital ward.

While he was away, she had studied hard and had already begun to work as a nurse, caring for the wounded and doing her part in the fatherland's difficult struggle. But this was different. This was something she might have to live with for the rest of her life.

Something in her nature had suddenly turned her feelings for Kurt into smoldering, loathsome discontent. She felt fearful of his scars to the point of never wanting to see him again. How could she make love to a man who had half a shoulder? She knew that ultimately she'd have to face it, but the trauma to his once fine body had completely blocked out any real compassion or sensuality she might have felt for him. Now she had to force herself even to lie to him, hating herself for feeling the way she did. Maybe they had been apart too long.

Kurt couldn't have suspected her innermost feelings. Playfully, he asked for a kiss. She responded bravely and pressed her lips against his while his good hand fondled the softness of her posterior.

It was at that precise moment she made the unalterable decision to leave Hamburg. Women of her profession were sorely needed in every part of Germany. Why not go to a hospital in Weisbaden or Munich? Of course, she couldn't tell him, but in a few days she would say she was needed in Berlin for a short time, then she'd simply disappear, leaving no trace. With all the confusion going on in Germany, it would be quite possible, in fact easy, to make a new life elsewhere.

It seemed Kurt Reinhardt was destined to suffer from not only the devastating pain across his chest and back but also the almost unbearable emotional loss of his childhood sweetheart. It would tear at his manhood, his smugness, permitting at best only a dimmed hope for a bleak future.

Now I could finally shut this arrogant enemy out of my fantasies and, like some omnipotent god, know that I handed the damned fool exactly what he deserved. I told you I'd get even!

→ ·━◆▆· ·→

With plenty of time to kill, J.P. and I attended a wonderful performance of *Tosca* performed outdoors by a Neapolitan opera company in Campobasso, a few miles from where we were bivouacked. We attended the matinee showing of this delightful Puccini masterwork, and I was totally amazed at the highly professional quality of voices and orchestra, especially in view of the fact that it all took place on a comparatively small wooden stage made of rough, unfinished two-by-fours.

I learned later that, in Italy, anything even slightly less than musical perfection, especially in their operatic performances, was tantamount to sacrilege. And as always, the Italian audience, unlike up-tight Americans, was quick to respond with either exorbitant, emotional applause or, when warranted, noisy, merciless derision. I found it wonderful that they were so expressive, always wearing their hearts on their sleeve when it came to music or anything else.

That day, the country's unusual brand of hospitality exhibited itself again as it had on so many occasions before. We offered a cigarette to a first violinist during intermission and spent the ten minutes chatting with him. Almost predictably, he invited us to his home in Naples for dinner the following night, after their short tour would be concluded. Regretfully, we had to decline because the distance to Naples from where we were camped would have been prohibitive to travel. I'm sure it would have been an evening to remember.

I had learned that, for J.P. and I travelling in Italy, learning as much as we could of the language and making an attempt to speak it rewarded us with some unforgettable, treasured experiences and memories.

After we returned to camp, we found out that a battalion formation was called for the next day. When it came time for the formation, Colonel Woods took me aside.

"Stay here and man the command post, sergeant, in case we get any messages from division," the colonel said. "We should be back in about an hour or so."

I watched as the rest of the battalion, in full dress uniform, fell in and marched off to the parade grounds.

That historic day was August 6, 1945.

I was alone in the tent, writing a letter home and tentatively listening to the radio as I waited for the battalion's return, when the music was suddenly interrupted by a static-filled special bulletin. I turned up the volume to hear what all the excitement was about but managed to catch only part of the broadcast, something about a science fiction kind of bomb, a formidable new weapon our Air Force had just detonated over the city of Hiroshima. They claimed it had the power of a thousand suns or some such unbelievable amount. The impassioned reporter continued in urgent tones that many thousands of Japanese civilians were assumed to be dead from the blast and thousands of others burned or mortally wounded from the radiation of this single atomic bomb.

Not sure that I heard correctly, I wasn't quite ready to believe my ears. Having personally heard Orson Welles' unsettling radio drama of Martians landing on our planet a few years back, I wasn't going to let myself be taken in again with this kind of fictional nonsense.

I kept my ear to the squawking signal that was coming in from who knows where. Reports continued to fill the airways depicting horrible scenes caused by this amazing weapon and the untold damage it was capable of doing. Announcers repeated the sensational news over and over again as it occurred in Hiroshima.

Wishfully, I had begun to believe it was true. If all this was really happening, it was bound to put a lid on the war in the Pacific. Not for one moment did I bother to think about the women and children, the more innocent victims of this holocaust, who were charred beyond recognition or made forever radioactive. Not until many years later as I matured did I consider the possibility that this first devastating bomb could have been dropped in a much less populated area with similar, but considerably more humanitarian, results.

Simply put, at that time I selfishly thought of myself only, idiotically dancing for joy with the thought that now I might not ever have to become part of the invasion force destined for Japan. If everything I had been listening to was factual, this new scientific widget should settle everything, and whatever accomplished that end couldn't be anything but great.

After listening for nearly an hour to the almost hysterical announcer's special bulletins, I finally assured myself that the fantastic news I was hearing was not a Hollywood stunt. I ran to the colonel as he returned to the command tent to tell him what I had heard. He looked at me oddly as if to ask, "Have you been out in the sun too long, sergeant?" Of course, his initial reaction had to be as dubious and unbelieving as mine was. After listening to a few minutes of the garbled voice of the excited newscaster, however, he paled and placed a call to division headquarters to confirm the report. I watched appreciatively as the expression on his usually brooding face turned to one of rare elation. His hands even began to shake as the shocking news from the G-2 officer at division headquarters confirmed the radio report.

It seemed to make more sense now, that with the onset of this bomb it wouldn't be very long before our crazy world would finally settle down to enjoy the peace, hopefully for a long, long while. That was, again, wishful thinking from one who had personally seen too much of the recent slaughter.

The commentator kept harping on the fact that the Soviets could still be a problem, atomic bomb or not, but we were all just too darned happy now to even consider that remote possibility. They must have been just as weary of war as we were, I thought.

With the dropping of the second bomb on Nagasaki a few days later, the emperor's expected surrender came quickly, ending whatever nightmarish fears I might have still entertained of one day having to invade the highly fortified Japanese mainland. This last bit of wonderful news exploded in my head like an all-encompassing answer to all my fearful questions about the survival of everything I held dear. I felt like saying a prayer of thanks to the god who had brought me this far until I thought of those thousands who hadn't made it. A few atoms of agnosticism were growing into my brain that day.

⊷ ⸭✦⸭ ⊶

The point system of discharge from the service was instituted almost immediately after the Japanese capitulation. While some of the greener troops would have to remain in Italy to occupy much of that devastated country, it appeared logical to the big wheels in the Pentagon that each medal earned and each month served in combat would count as points toward eligibility for discharge. When a soldier had tallied a high enough number of points, he would be eligible to go home.

Finished! Finito! Over! I had enough points!

The departure from Italy was surprisingly easy. Most of my regiment boarded ships, benignly forgiving and forgetting all previous gambling debts. A few others opted to remain, those who had decided to marry Italian women. They'd have tons of paperwork to do before returning home, poor souls, but I could easily empathize with their good fortune. Judging from the Italian women I had seen and those I had met, most of them could be considered a prize catch. I base this conjecture mainly on their delightful, forthright personalities and their great eagerness to please. I was sure that their future American husbands and their future mothers-in-law would be very lucky to have them.

On August 21, our battalion left Italy from Naples and arrived a week and a half later at Fort Patrick Henry in Virginia, our former debarkation point. For whatever reason, I didn't get seasick this time.

I wanted badly to kiss the ground of the good old United States of America, but anything more demonstrative than grabbing a handful of American dirt and watching it slowly trickle through my fingers would have seemed pretentious.

Now that I would have to say good-bye to my men, especially those who were almost like brothers, that last day became one hell of a gut-wrenching farewell. I had thought about attempting to avoid those trembling handshakes, the embarrassing hugs that were so final, hoping I could just take off without all the emotional anxiety. But I realized that it would be my last sight of these mentally exhausted comrades, men who, with me, had faced indescribable horrors. We had been through too much together. So I resolved to make it through that sentimental finale.

Afterwards, I remembered too late that I never got the chance to tell any of these men how proud I was to have served with them. If I had, intrepid Tom Miller of New Jersey would have been among the first of my squad to have been told of my undying respect. He was dedicated to remain in the thick of things and would join in climbing the highest peak and go about doing his job without griping more than necessary. There was no doubt in my mind that his IQ soared above mine.

Charles Lott, a shy kid from the heartland country of Wellsville, Missouri, almost always wore an indulgent grin that openly displayed his inner winsomeness. Yet, I would have bet my bottom dollar that had the occasion arisen, he above all my men had what it took to win the Congressional Medal of Honor.

Private First Class Lloyd Gallegos, a Native American from Denver, was always an enigma to me. After my arrival in boot camp, he had been assigned to teach me how to handle my M-1 rifle. His rough-and-tumble ways scared the hell out of me then, and I was sure he was some kind of high-ranking non-com. But a few years later in the Apennines, he was transferred into my squad and completely surprised me by accepting my stripes with perfect tolerance and approval. To this day his unusual calmness and military sense of what was needed in any situation still awes me. He would have made a great professional soldier.

Bob Gordon could very well have been a movie star with his handsome, dimpled cheeks and thick, wavy dark hair yet never once displayed any sort of vanity.

Harry Crooker, my man Friday, had sensitive mannerisms, but he served throughout the entire campaign by my side never once shirking the toughest, most miserable assignment.

I could go on and on about the magnificent others, but the memories are too bittersweet.

In recent years, I tried to get in touch with Crooker. To my great sadness, his wife told me that he had been in a convalescent home, his once keen memory the victim of Alzheimer's disease. She was certain he wouldn't know me.

I followed this news with a call to my buddy, Jess Dunnagen, whom I've stayed in touch with through the years by postcard and phone calls. I gleaned from his wife Pat that, although he probably wouldn't let on, he too had fallen victim to a badly debilitating chronic illness.

After I hung up, I poured myself a particularly stiff drink, convinced that I would make no more calls. While I wasn't looking, time had been taking its inevitable toll on my old comrades, and I would rather just remember them as the stalwart youths they once had been.

⊷ ⥊⊹⥋ ⊶

From that port in Virginia, I boarded a train to Fort Ord in Monterey along with others who had originally emanated from California. I did my best to restrain what was gradually becoming a wildly euphoric frame of mind and to keep it from leaping all out of bounds as our train neared the Rocky Mountains.

With enough points, considering my time spent overseas and my combat decorations, I realized that I could get out of the service almost as soon as my feet touched the ground at the separation area. I was right. It didn't take more than a few hours for them to process me out and hand me my long-dreamed-of discharge papers with a one-way train ticket to Los Angeles. My duffel bag was all that I had carried with me, and I had stowed everything I owned in it before I left Italy.

For less than twenty seconds I thought about the contents of that duffel bag, then reached inside for the little cardboard box that held some souvenir photographs. Every last bit of whatever else might have been left in that dilapidated, olive-drab bag I kicked out of my life forever, into the farthest corner of the old barracks. It included my once very precious telescope. Maybe I should have kept it for a souvenir, but at that point I could no longer stand the sight of anything military.

The realization of my newfound freedom and my great elation would remain forever indescribable. I was flying! The invisible chains had been removed. Once more a free man, I never wanted to see anything khaki, anything that even distantly reminded me of war ever again.

However, I had yet to face a few, unforeseen psychological complications as I set my feet on home soil. The first was that, every time a jet plane flew by, which in those days had become a daily occurrence in Los Angeles, I'd flinch and start to duck for cover. Our European support planes had always been prop driven, but these noisy, newfangled, rocket-fueled aircraft made roaring noises that sounded awfully similar to incoming artillery shells. Actually, it did take several years for me to get used to the jarring screams of the jets.

The second and probably more commonly shared enigma was the psychological fear of feeling like a stranger when I would finally come face-to-face with my young wife after all this forced separation time.

I struggled with the trauma in the taxi right up to the moment I leaped out to clasp my extraordinarily wonderful, Russian-born mother-in-law as she shouted my Hebrew name, Label, and ran ecstatically down from the front porch to greet me. Her exuberance calmed my troubled mind just as my wife appeared next, looking as lovely as I had remembered.

It was going to be alright.

⸺ ⫶⫶ ⸺

A few weeks after my arrival home, I received two packages from the War Department in Washington, D.C., each containing foreign medals and commendations. One was a royal decree beautifully written in Italian and sent to me by the Italian Minister of War, accompanied by its impressive medal, the Military Cross of Valor. The other was from the Polish exiled government in London, the Bronze Cross of Merit with Crossed Swords.

Needless to say, I highly prize these and my American award of Legion of Merit. They are each framed in a simple, six-by-ten-inch, glass-covered frame over my desk. When I occasionally chance to glance up, they challenge my aging, yet fortunately vivid, memory with both sad and sunny recollections, and for those few seconds, I'm twenty-three again.

No. 2605

WAR DEPARTMENT

Humbert of Savoy, Prince of Piedmont, Lieutenant General of the Realm, by His Decree under date of September 15, 1945, in view of Royal Decree No. 1423 of November 1932 and successive modifications; upon the suggestion of the Secretary of State for War, has conferred, on his own motion, the

MILITARY VALOR CROSS

upon   **S/Sgt Weckstein, Leon**

In the Italian Campaign he distinguished himself by valor and a splendid spirit of self-sacrifice.

The Secretary of State for War therefore issues the present document as proof of the honorific insignia conferred.

Rome, October 5, 1945.

Record Office   The Secretary
                                                          (Signature)

            19

Registry   Page

Numero d'Ordine 2605

MINISTERO DELLA GUERRA

Umberto di Savoia Principe di Piemonte
Luogotenente Generale del Regno con Suo Decreto
in data del 15 Settembre 1945
Visto il Regio Decreto 4 Novembre 1932 n. 1423 e successive modifiche;
Sulla proposta del Ministro Segretario di Stato per gli Affari
della Guerra;
Ha conferito di " Motu Proprio „ la

Croce al valor militare
al Ssgt Weckstein Leon

*"NELLA CAMPAGNA D'ITALIA SI DISTINGUEVA PER VALORE
ED ALTO SPIRITO DI SACRIFICIO..."*

Il Ministro Segretario di Stato per gli Affari della
Guerra rilascia quindi il presente documento per attestare
del conferito onorifico distintivo.

Roma, addì 5 Ottobre 1945

Registrato alla Corte dei Conti
addì   19
Registro   Foglio

Il Ministro

R E S T R I C T E D

WAR DEPARTMENT

THE ADJUTANT GENERAL'S OFFICE

WASHINGTON 25. D.C.

IN REPLY
REFER TO: AGPD-C 201 Weckstein, Leon
(16 Apr 46)   39 687 321

4 June 1946

Subject: Polish Award

To: Staff Sergeant Leon Weckstein
        543 North Brittania Street
        Los Angeles, California

1. There is forwarded herewith the Bronze Cross of Merit with Swords, and the order relating thereto, awarded to you by the former Polish Government in London.

2. Acceptance of this decoration is authorized since the award was made prior to the recognition of the present Polish Government by the United States. However, at the request of the Secretary of State, no ceremony or publicity is authorized in connection with the receipt of this decoration.

BY ORDER OF THE SECRETARY OF WAR:

Edward F—
Adjutant General

2 Incls
  1. Medal
  2. Citation

CITATION FOR LEGION OF MERIT

LEON WECKSTEIN, 39687321, Staff Sergeant, 363d Infantry Regiment, for exceptionally meritorious conduct in the performance of outstanding services in Italy from 4 July to 20 October 1944. As intelligence sergeant of the battalion intelligence section, Staff Sergeant Weckstein spent much time and effort in building up his section of replacements, through teaching and example, into one of the best in the regiment. On one occasion, through his observation, two enemy observation posts, two machine guns, and a convoy of six trucks carrying personnel were knocked out by artillery fire. On another occasion he picked out and aided in adjusting artillery fire on pillboxes that were holding up the advance of the battalion, and was the first to observe potential enemy counter-attacks and directed fire on them. His unceasing and tireless devotion to duty were an inspiration to the men in his section, and his actions were in keeping with the finest traditions of the Armed Forces of the United States. Entered service from Los Angeles, California

Epilogue

Whenever we could afford to, my wonderfully adventurous wife, Mimi, and I have always made it a point to vacation in Italy, not because I cared to relive the war but strictly for the immense pleasures that country offers its visitors.

In the spring of 1978, it happened that we were driving near Livorno (Leghorn) to spend the next few nights on the charming island of Elba, just a pleasant, one-hour ferry ride off the spectacular Italian western coast. We saw signs along the way designating Pisa, and Mimi suggested we visit it. I told her I had already seen it back in 1944.

"But you probably didn't see it up close," she protested, having already been familiar with my saga.

I couldn't argue with that. We went.

After we parked the car, she watched from a distance as I slowly walked to within a hundred feet of the crazily tilted tower. I stared openmouthed, amazed by the marvelously detailed historic structure and exquisitely carved architectural balustrades that I hadn't been able to see clearly through the eye of my telescope. She noticed my tears but didn't intrude.

"I wish I had brought the camera. We left it in the car," she said later, after my composure had returned. "I would have given anything to have caught your expression."

The moment could not be repeated.

But no camera, no mere words could ever express the thoughts that went through my turbulent mind during that fifteen-minute soliloquy. How could I ever forget it?

Yet, I could easily have been looking at shattered marble ruins, shards of splintered and unrecognizable quartz, if not for an improbable act of fate.

Index

CPSIA information can be obtained at www.ICGtesting.com
Printed in the USA
LVOW021135090112

263017LV00003B/7/A

9 781555 714970